The New Apostolic Reformation, Trump, and Evangelical Politics

Also Available from Bloomsbury:

American Evangelicals, Ashlee Quosigk
Neoliberal Religion, Mathew Guest
Religion in the Age of Obama,
Edited by Juan M. Floyd-Thomas and Anthony B. Pinn

The New Apostolic Reformation, Trump, and Evangelical Politics

The Prophecy Voter

Damon T. Berry

BLOOMSBURY ACADEMIC
LONDON • NEW YORK • OXFORD • NEW DELHI • SYDNEY

BLOOMSBURY ACADEMIC
Bloomsbury Publishing Plc
50 Bedford Square, London, WC1B 3DP, UK
1385 Broadway, New York, NY 10018, USA
29 Earlsfort Terrace, Dublin 2, Ireland

BLOOMSBURY, BLOOMSBURY ACADEMIC and the Diana logo are
trademarks of Bloomsbury Publishing Plc

First published in Great Britain 2023
This paperback edition published 2025

Copyright © Damon T. Berry, 2023

Damon T. Berry has asserted his right under the Copyright, Designs and
Patents Act, 1988, to be identified as Author of this work.

For legal purposes the Acknowledgments on pp. viii–ix constitute
an extension of this copyright page.

Cover image: Moussa81/ Getty Images

All rights reserved. No part of this publication may be reproduced or
transmitted in any form or by any means, electronic or mechanical, including
photocopying, recording, or any information storage or retrieval system,
without prior permission in writing from the publishers.

Bloomsbury Publishing Plc does not have any control over, or responsibility for,
any third-party websites referred to or in this book. All internet addresses given in this
book were correct at the time of going to press. The author and publisher regret any
inconvenience caused if addresses have changed or sites have ceased to exist,
but can accept no responsibility for any such changes.

A catalogue record for this book is available from the British Library.

A catalog record for this book is available from the Library of Congress.

ISBN: HB: 978-1-3501-7943-1
       PB: 978-1-3503-8484-2
       ePDF: 978-1-3501-7944-8
       eBook: 978-1-3501-7945-5

Typeset by Integra Software Services Pvt. Ltd.

To find out more about our authors and books visit www.bloomsbury.com
and sign up for our newsletters.

For Ray, the man who taught me everything worth knowing.

Contents

Acknowledgments — viii

Introduction: The Prophecy Voters — 1

1. Warfare and Dominion in the Second Apostolic Age — 15
2. Earthly Peril & Kingdom Promise — 43
3. "God's Chaos Candidate"—Prophecy & Trump's 2016 Campaign — 71
4. Cyrus versus the Deep State — 99
5. The 2020 Election—Spiritual Warfare by Other Means — 127

Conclusion: Prophetic Politics after Trump — 155

Notes — 171
Index — 204

Acknowledgments

Writing a book is often a solitary endeavor, but no book results from the efforts of a single person. This book develops further as it builds upon and expands greatly on what I have already written in an article published in *Nova Religio* in 2020 titled "Voting in the Kingdom: Prophecy Voters, The New Apostolic Reformation, and Christian Support for Trump." Since this is the case, I owe many debts to those who helped me so much to write that original article. First, special thanks Sabina Magliocco who, as the editor for that special edition of the journal, invited me to contribute to it. My friend, thank you for your kind words and generous spirit. Thank you to Catherine Wessinger, who worked tirelessly with me to prepare the article for publication. Your support and patient instruction benefited me greatly. Thanks also to Michael Ashcraft and others who reviewed the draft of the article and offered very helpful critiques. I also want to extend my gratitude to the editorial board of *Nova Religio* who so graciously awarded the article with the Thomas Robbins Award For Excellence in the Study of New Religious Movements for that year. Writing with and for those associated with the journal was certainly one of the high points of my relatively young career.

I want to thank Hugh Urban, from whose advice and friendship I have benefited since I was his student till now. I want to also thank all my colleagues at St. Lawrence University who continue to create such a wonderfully collaborative and supportive environment. I want to offer special thanks to my colleagues in the religious studies department, Arun Brahmbhatt, Mark MacWilliams, and Kathleen Self. Professor Self was particularly helpful, serving as our department chair throughout the pandemic and as I was producing this manuscript, teaching, and going through the tenure process. We all owe you a debt, my friend, for seeing our department through this difficult time. I owe you, too, for your consistent willingness to pull up a chair and if nothing else just to listen. Finally, I want to express my gratitude for all the hard work of our department administrator, Mary Ann Gera. So much of what we need to do our work would simply not happen without you. You are truly the heart of the department, my dear friend. Thank you so much for all you do for us.

I also wish to thank the wonderful people at Bloomsbury for inviting me to publish with them. Lalle Pursglove, Lily McMahon, and Kaveya Saravanan have been especially helpful, patient, supportive, and kind as I produced this book. It is one thing to have ideas and quite another to communicate them effectively. Thank you for your help in that regard.

Finally, I want to thank a few friends and family for their support and kindness. It is certainly an understatement to say that the past three years have been difficult. However, even remotely, I have enjoyed the fellowship of several wonderful people. Among these friends are Asbjørn Dyrendal, Allison Melnick, Yvonne Chireau, Genine Gehret, Bill & Jessica Schneider, Justin Woods, and so many others. My family, too, has been so comforting. Heather, Livi, and Aidan, you are everything that drives me to be better in all aspects of my life. Pam & Ray Riffle, I hope I continue to make you proud. Lastly, to Benny. You always make me smile. Thank you all for who you are.

Introduction: The Prophecy Voters

How could Donald Trump, who seemed the least likely champion of Christian values, win such incredible support among conservative Christians in 2016 and maintain that support through his tumultuous presidency, into the 2020 election, and even after he lost his bid for reelection? I argue that this answer is complex, and the specifics of that answer vary depending on which Christians one asks. Christian support for Trump not only represented large numbers of voters but also crossed denomination lines and included Catholics, Mormons, and a broad spectrum of evangelical Protestants, many of whom would not agree on significant theological issues. Among Trump's base of Christian support were independent Christian leaders not associated with a denominational hierarchy or established convention or fellowship, like the Southern Baptists or Grace Brethren Churches. Among these independent Christian leaders were charismatic Christians, including controversial ministry leaders like Paula White, President Trump's spiritual advisor, who is most associated with the prosperity gospel movement. Among these independent, charismatic Christian leaders who supported Trump was a less recognizable but influential network of self-proclaimed prophets and apostles associated with a movement known as the New Apostolic Reformation. This book is about this lesser-known movement and the reasons those associated with it gave for supporting Trump.

The first thing to note here is that the New Apostolic Reformation (NAR) is not a formal organization or denomination to which people can belong. The NAR is, in fact, specifically anti-denominational. Former Fuller Theological Seminary Professor C. Peter Wagner (1930–2016), who is responsible for coining the term New Apostolic Reformation, stated explicitly that the focus of the NAR was to create "extra-denominational networks."[1] Churches associated with this movement are not led by elected leadership or a board of directors but by modern-day apostles chosen by God, as demonstrated in the New Testament. He also said of the NAR in an article from 2001 that the NAR "is not an organization," that one does not "join or carry a card," and that it "has no leader."[2] As we will see more fully in Chapter 1, the NAR is better described as a network of like-minded individuals more in line with independent charismatic Christian movements than any specifically organized hierarchy or ministerial organization.

Individuals associated with the NAR, as did Wagner, believe in the continuance of the office and gifting of apostles as the proper leaders of Christ's church on Earth as described in the New Testament and the perpetuation of the gifts of the Holy Spirit, including prophecy. Deriving much from Pentecostal and charismatic traditions and movements, the NAR adapts trends that have come to define the prosperity gospel movement as well as spiritual warfare prayer practices common in charismatic Christian praxis. Those associated with the NAR also believe in a particular expression of dominionism, often referred to as the Seven Mountains Mandate or the Dominion Mandate. This mandate explicitly calls for God's people, as Wagner puts it in his 2008 book *Dominion! How Kingdom Action Can Change the World*, to establish dominion over the "seven supreme molders of culture—namely, religion, family, government, arts and entertainment, media, business, and education."[3]

The networked orientation of the NAR, their belief in the continuation of revelation through prophets of God's work on Earth regarding human affairs, combined with their understanding of a dominion mandate, gives shape to a particular understanding of what it means for one to engage in politics. I have elsewhere referred to those so motivated as *prophecy voters* and argued that they supported Trump because they believed, as they were informed through prophetic visions, that God chose him to save America from alleged demonic conspiracies aligned that seek to destroy America, keep it alienated from God's purpose and calling for the nation, thereby hindering the church's effort to establish the God's rule over all nations.[4] Prophecy voters' narratives imagined Trump as a vessel through which God was going to lead America into revival and correct covenant relationship with Him, and thereby make America the foundation for a global movement that would eventually, through Christians' dominion over social and political institutions, lead to the establishment of God's Kingdom on Earth.

Prophecies that Trump was God's choice for president were deeply informative to the political activity of those associated with the NAR, but that did not mean that social issues that had historically motivated conservative Christian voters were unimportant. On the contrary, although Trump did not embody the kind of character Christians expected from religious leaders, he possessed the correct temperament as a warrior who would fight on their behalf for social causes, they believed God anointed him to address as president. Moreover, Trump signaled to these voters repeatedly throughout the 2016 campaign that he would be their champion on critical issues and that he would appoint judges and cabinet members that shared their vision. Key issues included abortion, gay marriage, religious freedom, unequivocal support for Israel, and free-market economic prosperity. Precisely because of their commitment to ending abortion, for example, the prophecies that promised that Trump would disrupt the political status quo to appoint pro-life judges and thereby put an end to abortion, supporting Trump made even more sense from their perspective.

The prophets associated with the NAR revealed that God was using this seemingly un-Christian man to accomplish His goals. Moreover, Trump would fight the secretive forces seeking to subvert America's unique place in the world and God's divine plan for the nations. Trump's brazenness and antagonistic demeanor were assets that God would use to enable him to stand up to Leftists, support godly legislation, and reverse the course of the nation from God's judgment to move toward His divine favor, making America great once again. As such, Trump came to represent the type of leader religious conservatives need to accomplish their goal of social transformation—a brash warrior, a chaotic wild-card, a wrecking ball, a new King Cyrus.[5]

I argued before the 2020 election that "the conspiratorial and millennialist narratives propagated by those associated with the New Apostolic Reformation [would] continue to hold influence among the Christian Right in the United States through the 2020 presidential election," in part because of the NAR's "dualistic and conspiratorial vision of politics is not confined to the margins of charismatic Christianity, but is common among Trump's most vocal Christian supporters."[6] The chapters of this book further develop this thesis and expand on the conclusions to include a discussion of the 2020 election, the aftermath of Trump's loss, and its effects on the NAR. The main conclusions I reach in this regard are that prophetic ministries, especially those associated with the NAR, had to address their failed prophecies that Trump would win reelection, which led to a crisis in the meaning of prophetic ministry going into the post-Trump years. Moreover, this moment of concern for and debate over the future of prophetic ministry did not mean that they would abandon their commitment to social change through dominion over the main spheres of political life, far from it. Even when the prophets confessed that they were wrong in their predictions about the 2020 election, they reaffirmed their commitment to their political and social agendas. I argue further that because of their commitment to dominionism, those associated with the NAR will continue to be relevant to the development of the American Religious Right for the foreseeable future.

Prophecy Voters in Context

Donald Trump, a former reality show host who battled on pay-per-view television the World Wrestling Entertainment's then-owner Vince McMahon, a former casino owner, a multiply bankrupted businessman who regularly boasted of his sexual conquests and went through two rather messy divorces, did not fit the mold of the "values voters" candidate. Yet, like the relatively unreligious Ronald Reagan, Trump managed to signal that he was going to be the champion that Christian conservatives needed and promised, as did Reagan, to "make America great again."[7] However, early in the running for the Republican nomination for the 2016 election, conservative Christian voters seemed more likely to support candidates who had groomed their Christian Right bona fides more carefully. In December of 2015, *The Washington Post* reported, "While Trump gets all of the attention for his over-the-top statements, Cruz has staked out a position on the far right on virtually every major hot-button issue—from immigration to Obamacare to national security and the fight with ISIS. And, tonally, Cruz comes across as aggressively and unapologetically conservative—a less controversial and unelectable version of Trump."[8] The hesitation in supporting Trump among some conservative Christians did not hold as the campaign for the GOP nomination continued.

In July 2016, Pew Research released a report explaining that the aggressive newcomer was heading into the 2016 election with the support of "churchgoing Republicans," some of whom were not previously supportive of his nomination. The report stated at that time "Churchgoing GOP voters were as supportive of Trump in the general election as Republicans who attend religious services less than once a week," and that "[n]early nine-in-ten GOP registered voters who attend religious services weekly say they would vote for Trump over Clinton if the election were held today, including 40% who say they would 'strongly' support Trump in the general election."[9]

It is difficult to be sure precisely what caused this change in support but what is known is that in his pursuit of the GOP nomination in 2016 and the ensuing campaign for the presidency, Trump specifically spoke to the issues that had motivated conservative Christian voters while maintaining his belligerent attitude toward anyone who challenged his path to the White House. While his attacks on political opponents and critics seemed perfectly in character for Trump the businessman and reality show star, his relatively new positions on abortion and other social issues seemed to be at odds with statements he made earlier in his public life. In 1999 in an interview on *Meet the Press*, Trump said that he was, even in the context of so-called partial-birth abortion, "pro-choice in every respect," though he did say that he did not like abortion.[10] Contrast that statement with his claim in 2011, when he first seemed to seriously consider a run for the presidency, that he was pro-life, and in August of 2015, again, he said that he was "very, very proud to say that I am pro-life."[11] Finally, in a statement that he later attempted to qualify differently, he claimed regarding women who choose to have an abortion that "there has to be some form of punishment."[12]

In addition to this confessed change in personal outlook on abortion, Trump promised to appoint conservative justices to the Supreme Court who would overturn Roe v. Wade.[13] During his term, Trump appointed three judges to the Supreme Court who did vote to overrule Roe, to the delight of his Christian supporters.[14] Christian author and journalist Daniel Silliman concludes that this was a demonstration that at least some of Trump's Christian base, who might have had reservations about his candidacy, saw him as the right person for the presidency. He writes, "While abortion was never evangelicals' only issue, in the voting booth it often outweighed all other concerns," and while some of them supported Trump "despite moral misgivings," considering his promise to appoint pro-life justices to the court, "The political calculation appears to have paid off."[15]

Trump's appeals to issues like abortion and gay marriage seemed insufficient to explain Trump's support from white Evangelical Protestants formerly described as "values voters." Robert P. Jones, founding CEO of Public Religion Research Institute (PRRI), and his team of researchers are primarily responsible for the much-referenced datum that 81 percent of white evangelical Protestants voted for Trump in 2016, stating, "No religious group is more strongly backing Trump's candidacy than white evangelical Protestants."[16] In *The End of White Christian America* (2015), Jones explains how, in the words of his article in *The Atlantic*, values voters had become "nostalgia voters."[17] He argues that the white evangelical Protestants had found themselves "in the position of having lost much cultural power while still retaining—at least in the southern enclaves—the remains of significant political clout" and that, in that sense, were prepared to "mortgage the future in a fight to resurrect the past."[18]

Other researchers and observers, however, saw more going on with the Evangelical vote in 2016 than racial dynamics or nostalgia. Popular Christian writer and speaker Stephen Mansfield wrote in 2017 that the motives for such incredible Christian support for Trump were reactionary and emotional. "By the dawn of the 2016 presidential race," he argues, "religious conservatives were traumatized by the Obama years and fearful of a second Clinton presidency would mean more of the same." In this reaction, Mansfield claims, "They would back anyone who could win," even "a nonbeliever" or someone "of doubtful morality."[19] In May of 2022, in an affirmation that Silliman was perhaps correct, a guest on Lance Wallnau's podcast explained that while she had supported Trump, some Christian "held their nose" and voted for him "to put conservative justices on the Supreme Court to overturn Roe v. Wade."[20]

Similarly, in a 2018 article for *Christianity Today*, Ed Stetzer, Executive Director of the Wheaton College Billy Graham Center, and Andrew MacDonald, Associate Director of the Billy Graham Center Institute, argued that Jones's explanation was incomplete. They write that faced with the choice of Hillary Clinton or Donald Trump, conservative Christians felt compelled to vote for the Republican nominee and thereby stay consistent with their voting history rather than support a candidate with whom they had no agreement on any significant issues.[21] Stetzer and MacDonald argue further from a 2018 Pew study that "evangelicals voted more along Republican values than traditional social conservative values," especially concerning abortion. "Some Trump voters legitimately wrestled through his personal immorality for national policies they believed in," they argue. In contrast, others "seemed oblivious to Trump's personal life, and a sizable group justified and even embraced his controversial character as a sign of toughness."

During his term of office, Trump maintained this loyal following among conservative Christians. In March of 2018, Pew Research released a report that revealed Trump held his support among evangelical Protestants even as other religious groups seemed to sour on his presidency.[22] At the very start of his 2020 reelection campaign, Trump sought to secure his base of Christian support by continuing the talking points that had gained him conservative Christian support, represented in his continued appeal to his promises to defend religious freedom, his support for Israel, and his commitment to being their champion if reelected. Even after the riots on January 6, 2021, support for Trump among his Christian base seemed little affected. Steadfast support for Trump, seemingly despite all that had transpired, was especially prevalent among those prophecy voters who continued to insist that the prophecies that Trump would remain president were still accurate.[23]

In June of 2021, *NPR* reporter Danielle Kurtzleben wrote that while Trump faltered on fundamental points of Evangelical discourse, including the statement that he was not sure if he ever asked God for forgiveness or when he referred to Second Corinthians as "two Corinthians," support from conservative Christians was forthcoming as he "he wrapped more traditionally conservative Christian issues like abortion in with his own particular cultural fixations, such as race and grievance politics."[24] This conclusion is quite close to what Stetzer and MacDonald argue in that Kurtzleben contends that support for Trump even after the election dovetails with issues associated with cultural issues that long motivated Christian conservatives in America.

One must consider, too, that Trump's boorishness and bellicosity were not terribly far from the kind of personality that conservative Christians had come to embrace. For the Trump supporters among the networks of apostles and prophets associated with the NAR, Trump's belligerence was an asset, even if later some expressed concern that it could go too far. Historian Kristin Kobes

Du Mez wrote in *Jesus and John Wayne: How White Evangelicals Corrupter a Faith and Fractured a Nation* (2020), "In 2016, many observers were stunned at evangelicals' apparent betrayal of their own values." However, she argues, these observers failed to notice that Trump's evangelical supporters "did not cast their vote despite their beliefs but because of them." Du Mez argues that there had already been a militant turn among this demographic who had "replaced the Jesus of the Gospels with a vengeful warrior Christ," and that support for Trump from this demographic should not surprise us. "Donald Trump did not trigger this militant turn," she argues. Instead, "his rise was symptomatic of a long-standing condition."[25] Remarking in an interview in June of 2022, Du Mez states, "At a time when many evangelicals perceived their values to be under fire, they looked to Trump as their 'ultimate fighting champion,' a man who would not be afraid to throw his weight around to protect 'Christian America' against threats both foreign and domestic."[26]

One should conclude that the motives for Christians' support for Trump were complex and varied. These reasons included party loyalty, resentment, and continued support for social and political issues that have long motivated conservative Christians, like abortion and gay rights, mingled with a sense that Christian America was in peril if Christians failed to support Trump and his mission to make America great again. Of course, we cannot ignore the racialized elements of Trump's messaging, specifically, the way that white identity politics formed a core component of his rhetoric and that white nationalists, especially those associated with the Alt-Right, saw him as a champion for their cause. In that regard, there was no small overlap with the broad base of Trump's supporters and evangelical Christians on issues like immigration, pointing to the anxieties of demographic changes and cultural shifts shared by white evangelicals and others in Trump's base of support.

Adding to this complex picture is the work of sociologists Andrew L. Whitehead and Samuel L. Perry in *Taking Back America for God: Christian Nationalism in the United States* (2020). They describe how support for Trump was shaped by Christian nationalism, which they describe as "a cultural framework—a collection of myths, traditions, symbols, narratives, and value systems—that idealizes and advances a fusion of Christianity with American civic life."[27] Further, they claim that Christian support for Trump, "[c]ontrary to the dominant narrative offered by pollsters and pundits, the answer isn't simply 'white evangelicalism' or 'conservative Christianity,'" but "that Christian nationalism motivates Americans—whether they are Evangelicals or not—to see Trump as the defender of the values they perceive are being threatened."[28] They conclude that "[a]t least since the early 1800s, Christian nationalism has provided the unifying myths, traditions, narratives, and value systems that have historically been deployed to preserve the interests of those who wish to halt or turn back changes occurring within American society."[29]

Analyses by Stetzer, MacDonald, Kurtzleben, Du Mez, as well as Perry and Whitehead list several motives for Christians' support for Trump and highlight the complexity among the broader population of Christian voters who supported Trump. Their perspectives shed light on the various responses that led to their support for Trump, triggered by racial and xenophobic anxieties, as well as or at odds with possible pragmatic concerns and specific interests of those who feared demographic and cultural shifts in American society. In this book, I want to expose further complexity by drawing attention to Christian support for Trump articulated by the network of charismatic Christians associated with the NAR. In the complexity of Christian nationalist mythological tropes, resentment, white racial anxiety, and support for conservative issues, among the reasons noted for Christians' support for Trump was also the conviction among the prophecy voters who regarded Trump as anointed by God, as confirmed by their prophets and apostles, to reverse the fortunes of America and to put the nation on track to play a significant role in establishing the Kingdom of God. This disposition brought with it a sense of inevitability that God's will be done but simultaneously a combative approach that articulated the political drama of the Trump years as a battle between the spiritual forces of good and evil.

Pentecostal theologian Amos Yong wrote concerning the kinds of spiritual warfare practices among those associated with the NAR meant a demonization of the political opposition and designating that demonic opposition as possessing control over a specific domain, whether that be geographical or over an entire people-group. This practice came to be called spiritual mapping. In his 2010 book titled *In The Days of Caesar: Pentecostalism and Political Theology*, Yong wrote, "This kind of spiritual warfare prayer includes but goes beyond New Testament injunctions to pray for leaders of governments (e.g., 1 Tim. 2:1–2) since there is a more proactive agenda of countering the political effects of alleged spiritual entities."[30] He goes on to say that in "today's political environment" such practices "have translated into what might be considered as 'politically incorrect' pentecostal political practices," and as such at each level "involves a demonization of the political 'enemy,' whether understood in terms of social problems or in terms of the political opposition."[31]

In the context of support for Trump, those associated with the NAR frequently expressed this attitude toward framing political events in terms of spiritual warfare in the form of intercessory prayer to shield Trump from demonic attack, which could take the form of illness, threats to his life or his family, or even political opposition and criticism. For these Christians, the very notion of supporting Trump meant to be engaged in active spiritual warfare on his behalf as they were led through the directives of prophets and apostles. Political activism, especially voting, was itself seen as an extension of these activities, informed by prophetic and apostolic leaders and teachers.

The results of the 2020 election presented a significant challenge for the prophecy voters. Despite the assertion of the same prophets that claimed Trump would win in 2016 and claimed he would win once again through divine intervention, he lost. What followed was a period of denial, concern, and reflection on why the prophets got the election wrong and what that meant for prophetic ministries in the future. However, in whatever ways the failed 2020 prophecies contributed to a moment of self-reflection among the prophecy voters, it did not lessen their commitment to the social and political causes they identified as central to God's concern. Moreover, there seemed to be a deepening of the political alliances between socially and politically conservative Christians still loyal to President Trump's vision and the cross-denominational cooperation, even among those Christians whose traditions were historically at odds with one another over critical theological issues. This tendency to prioritize political orthodoxy has also plunged churches in America into a crisis concerning their doctrinal and political allegiances. As Kristin Kobes Du Mez argues, "In the past some issues that divided evangelicals, such as speaking in tongues, End Times theology, Calvinism—all of those things have receded, and it's now these social and political issues that define allegiances."[32] In this context, political alignment seemed to inform the boundaries of what it meant to be an authentic Christian rather than theological positions or ecclesiastical affiliation. Christians who share little theological affinity are finding communion over a political vision for America, and this coalition includes those associated with the NAR.

Framing the Book

My approach to this book is as a historian of religion. This approach is rooted in what the historian of religions Bruce Lincoln describes in "Theses on Method" as one that focuses on "discussing the temporal, contextual, situated, interested, human, and material dimensions of those discourses, practices, and institutions that characteristically represent themselves as eternal, transcendent, spiritual, and divine."[33] As a historian of religion, to quote historian of religions Hugh B. Urban, my goal is to "situate this complex spiritual movement very concretely in its specific historical context."[34] In this book, therefore, I aim to contextualize the various claims of those associated with the NAR and the form of Christianity it exemplifies to add clarity and specificity to the complex picture of Christian support for Trump. I will also demonstrate that the prophecy voters were not simply on the periphery of Trump's Christian base but incorporated the language of the established Religious Right and contributed to its deployment in the Trump years.

To accomplish these goals, I focus on primary sources to structure the chapters to establish familiarity with the history and specific teachings of the New Apostolic Reformation and the theological perspectives of those associated with the movement. Once we have introduced the NAR in the first two chapters, we proceed chronologically from the 2016 campaign, through Trump's presidency, into the 2020 election, and finally, to the first two years after the 2020 election to chart how leaders associated with the NAR responded to changing political and social conditions, including the Trump's defeat in 2020.

In the first chapter, I describe the historical origin of the NAR and the accompanying development of the ideology of dominionism associated with it. Further, I elaborate upon the role of specific spiritual warfare practices associated with how those associated with the movement understand how to achieve dominion. I explain how the missionary mandate to establish political and social dominion so prioritized within the networks of apostles and prophets associated with the NAR necessarily incorporates a progressive vision of making the world better by destabilizing demonic strongholds over geographical spaces, or even entire nations, to make way for the establishment of the Kingdom of God.

In Chapter 2, I further elaborate on the ideology of the NAR as it relates to the millennialism associated with the dominion mandate that the movement emphasizes. Related to this millennialism that posits that Christians, through the power of the Holy Spirit, are taking back earthly dominion from Satan are apocalyptic warnings that should Christians fail to do their duty, catastrophe will befall them, their communities, and their nations. Necessary to these conceptions of taking dominion from Satanic forces is the conviction that Satan and his allies are at war with Christians and with God to retain control over crucial geographical spaces and social institutions. Narratives concerning a conspiracy of malevolent entities behind the machinations of destructive governmental and extra-governmental agencies that seek to subvert God's Kingdom are a necessary component of the thought of those associated with the NAR and deeply inform their political discourse. In this context, long-standing conspiratorial tropes of communist and leftist subversion of America and the Christian faith blend with the NAR's dominionism to shape the reasons they support Trump as God's chosen leader.

Chapters 3 through 5 follow the deployment of the discourse from the 2016 campaign through Trump's failed attempt at reelection and describe how this shifted from Trump's victory in 2016 to his defeat in 2020 and how prophecy voters coped with the election loss and their failed prophecies. In Chapter 3, I argue that if we want to understand the dynamics behind the Trump prophecies that inspired so much support from those associated with the NAR, we should approach prophecy in the NAR, especially as it relates to Trump, as a project of imaginative world-building. That is the prophets narratively constructed the election to have a specific prophetic spiritual significance for America and the fate of the world. This chapter will build upon the contextualization of the previous chapters to describe NAR's support for Trump's candidacy for the Republican nomination and then for the presidency.

In Chapter 4, I describe how a sense of avertive apocalypticism, hopeful millennialism, and the emphatic dominionism of key figures associated with the New Apostolic Reformation molded how they understood and described Trump's presidency. Of particular concern in this chapter, too, is the significant role of conspiratorial narratives about evil forces working to subvert Trump's efforts to save the nation in shaping their defense of the president. NAR leaders argued that God specifically chose Trump and anointed him for the task of restoring America to Himself, which meant that satanic forces seeking to undermine or even destroy what he was going to do for America would attack Trump. Every political attack or legal challenge demonstrated that the enemy was indeed frightened of what God would accomplish through Trump.

In Chapter 5, we look closely at the narratives presented by prophets associated with the NAR before, during, and after the 2020 election to see how, in some ways, these narratives were a continuation of the claims in 2016 and throughout Trump's presidency, but also that these prophecies differed in that they continually adapted to the tumult of the months leading up to the election and after to adjust their prophetic outlook to challenging and ever-shifting circumstances during the pandemic and the increasingly bleak prospect that Trump would be reelected. The 2020 election was expected to confirm the ambitions of those prophets who saw Trump as God's anointed leader for this moment in American history. Yet, it became a moment to question their own prophetic vision and, in some cases, the future of prophetic ministries. While some concerned themselves with the future development of prophetic ministries, none of the leaders among the prophecy voters seemed willing to abandon their dominionist commitments or the political activism or spiritual warfare that would ultimately bring God victory.

In the conclusion that follows, I summarize what I have learned in studying the NAR's support for Trump and contextualize that with the broader shifts among American Christian organizations politically and demographically in part because of the deepening partisan political divide in the United States today relative to the Trump years and the 2020 election. One of those main lessons is that there persists a theological elasticity to political cooperation among the Religious Right in America. As religion scholar Anthea Butler noted in her 2012 article, "From Republican Party to Republican Religion: The New Political Evangelists of the Right," connections across theological and denominational lines are not unprecedented in the Republican Party.[35] I argue that her point remains especially prescient now, and I would add that it is certainly no longer something we should consider anomalous.

Those who supported Trump from among the broad spectrum of traditions and persuasions of American Christianity, no matter how bitter his defeat or controversial his actions or legacy, regarded him as a gift from God. Some meant that more literally than others, but with the Supreme Court's ruling on Roe, Trump's legacy was solidified for his Christian supporters regardless of their theological or denominational affiliations. For the prophecy voters in particular despite his flaws and loss in 2020, no matter how they individually responded to the failed prophecies concerning the recent election, Trump was God's anointed leader and was indeed their American Cyrus.

1

Warfare and Dominion in the Second Apostolic Age

Though the New Apostolic Reformation is obscure to the general public, scholars of religion, journalists, and critics of the movement have been writing about and discussing this network of prophets and apostles for over a decade. There have been two scholarly books; one by historian John Weaver (2016), which focuses on the movement's history, and another only available in French by religious studies scholar André Gagné (2021) that broadly addresses charismatic Christians' support of Trump's presidency with references to the NAR.[1] There are now a few academic articles on the topic, including my article published in 2020 and a theological assessment by Arne Helge Teigen in an article that addresses the Trump prophecies phenomenon and the NAR.[2] The NAR is also discussed in the broader scholarship on the religious right in America and the recent history of Pentecostalism and charismatic movements. Religion scholar James Davidson Hunter, for example, in his 2010 book *To Change the World: The Irony, Tragedy, & Possibility of Christianity in the Late Modern World*, writes that the "Christian Right is far from dead as a movement," but that it is "undergoing a crisis and a transformation."[3] He argues that NAR-affiliated groups, in particular, have emerged with a focus on transforming culture in a holistic sense and not necessarily focused on strictly political reforms in the way the former religious right in America was. Hunter quotes at length from Reclaiming the 7 Mountains Culture, one of the groups in the orbit of the NAR networks, to prove his point that the movement emphasizes dominion over these strategic "mountains," or spheres of social and political life, to eventually themselves "control what influences our culture."[4]

The NAR has also been the focus of journalistic reports, especially in the context of presidential politics in the United States. In 2011, NPR's program

Fresh Air featured an interview with C. Peter Wagner, focusing on the movement's relationship with Rick Perry's prayer rally.[5] That same year, Sarah Posner also wrote concerning Perry's prayer rally and its associations with those associated with the NAR.[6] In both cases, the focus was on understanding the movement, its doctrines, its significant leaders, and, most importantly, what their associations were with politicians like Rick Perry and Michelle Bachmann. Posner references a story in *The Texas Observer* by Forrest Wilder about Perry's relationship with charismatic Christians, particularly those associated with the NAR.[7] She notes that while a broad coalition formed around Perry during the prayer rally, it represented a "cross-pollination" of ideas among charismatic Christians and politics, which for her was not entirely novel as a phenomenon. Posner writes:

> Taking dominion of government and other social, cultural, and political structures has long been the overtly stated goal of the religious right, long documented by scholars and journalists from Sara Diamond to Fred Clarkson to Michelle Goldberg. The NAR might have coined the "Seven Mountains" terminology, but it's just a different way of presenting what the religious right has wanted all along.

The point for Posner is that the NAR is a further expression of the American Religious Right's ambitions to transform the American political and cultural landscape.

Rachel Tabachnick, an independent researcher focused on the Religious Right, has also written extensively on NAR. In an interview on September 12, 2011, she describes the main features of the NAR, noting the significance of its dominionist ideology and its connections to political figures like Rick Perry, who was actively seeking the Republican nomination at the time.[8] In March of 2013, Tabachnick wrote for Political Research Associates, restating much of what she shared in the 2011 interview, this time focusing on the anti-gay agenda in the movement.[9] Of particular interest here is that as she once again affirms the importance of the ecclesiastical reform the NAR wants to enact, she also notes that this movement has, in a sense, moved beyond its own brand. Tabachnick notes, for example, a shift away from "democratic governance" within churches, advocated by influential pastors like Rick Warren, whose famous Saddleback Church was affiliated with the Southern

Baptist Convention, had "echoed" the point of the ecclesiastic reforms of the NAR in stating the church leaders should possess "spiritual gifts." Tabachnick reminds us that Warren wrote in his dissertation concerning the apostolic office, "You don't find anybody getting elected in the New Testament."[10]

The NAR has had its critics from within Christian communities as well. For example, the late pastor and Christian apologist Ken Silva noted with disapproval on his ministry's website the connection between Rick Warren and C. Peter Wagner.[11] Silva's report relates information from another critic of the NAR, Sandy Simpson, who describes Wager's association with the Latter Rain movement, which Silva flatly calls a heresy. For Silva and other critics of the NAR, the movement is simply heretical. For others, the concern about the NAR reflects suspicion of the movement's potential for abuses of ecclesiastical offices to go unchecked.

R. Douglass Geivett, a professor of philosophy at Biola University, and Holly Pivec, an independent Christian writer, have coauthored two books on the NAR.[12] They contend that the movement presents certain dangers, particularly in that it fosters dependency on "apostles and prophets who exert unhealthy and unbiblical control" over the lives of their followers, and that "[w]hen promises made by NAR leaders don't pan out … many people grow disillusioned," assuming that that "God had failed them."[13] For them and other Christian critics of the NAR, the movement distorts essential Christian doctrines, supports an undemocratic and unaccountable ecclesiastical hierarchy, and provides misleading and often-incorrect prophetic advice and assertions.

The objections noted by Gievett and Pivec fit within the broader critique of what other critics perceive as the excesses of certain charismatic Christian movements, particularly the prosperity gospel movement; most notably criticisms emerging from influential figures like Costi Hinn, the nephew of the well-known faith healer Benny Hinn, and Pastor John MacArthur. MacArthur's criticism of the NAR is rooted in his earlier criticism of what he regards as excesses and even heresies in Charismatic movements in his 1978 book *The Charismatics*, which was later revised and republished as *Charismatic Chaos* in 1992.[14] In this revised version, MacArthur argues that C. Peter Wagner's notion of "power evangelism," a key component of how the NAR comes to understand itself as using signs and miracles to augment the effect of the Gospel message, is in fact "hardly evangelism at all," and that accusing its proponents of "badly corrupting the saving message."[15]

In his 2013 book *Strange Fire: The Danger of Offending the Holy Spirit with Counterfeit Worship*, MacArthur calls the New Apostolic Reformation a "fraud" and remarks with concern that it had become increasingly popular among charismatic churches.[16] MacArthur and other critics of the NAR and its related charismatic expressions, including influential theologians and evangelical figures like R.C. Sproul and Joni Eareckson Tada, met in 2013 at his Strange Fire conference to evaluate and critique "the doctrines, claims, and practices of the modern charismatic movement, and [to affirm] the true Person and ministry of the Holy Spirit."[17] Among the movements discussed was, of course, the NAR.

Costi Hinn and pastor Anthony G. Wood express similar criticisms in a 2018 book that includes John MacArthur's foreword. Hinn and Wood's denunciations of the NAR and other charismatic excesses are direct; however, they argue that while one might criticize the ideas and practices of figures like Wimbur and others associated with certain charismatic traditions, they contend that not all of them are necessarily heretical. On the other hand, Hinn and Wood describe C. Peter Wagner as having "embodied the essence of a false teacher."[18] Echoing the criticisms and concerns of Geivett and Pivec, they argue the NAR is creating a "new breed of self-proclaimed apostles" who operate outside any "accountability structures."[19]

These Christian critics of the NAR were not alone in their concerns. In an early critique of the NAR from 2009, prominent scholar of religion Anthea Butler questioned if the movement was a problem for charismatic and Pentecostal Christianity.[20] She noted:

> For a movement that started out with a millennial orientation, it has certainly become enamored with the world, and remaining powerful within it in every way. Whatever these new tribbles of Prosperity and Apostolic leadership are, it is time to pay them even closer attention, before they overrun the ship entirely.

Using the analogy of the tribbles from Star Trek, she worries that the NAR and prosperity gospel ideologies and practices are, in fact, becoming problematically popular among charismatic Evangelicals in the twenty-first century. In an interview with Sarah Posner in 2012, Butler noted concern that commentators erroneously minimized the importance and influence of the NAR. "Yes, the NAR isn't in a vacuum and more powerful than other movements, but it should not be dismissed either."[21] She adds, "For the last 30 years, journalists have had an easy time reporting on the religious right, because all they did was pay attention to white male leaders of big organizations like Focus on the Family, National Association of Evangelicals, or Family Research Council." She goes on, "The days when a nice soundbite from Jerry Falwell, James Dobson, or Ted Haggard would suffice are over," and that if "journalists and others want to understand the last 10 years of the religious right movement, they will need to pay attention to the theological, religious, and ethnic diversity among evangelicals, Pentecostals, and non-denominational churches." For Butler, the NAR was not only affecting churches but also adding more theological and organizational diversity within the Religious Right.[22]

The descriptions and criticisms of the NAR mentioned above are important for us to consider as we proceed through the chapters in this book. One of the aspects of the support Trump enjoyed from the NAR that we must consider is that in supporting Trump, leaders associated with the NAR politically allied themselves with their conservative Christian critics. This point certainly relates to Posner's cross-pollination in her Religion Dispatches article. Moreover, as Anthea Butler worried even before the 2011 Perry-led prayer rally that focused so much journalistic attention on the NAR, there is something to be said about the popularity of this expression of Christianity in general. There is, in short, no misunderstanding that the NAR is significant to developments within Christian support for Trump, especially within the context of the influence of an increasingly theologically diverse yet politically allied Religious Right in America.

In this chapter, we will begin to lay the groundwork for understanding the NAR's support for Trump. Crucial to this understanding is the origins of the movement's name in emphasizing its efforts at popularizing a particular understanding of ecclesiastical reform and how this has been tied to a perceived mandate to establish social and political dominion over communities, states, and local jurisdictions, and even entire nations. Further, we should understand that this mandate for dominion is bound to specific practices of spiritual warfare and intercessory prayer. In the next chapter, continue providing more context for NAR support for Trump by describing the peculiar eschatological vision that sets the movement apart from the more familiar dispensational eschatology expressed, for example, in the popular *Left Behind* series and the Christian Zionism of John Hagee. Further still, in the following chapter, we will discuss how conspiratorial narratives among those associated with the NAR overlap with the broader spectrum of Trump's supporters and how these narratives tie directly back to their understanding of the place of spiritual warfare and intercessory prayer in relation to their dominion mandate.

The Origins of the NAR

Defining the membership of the NAR presents difficulties. First, it is not a formal organization, or a denomination, to which people can belong on official rolls. It is specifically anti-denominational. C. Peter Wagner explicitly states that the NAR's focus was to create "extra-denominational networks."[23] Wagner also said of the NAR in an article in 2011 published in *Charisma News*:

> The NAR is not an organization. No one can join or carry a card. It has no leader. I have been called the "founder," but this is not the case. One reason I might be seen as an "intellectual godfather" is that I might have been the first to observe the movement, give a name to it, and describe its characteristics as I saw them.[24]

To accurately picture the NAR, we must imagine a network of like-minded Christians who share a similar vision of the church's organization and its role in transforming society but do not organize themselves into formal associations. It is far more accurate to think of those associated with the NAR in terms of a network of apostles, prophets, ministry leaders, and public personalities who affiliate with one another in relation to a set of mutually held ideas.

Additionally, some of those who have been associated with the NAR by its critics have denied connections or that the NAR exists. An influential charismatic teacher and writer named Michael Brown has argued that the NAR is neither an organization nor a movement. Referring to Gievett and Pivec's criticism, he writes, "they included Charismatic leaders who believe in five-fold ministry today (as I have, for decades) and grouped them together as part of NAR." He complains that Gievett and Pivec "also painted an extremely negative picture" of the movement, "although [he believes] that the authors were sincere in their writing and sought to do solid research." He goes on, "In the end, we are left with a totally ambiguous picture of what NAR actually is, making it all the more dangerous in the minds of the conspiratorial critics, who inevitably believe the worst."[25]

Brown further points to the statement by The International House of Prayer, pastored by Mike Bickle, in which they refute any connection to the NAR. The statement argues:

> In much of the writing against NAR, there are strong implications that NAR is an organized movement with such things as "leaders," "spokespeople," "theology," "interpretations of the Bible," and even a NAR translation of the Bible. This presentation is misleading and disingenuous at best, as these same writers will add caveats that no such organizational apparatus or agreement between leaders and spokespeople exists.[26]

Brown further argues in his article, "In short, what the critics have basically done is take whatever trends they differ with in [sic] the worldwide Pentecostal-Charismatic movement, group them all together, and put them under the heading of NAR—even though this is not what NAR has ever meant."

I am sympathetic to Brown's contention and agree to an extent that those involved in what Brown calls the worldwide Pentecostal-Charismatic movement might be mistakenly lumped into the category of the NAR by its critics. Not all those referenced in this study would self-identify as part of the NAR. However, I want to refer here to what sociologists Brad Christerson and Richard Flory describe as a new form of organizing focused less on the denominational hierarchy than on networks of independent churches existing outside formal organizations that they call "Independent Network Christianity," or "INC Christianity." They explain that this form of Christian organizational practice comprises "networks of dynamic individual leaders rather than of congregations and denominations."[27] Their study references the NAR and those associated with Wagner but, like Bickle, parted ways from Wagner as the NAR developed. However, while Christerson and Flory opted for the INC designation for their more broadly focused study, I find the term "New Apostolic Reformation" useful, despite the controversy around the term's usages, to center our attention on figures who contributed significantly to developing its teachings and practices, and who felt that these teachings and the apostolic framework were essential for the future development of the church and fulfilling its earthly mission.[28]

Primarily, the NAR signifies a change in ecclesiastical structure that at once resembles more closely the New Testament paradigm, its proponents argue, and something more fitting for the further working of God on Earth. For example, apostle Ché Ahn, Wagner's protégé, describes Wagner as his "spiritual father," quotes Wagner in the prologue to his 2019 book *Modern-Day Apostles: Operating in Your Apostolic Office and Anointing* to explain what this reformation means. According to Wagner, the NAR represented a "paradigm shift" in that the church was "moving from bureaucratic authority personal authority; from legal structure to relational structure; from control to coordination; and from rational leadership to charismatic leadership." He argues that the church's success relies not on rational, effective bureaucratic governance but "on the personal leadership of apostles rather than organizational systems."[29]

The NAR emerged in the late 1990s from earlier charismatic Christian movements. Weaver calls particular attention to the importance of the Latter Rain movement (1948–52) that helped to popularize the growth of independent charismatic churches. He notes that charismatic and Pentecostal movements were encouraged by a "flourishing network of leaders" that guided a further "Charismatic renewal," offering prophetic visions, demonstrations of spiritual gifts, and instruction on how they might establish the Kingdom of God.[30] However, some of these movements were controversial, as is the NAR today, even among Pentecostals and charismatic Christians.

In his 1988 book, *The Third Wave of the Holy Spirit: Encountering the Power of Signs and Wonders*, Wagner described the "Third Wave," a term he says he coined as a matter of convenient reference, as a "new moving of the Holy Spirit among evangelicals who, for one reason or another, have chosen not to identify with Pentecostals or charismatics," but who accept that the "Spirit of God" is working in similar ways that Pentecostals and charismatics have already taken as proper to Christian thought.[31] This Third Wave movement grew out of the Kansas City Prophets movement, rooted in the ministries of charismatic Christian leaders like Mike Bickle, founder of the International

House of Prayer based in Kansas City, Missouri. It influenced both the prosperity gospel movement and NAR. The 1994 Toronto Blessing, named after the city in which participants associated with the Vineyard Churches exhibited potent responses to prayer, including weeping and uncontrollable laughing, also became a significant factor in the birth of the NAR.[32]

These early connections between the various expressions of charismatic and Pentecostal Christianity are at the core of what eventually became the NAR. Indeed, before they parted ways over differences of opinion regarding spiritual warfare practices, John Wimber (1934–97), the influential former leader of the Vineyard Movement, wrote the foreword to Wagner's *The Third Wave of the Holy Spirit*.[33] Further, As Wagner counted himself as among those Christians with no previous connection to charismatic Christianity, he credited Wimber, whom he regarded as a close friend, for having aided his "own spiritual pilgrimage" to accept the working of the Holy Spirit.[34]

Wagner fully expressed the meaning of the NAR in his 1999 book *Churchquake! How The New Apostolic Reformation Is Shaking Up the Church as We Know It*. However, that was not the first place where he described it. In a collection of essays titled *The New Apostolic Churches: Rediscovering the New Testament Model of Leadership and Why It Is God's Desire for The Church Today*, which Wagner edited, he contributed an essay titled "The New Apostolic Reformation." Referencing Matthew 9:17, Wagner argues that throughout the ages, the church has changed or adapted and put into "new wineskins."[35] Wagner further explains that this new vision of the church came into view in 1993 as he was, as a missiologist, "picking up certain tidbits and pieces of information" about what was happening in the world related to evangelism.[36] Among these "tidbits" were the tremendous growth and success of African Independent Churches, Chinese house churches, and Latin American grassroots churches, all of which seemed to demonstrate the popularity and potency of independent churches that worked in networks with other church organizations and who sometimes exhibited the qualities of charismatic Christian worship and praxis. What at first seemed to be unrelated events became the groundwork for Wagner's effort to define what these churches had in common.[37]

In this essay, Wagner goes on to summarize what he later elaborates upon in *Churchquake!*, and to explain that the name NAR was, in fact, a neologism for what he saw in the examples that he mentioned. He had studied Pentecostalism and other charismatic movements for years before this. Still, he explains, as he was preparing to teach a course at Fuller Theological Seminary on the topic of this new ecclesiastical movement, it required a name. He did not like the initial phraseology of "independent charismatic" churches because, as he argues, they saw themselves as "interdependent, as opposed to independent," and they were "not all charismatic in orientation."[38] Finally, the name he "settled on for the movement is the New Apostolic Reformation, and individual churches being designated as new apostolic churches."[39]

In his 2010 memoir, Wagner again explains that he devised the NAR to describe what he was observing as an ongoing work of the Spirit of God among churches attuned to this recent development of how God was directing the church. He explains further, "I used the word 'reformation' because, as I have said, these new wineskins appear to be producing at least as radical a change as those of the Protestant Reformation 500 years ago."[40] He goes on to explain that the word "apostolic" speaks to the "strong focus on outreach, plus a recognition of present-day apostolic ministries," along with "the affirmation of the contemporary gift of and office of apostle," which he argues is the most distinguishing factor of the movement from what has come before in the mold of the "old wineskin" making it "new."[41] He goes on in this section of his memoir to exclaim how thankful he is that God allowed him to be a "participant observer" to what he describes as the "Second Apostolic Age."[42]

"The First Apostolic Age," Wagner argues, "took place in the first couple of centuries after Christ," after which, "for some 1,800 years the biblical gift and office of apostle was virtually neglected by the wider body of Christ." He argues that he does not mean to say that no apostles existed during that period. On the contrary, he counts Martin Luther, John Wesley, and others as having functioned as apostles. Still, he explains that the church was "not prepared to interpret literally Ephesians 4:11 and affirm the gift, office and ministry of apostle in our days." However, since 2001, which he marks as the beginning of what he calls the Second Apostolic Age, "a critical mass of the Body of Christ began to agree the foundation of the church is, indeed, apostles and prophets and that they should be openly recognized as such in the churches today."[43]

Wagner mentioned in his 1988 essay that he was preparing a "textbook" that would go into greater detail on the movement and suggested the title *Churchquake!*, which he did publish the following year.[44] In that book, he reiterated the origin of the term "New Apostolic Reformation." He explained that this movement was most significant because it sought to establish "extra-denominational networks."[45] He concluded that God was doing something to usher in a new age of Christianity.[46] In *Churchquake!*, Wagner argues that these churches are apostolic because of how their leadership structures were led by apostles, which he defines as one whom God has called for the work of "planting and overseeing new churches," who demonstrates a prophetic anointing confirmed by "a word from the Lord," is approved by the congregation for the position, and who exhibits godly character and spiritual maturity.[47] In addition to the particular form of ecclesiastical leadership in the movement, Wagner placed heavy emphasis on the growth of such independent, or interdependent, churches, operating in networks led by charismatic leaders who were recognized as being gifted by the Holy Spirit for the office, who were focused on evangelism, and were characterized by theological soundness and eschatological optimism.[48]

By eschatological optimism, he means that those associated with the NAR hold as a "compass-point value" that "Satan is being defeated, that things are going well for the Kingdom of God and spiritual victories will continue to exceed spiritual defeats."[49] Far from expecting a rapture of the church before the world descends into extreme violence, chaos, and judgment, those associated with the NAR opt for an eschatological vision of progressive dominion as demons are defeated, and God's Kingdom more fully manifests. Though, he argues, those among the NAR "recognize that society is crumbling, that demons infest our environment and that people are hurting more and more," they believe that "more souls than ever are being saved, that churches will continue to multiply, that demonic strongholds will be torn down, that the powers of darkness will crack open and that the advance God's Kingdom is inexorable."[50] In short, the NAR is, in Wagner's understanding, a reformation in how churches are organized, but also a theological reformation that emphasizes aggressive evangelism and a revaluation of eschatology oriented around the notion that Satan is being presently defeated and that the church is undergoing a revolution in this regard to progressively establish the Kingdom of God.

Apostles Today

We have already discussed what an apostle was for Wagner concerning church leadership in what he calls the Second Apostolic Age. It bears mentioning, however, that he develops more details concerning the office of apostle, particularly in his 2006 book *Apostles Today: Biblical Government for Biblical Power*. He mentions in that book that though it was his fifth book on the topic to date, he yet neglected to offer a thorough definition of what an apostle was. Wagner explains that this is because he was "on a learning curve," and any definition he might come up with "would probably soon have to be revised—perhaps many times over."[51] He writes, however, that he had "been able to craft a definition that is beginning to stand the test of time and has been accepted as the official definition of the International Coalition of Apostles," one of the many organizations in the global network of the Apostolic movement. This definition reads:

> An Apostle is a Christian leader, gifted, taught, commissioned, and sent by God with the authority to establish the foundational government of the church within an assigned sphere of ministry by hearing what the Spirit is saying to the churches and by setting things in order accordingly for the growth and maturity of the church and for the extension of the kingdom of God.[52]

After this "bare-bones definition," he goes on in the following seven pages to list detailed points about what apostles do. Among these functions are that they "receive revelation" from The Spirit of God for the churches, governing and alongside prophets laying "the biblical foundation of the Kingdom," acting as "generals in the army of God," leading the church "in spiritual warfare."[53]

For Wagner, the qualifications for apostolic leadership are "formidable," requiring much from those with such a calling and gifting precisely because their authority over the churches they govern is equally profound.[54] Indeed, one of the objections to the NAR is what critics perceive as an undemocratic and unaccountable form of control that apostles hold over congregations. This measure of authority, however, is for Wagner justified in the New Testament and is a logical conclusion from the fact that apostles, as he understands them, act on what they believe God is doing in the world. That is to say that apostles can understand God's will as part of their gifting for that office. Wagner states further that he uses a "phenomenological approach" that leads him "to employ terms not found in the Bible" because he believes that "it is not necessary to only use the *Word* [sic] of God," referring to the text of scripture, "but to also combine the Word of God with accurate observations of the present-day *works* of God."[55] Therefore, apostles govern partly via the correct understanding of what God is currently doing and not by denominational bylaws, the vote of the congregation, or even by precedent or scripture alone.

Wagner goes on to describe three categories of apostles—vertical, horizontal, and workplace apostles.[56] The vertical apostles are, according to Wagner, the most common type. They are the leader to whom other subordinate church leaders in the relevant "network of churches and ministries" are accountable.[57] His example is the Apostle Paul and even the "18 apostles" he invited to contribute to his "first book on the subject of apostolic ministry," *The New Apostolic Churches*, which we have already discussed.[58] In keeping with how Wagner defines the category, each one of these apostles oversaw a network of ministries and churches.

The second category is the horizontal apostle. This category differs from the first in that these apostolic leaders "do not have churches or ministries or individuals under them," but rather "they serve as peer-level leaders in helping them [their peers] to connect each other for different purposes."[59] His example, in this case, is James's actions described in the Book of Acts, where the early apostles debated the issue of gentiles becoming followers of Jesus. As Wagner sees it, James, the blood brother of Jesus, who was not one of the twelve original apostles, coordinated a meeting of the "vertical apostles Peter, John, Paul, Matthew, Apollo, Barnabas, Thomas, and the rest."[60] Since, Wagner argues, vertical apostles "are not ordinarily inclined to seek each other out and spend time with each other," horizontal apostles serve the purpose, like James, to bring vertical apostles together when need to make crucial decisions or perform other functions that require a broader network of apostolic leadership.[61]

The third and final category is the workplace apostle. This role is developed in an entire chapter of its own in *Apostles Today* and remarked upon elsewhere as Wagner develops his idea of the church in the workplace in other works. Significantly, the premise under which the notion that a specific apostolic calling is for the workplace is that "God's plan for His people extends far beyond the four walls of the local church."[62] Wagner explains that one of the "debilitating tendencies" among Christians is that they "identify the kingdom of God with the Church" when they are not, in fact, identical.[63] The church is part of the Kingdom of God, he argues. Still, the Kingdom itself extends far beyond "geographical or political boundaries," which he concludes from Jesus's words in Luke 17:21, "that the kingdom of God is within you."[64]

For Wagner, bringing the Kingdom to earth and ensuring that God's will is done here as in heaven means that much of the work of building the kingdom is taking place outside the church building itself and in the marketplace, literally and figuratively. As such, apostles in the workplace, though they have in Wagner's view, operate on the "same plane" as other apostles, function under different rules and with a different set of characteristics as they "set things in order in the workplace and equip the saints there" for the work of building the Kingdom of God.[65] They are people who "command respect from associates" based on their "effectiveness in their field of endeavor," respect which they command through their financial acumen.[66]

Money holds a particular significance for the NAR and not just for the work of workplace apostles. For Wagner, who quotes Rich Marshall, the author of the popular *God @ Work* series of books and supplemental materials, "money is a tool God gives to businesspersons to gain authority in their city—which means money to carry out tasks that will benefit society."[67] Workplace apostles still offer more particular skills as they are accustomed to taking risks, have command of a "spectrum of interests," can navigate "legal structures" that might otherwise "set boundaries on what God can do," and, importantly, they hold influence in what he calls the "seven molders of culture."[68] In keeping with the calling of the workplace apostle, Wagner argues further that these apostles will have a "Kingdom mentality—meaning that their driving passion is to see God's kingdom values permeate society at every level." They are "actively involved in city or nation transformation as well as setting in order the 'church' in the workplace."[69]

The workplace apostle is the individual most intimately connected to the fulfillment of the dominionist vision of NAR as it is understood within the context of the "optimistic" eschatology of Kingdom building that Wagner articulated. The importance of workplace apostles does not diminish the role of other apostles. Still, it demonstrates that those associated with the NAR share a vision of the Kingdom of God that exists beyond the church itself and seeks to permeate society and control the seven spheres of social and political life. Workplace apostles are particularly important to their achieving that vision.

In *Modern-Day Apostles*, Ahn repeats much of what Wagner described concerning apostles, including the three categories and the characteristics of an apostle doing this work. He specifically keeps the emphasis that Wagner placed on money and influence for the sake of building God's kingdom. This sense permeates every other articulation of how NAR affiliates see apostles today, and at the center of this understanding of what an apostle is the larger mission of bringing dominion over every aspect of society. As Wagner says in his memoir, the workplace apostles are essential for the social transformation the NAR is working to accomplish. He argues, "only by activating apostles in the extended church will we hope to see the necessary gates to reformation and wealth transfer effectively opened."[70]

The Seven Mountains Mandate

One of the most critical aspects of the NAR, especially as it relates to their support for Trump, is a particular form of Christian dominionism known as the "Seven Mountains Mandate," sometimes written as "7 Mountains" or simply "7M". In his memoir, Wagner credits Lance Wallnau for having shaped his perspective on dominionism, particularly in how he understands what he calls the "battlefields" or "the vital pieces" of the whole picture of social reform that Wagner felt were necessary to begin taking control over. "I knew that apostles in the workplace would be the general," he wrote, "but apostles have spheres." He goes on to explain that it was his friend Lance Wallnau who developed "insights from leaders like Bill Bright and Loren Cunningham," who popularized what Wagner calls Wallnau's "warfare strategy."[71] Wagner quotes Wallnau, who says, "If the world is to be won, these are the mountains that hold the culture and the minds of men," and he goes on to explain that whoever "controls these mountains controls the direction of the world and the harvest therein."[72] Those "mountains," according to Wagner and Wallnau, are: religion, family, education, media, government, arts and entertainment, and business.[73] For Wallnau, Wagner and others associated with the NAR control over these "Mountains" is nothing short of a directive from God to exercise dominion over this world, defeat the schemes of the Devil, and eventually establish the Kingdom. Therefore, their dominionism is intimately connected to their optimistic eschatology and their emphasis on spiritual warfare practices.

Wallnau describes this dominionist mandate in an aptly titled essay "The Seven Mountain Mandate." He argues foremost that this is a metapolitical project that relies less on winning individuals to Christ than on seizing those points in a culture that can affect the most change from the top down, as it were. "The business of shifting culture or transforming nations does not require a majority of conversions," he argues, but instead requires that Christian take control of the levers of power in the "Seven Mountains."[74] This taking of dominion, of course, has a practical side related to Wagner's description of workplace apostles. However, this mandate is never described in the literature or sermons as something done separately from spiritual warfare and intercessory prayer. Quoting from Ephesians 6:12, Wallnau claimed, "we do not wrestle against flesh and blood, but against principalities, against powers," and that he and his fellow believers carry a "combat anointing" that empowers them to take control of the Seven Mountains.[75]

Attacking the demonic entities who control the mountains was not a suggestion for better Christian living, as he explains, but rather a prophetic, divine mandate to tear down Satan's hold over entire societies. To act spiritually, therefore, meant acting politically, and for one to act in a politically effective way required one to have the proper spiritual disposition and divine empowerment to take down demonic strongholds in the effort to establish Christian dominion over the various spheres of society to then continue building God's Kingdom on Earth.

In *Invading Babylon: The 7 Mountain Mandate* (2013), a collection of essays edited by Lance Wallnau and Bill Johnson, the controversial leader of Bethel Church in Redding, California, we can see the concept of dominionism developed further, as well as the relationship it has to spiritual warfare. "If we are to have any hope of reaching this world with the Gospel, we must understand that there is a spiritual component to influencing our world," the introduction states. "We must first recognize demonic spiritual powers and displace them through prayer and fasting."[76] The introduction also specifies that the "Seven Mountain revelation helps us strategically identify aspects of society so that cultural transformation can become a manageable task."[77] For the advocates of this mandate, social transformation through dominion blends spiritual warfare into the practicalities of financial, political, and metapolitical strategies in the effort to "bring the Kingdom of God into every aspect of society."[78]

This form of dominionism draws upon and yet differs from other forms of dominionism, particularly that of Rousas John (R.J.) Rushdoony (1916–2001) and his understanding of what came to be called Christian Reconstruction. As Michael J. McVicar notes in *Christian Reconstruction: R.J. Rushdoony and American Religious Conservatism* (2015), Rushdoony rooted his dominionist thought in a "creation mandate" that required strict adherence to biblical law to "reconstruct" by replacement "secular forms of governance with decentralized theocracies and rule as Christ's viceregents on Earth."[79] McVicar argues that C. Peter Wagner combined elements of Rushdoony's "theonomy," or rule according to God's Law, and the notion that Christians have a mandate to "Christianize" all aspects of life, with Abraham Kuyper's (1837–1920) notion of "sphere sovereignty," to develop the Seven Mountains strategy.[80]

Wagner defines his dominion mandate most thoroughly in his 2008 book, *Dominion! How Kingdom Action Can Change the World*. He describes this dominion as control over the "seven molders of culture," which, of course, he understands as Wallnau's Seven mountains, explaining the scriptural justification for direct control over these spheres, which forms the basis of his "dominion theology."[81] Tracing the history of this theology through Calvin, Kuyper, and Rushdoony, Wagner argues that dominion theology seeks practical measures to transform society.[82] Connected to this, too, for Wagner, is the notion that Satan currently exercises a measure of temporary dominion over this world since it was given to him when Adam sinned. This line of reasoning is demonstrated for Wagner in Satan's temptation of Jesus in the gospels of Mathew and Mark, wherein Satan stated that he had been given the kingdoms of this world and could, in turn, give them to whomever he chose.

However, Wagner argues that Satan's dominion is being eroded since Jesus's resurrection until now as Christians, empowered through the Holy Spirit, assert their authority to claim that dominion back from Satan in the name of Jesus. Through this divine empowerment, Christians work to destabilize Satan's hold on this world and continually establish the Kingdom of God through "spiritual and social" activism. They will continue to do so "until Satan's dominion is ended."[83] For Wagner, this conflict over dominion is the more complete meaning of the Great Commission. He understands the fullest sense of the Gospel to not simply mean evangelizing individuals, though that remains important. He argues that "disciplining the nations and transforming society" through the power of the Holy Spirit is the fullest calling upon Christians. They are to establish dominion to engage in social transformation to finally realize the Kingdom of God, a mission which he calls "the battle cry of the Second Apostolic Age."[84]

The social transformation Wagner speaks of specifically means, in his terms, "*sociologically verifiable transformation* [emphasis in original]," and not simply anecdotal stories about "porn shops being closed, or school district has improved, or a bank prays for its customers, or the rate of AIDS has been reduced," et cetera.[85] To give an example of what he means, Wagner copies at length a 2005 story from *Christian World News* that describes the changed conditions of Almolonga, Guatemala, on which George Otis Jr. had also produced a documentary. The report states that the town was, once, in the words of Pastor Harold Caballeros of El Shaddai Church in Guatemala City, a "culture of death, a culture of alcoholism, idolatry and witchcraft, to a culture where they [the people] think only about expanding the kingdom of God—prosperity, blessing, healing."[86] The report claims that the population was now estimated to be 90 percent "born again Christians" and that the farmers there have experienced tremendous crop yields and economic prosperity, making special note that trailers of vegetables are often pulled by Mercedes Benz trucks. For Wagner, this is proof that such transformation is possible but also demonstrates what he says the Spirit of God demands of Christians today.[87]

It is evident at this point, but it is worth noting that if established this form of dominion would not allow for what these Christians regard as violations of the will or word of God. Wagner is deeply critical of what he sees as the excesses of tolerance in the United States regarding homosexuality and the presence and prominence of non-Christian religions. The kinds of behavior that would be prohibited or curtailed are the abuse of alcohol and drugs, various forms of sexual immorality, and non-Christian forms of religious practice. However, apart from the ethical and legal demands, this form of dominion would impose economic reform through free-market capitalism.

Economics plays a particular role in Wagner's thought, as we have noted. Wagner and others associated with the NAR frequently mention what they call "The Great Transfer of Wealth."[88] Weaver notes that this idea is wedded to workplace apostles, Wagner's notion of "church in the workplace," and is "the real centerpiece of the economic ideology of the NAR."[89] Wagner, in particular, argues that lack of money is a "significant reason why we have not yet taken any of our cities for God," and that, quoting John Kelly and Paul Costa's 2006 book *The Power to Get Wealth*, "There is no doubt that if the Kingdom of God is going to be established on earth, it is going to take a lot more money than the church has at present."[90] The need for money, Wagner argues, is to put Christian candidates on ballots, that "winning democratic elections fair and square does cost money," and that "the more serious we get about social transformation, the more serious we need to get about the realistic price tags."[91]

Wagner, of course, is not alone in this discussion of a transfer of wealth for the purposes of building the Kingdom of God. Johnny Enlow, in his 2008 book *The Seven Mountain Prophecy: Unveiling the Coming Elijah Revolution*, discusses the possibility of using "apostolic strategies" to accomplish a shift of resources by exploiting what he calls "Babylon's system," but turns away from that in favor of more "prophetic" means of controlling this "mountain of the economy."[92] He argues that God has "specific power" that he grants to his followers "to *get* [sic] wealth," not just "make" it.[93] "The transfer of wealth is not going to come through our Christian brainpower," he argues, but as the result of making the priority of one's life "the One who is wealthy."[94] For Enlow, this "mountain of economy and wealth" is conquered through direct spiritual warfare against the demonic spirit he calls Mammon engaged in by the "Elijah revolutionaries [who] hear the call of God and take this mountain."[95]

Prophet Cindy Jacobs, the author of *Possessing The Gates of the Enemy: A Training Manual for Militant Intercession* (1991), which Wagner called a "classic" in the genre of spiritual warfare manuals, posted in a blog for her and her husband's website Generals International on behalf of the word of prophecy received by The Apostolic Council Prophetic Elders, an organization founded by Wagner, and now under her leadership, a "prophetic roadmap" 2022 and beyond.[96] She writes that the prophets gathered at the meeting were told of a "shaking" that "will result in a wealth transfer that can be used for the great harvest of the nations." She goes on to say that this will result in "many prodigals" coming "back to the Lord" and that "God will give His people new ideas on how to create jobs and be on the cutting edge of developing jobs that will result in the promised transfer of wealth." And here, once again, the goal of such wealth is to establish God's Kingdom, even to the point of involving the latest innovations of cryptocurrency. She writes, "God will raise up a young generation who are 'futurists', or are very prophetic in their abilities to function in the world of crypto-currency, and great wealth will be created for the Kingdom of God."

We need to note at this point that Wagner explicitly rejects the idea that his dominion theology means the establishment of a theocracy. As Weaver notes in his history of the movement, the NAR's mission of "cultural conquest," in the estimation of Wagner, Wallnau, and others, does not translate to a theocracy but a rather loose understanding of "national and corporate transformation."[97] He argues in the introduction to *Dominion!* that contrary to a theocracy, which he describes as "a government headed up by God," dominion means the infusion of the Kingdom of God into society by democratic means.[98] He argues that since democracy means "a government for the people, by the people," any society that Christians have shaped would function democratically as they participate in democratic processes to infuse Christian principles at every level of that society. "The rules of the democratic game open the doors for Christians, as well as for non-Christians who have Kingdom values, to move into positions of leadership influential enough to shape the whole nation from top to bottom," he argues.[99]

The wording of dominionist claims is crucial, especially if we want to understand why NAR Christians would support someone like Trump for president. For Wagner and others associated with the NAR, it is not necessary for one to be a Christian to express what he calls Kingdom values. In a discussion of the dominion mandate, Wagner argues the general social stability in places like Japan and Singapore, where a small number of Christians live, have nevertheless applied principles that result in prosperity demonstrated by the "eradication of systemic poverty." This stability and relative prosperity were "not brought about by overt Christian action," but the actions that always result in favorable social conditions.[100] So-called Kingdom values are a matter of enacting the processes by which society prospers. Someone who exercises those principles may find success and prosperity even if they have yet to be born again.

The focus on broad social transformation, which Wagner describes as God's "desire" and "plan," is not to say that NAR Christians neglect the gospel of personal salvation. They still place a great deal of emphasis on saving souls by having people confess Jesus is Lord and acknowledging that he has given himself in our place so that we might be reconciled to God. However, they claim that this is not the whole picture of the purpose of Jesus' life, ministry, death, and resurrection. In a presentation from 2010, while discussing the "dominion mandate," he describes the "Gospel of the Kingdom."[101] The mandate means "casting out of demons," "healing the sick," and "transforming our society." As he presents his view in this talk, God intends Christians to rule as kings precisely because this is what God established for humanity with his command to Adam and Eve in the Garden of Eden and reestablished in Jesus's command for them to make disciples of all nations. Though Wagner expresses confidence and joy in the future coming of Christ, in his view, this does not allow Christians to abdicate their responsibility in the mandate that God gave them.

Considering what we have discussed so far, the distinction between theocracy and dominion may seem like a distinction without a difference; however, for Wagner, theocracy is the direct rule of God that will come about at a later point. Until God comes to rule the earth Himself, Christians should continue the struggle to establish dominion by "gaining influence in the seven molders of culture to ultimately benefit a nation and open society for the blessings, prosperity and happiness God desires for all people."[102] And as Wagner explains, though it is unknown at what time Jesus will return to establish a direct theocracy, which Wagner believes will happen, Wagner's dominionism advocates for "transforming society ... as if Christ were not coming for a long time"; elaborating on the logic of dominion theology by arguing that whether Jesus comes "sooner rather than later, we have not lost anything in our efforts to take dominion," concluding that by either dominion or through the theocracy established by Jesus upon his return, "We win either way!"[103]

Warring in the Spirit

Perhaps it is clear by now that one cannot overestimate the importance of spiritual warfare to the NAR's discourse and practices. Throughout articulating the meaning of the Seven Mountains Mandate, one finds repeated references to the need for spiritual warfare to achieve dominion. Wagner's teaching about the dominion mandate specifies that behind the efforts to control the various spheres of social and political life lies the real battle against Satan for dominion of this world. More than this, however, is the teaching among those associated with the NAR that there are spiritual entities behind all the negative phenomena that bring suffering. To return to how Enlow, Wagner, and others associated with NAR, talk about economics concerning the transfer of wealth, the phrase "spirit of poverty" is meant to denote the actual demonic nature of poverty and not simply that it is a social ill related to policy. In the foreword to Jacobs's *Possessing The Gates of the Enemy*, Lou Engle writes that he believes that the book will help believers "move into courageous faith to possess the gates of humanism, false ideologies, world religion, sex-trafficking and strongholds that create poverty."[104]

Issues like poverty, addiction, sexual immorality, and any ideologies opposed to Christ are demonically caused evils that result in a social condition of suffering that must be dealt with through specific practices of prayer as well as social reform. In her post about the prophetic roadmap for 2022, Jacobs emphasizes the urgency of spiritual warfare. She writes, "It is time to do spiritual warfare to see our nations come into revival and reformation. We will not change nations through solely natural means." The point of the particular form of spiritual warfare practiced and embraced by those associated with the NAR is to discern the alleged spiritual realities behind the material conditions of the world and to overcome them to manifest the will of God in the domains of politics, economics, and society at large. With this insight, Christians can effectively act to possess the "mountains." In this way, Christians can establish dominion.

Those associated with the NAR are known for their emphasis on spiritual warfare, which is not common among charismatic Christians more broadly; however, they engage a form of spiritual warfare that is quite controversial among other Christians, a practice known as "spiritual mapping." Wagner himself edited a volume in 2015 titled *Breaking Spiritual Strongholds in Your City* that focused on this practice and featured notables among NAR networks, like Cindy Jacobs, George Otis Jr., who is credited for coining the term "spiritual mapping," and Wagner himself. In the preface to the volume, Wagner notes that this is an updated edition from the original 1993 edition and that since that time, Christians have become "more aware of the Kingdom of God than [they] used to be," tying the insights into spiritual warfare in the volume to the Dominion Mandate.[105] In connecting this mandate to "transform" nations, and not just individual lives through the Gospel, Wagner argues that spiritual mapping allows for targeted prayer for entire communities, thereby "identifying and neutralizing the spiritual strongholds which attempt to hinder the work of God" to bring the entirety of communal life under God's rule.[106]

In chapter 1 of the volume, George Otis Jr. describes the practice primarily as "a way of seeing" the spiritual realities otherwise hidden from our view. He argues that it involves "[s]uperimposing our understanding of forces and events in the spiritual domain onto places and circumstances in the material world."[107] Otis specifically ties spiritual mapping, as do others engaged in the practice, to successful evangelization. He argues that because "spiritual darkness is increasing and becoming more sophisticated," which signifies "a geographical pattern to evil and spiritual oppression," and that so few "understand the spiritual dimension as well as they thought," there is an awakening to the need for this practice among some church communities.[108] To make way for the Gospel of Salvation, one should engage in spiritual mapping to destabilize demonic influence over the targeted area. This practice is becoming more critical to how some Christian communities engage in evangelism. For Otis, demonic powers operate in particular ways in particular geographic locations, often through cultural celebrations, like the summer Bon celebrations in Japan, which tie communities and geographies to demonic powers. He argues that such customs and practices bind the people of that location to the "lie" and that these practices are "fueled by demonic magic," called "tradition," which in turn "sustains territorial dynasties," or demonic control over given space.[109]

The practice of spiritual mapping identifies these demonic elements. It describes how they are given authority to operate in a particular space so that specific prayer practices can be used to target the correct entities and their "strongholds," and finally root them out and make available that area for the Gospel and eventual Christian spiritual dominion there. The practice of spiritual mapping ties directly to the theology that Wagner describes concerning the Dominion Mandate. Satan took authority to exercise dominion over the world by Adam when he sinned. That authority remained absolute until Jesus was resurrected and empowered believers by the Holy Spirit to take that dominion back. Spaces where demonic spirits are allowed to operate freely, uninhibited by spiritually aware Christians, are vulnerable but also spaces that must be conquered through this form of prayer. Spiritual warfare in the form of spiritual mapping is how Christians destabilize demonic strongholds so that God's people can take that dominion to establish God's Kingdom.

In the following chapter of *Breaking Spiritual Strongholds in Your City*, Wagner restates much of what Otis says in chapter 1. Wagner affirms that the core of the practice of spiritual mapping is the "assumption … that reality is more than appears on the surface."[110] He also reiterates the point that traditions within cultures often are how demonic forces control space through a community's practices. However, he wants to walk a fine line in that he wants to affirm the positive value of multiculturalism without "exaggerating" the value of tolerance. He argues that the danger is that "the effort to reassert cultural pluralism, tolerance becomes a high value," but that if that value "becomes exaggerated," it may cause more harm in that it then makes "politically correct" attitudes dominant so that "the only thing not to be tolerated is intolerance."[111] Tolerance is dangerous in his view because "Christianity is anything but politically correct," meaning that the values of tolerance coded as political correctness are seen as a form of spiritual attack, eroding even Christians' commitment, especially in the United States, to the values that Wagner associates with the Kingdom of God.[112]

Referencing some of what we saw in the Seven Mountains framework, Wagner argues that Christians ought to "recognize that Satan has so corrupted cultures that some of their forms, such as art and architecture and particularly some of their behavior patterns such as dances and religious rituals, are clearly intended to glorify the creature rather than the creator," and that such practices "exalt demonic spirits."[113] Referencing the consequences of such practices and not rooting out the demonic activity in a nation, he argues that God "will not stand for the spiritual harlotry in the United States any more than He did in Judah in Jerimiah's time, and divine judgment is the predictable outcome."[114]

This is a notion we will see come up repeatedly in prophecy voters' claims about Trump. Anointed by God, Trump will, by his actions as president, they claim, bring America back from the precipice and back into right relationship with God. That is if the demonic strongholds over the nation and in key places can be sufficiently destabilized.

We can see that the practice of spiritual mapping is deeply connected to the way that Wagner and others associated with the NAR understand evangelism and the practice of taking dominion in a given territory and that it is not simply a matter of saving individuals through a reasoned argument or the simple presentation of the Gospel. However, they do not entirely abandon these efforts either. Instead, through specific, insightful, and targeted prayer activities, they attempt to prepare an entire community, city, or even nation for evangelism and transformation by attacking the demonic spirits they regard as controlling that space. Further, as we can see from the way Wagner defines these connections between the dominion of space by demons and the role of spiritual warfare as seeing the spiritual realities behind material representations, including art, architecture, and even dance, that cultural representations themselves are part of the way demons gain their dominion and conversely what Christians should seek to gain control over. In other words, the Dominion Mandate, as understood by Wagner, Wallnau, and others, is necessarily connected to what they see as the reality of demonic spirits acting to subvert the will of God through aspects of culture like the toleration of homosexuality, abortion, addiction, poverty, and political correctness.

This connection between the practice of spiritual mapping and the NAR's particular form of dominionism should therefore be understood as part of the reason why so many associated with the NAR supported Trump when it seemed to make no ethical sense to do so. Supporting Trump was not an ethical choice but rather a strategic course of action described by the prophets who promised Trump would challenge the status quo and provide a window of opportunity for social transformation in the United States. What seemed to others to be a political battle between two vastly different politicians in the 2016 presidential election was, for those associated with the NAR, in fact, a spiritual battle between God and his spiritual warriors on one side and demonic spirits striving to maintain control over the nation on the other. Joining the dominionist logic and spiritual warfare practices of the NAR, support for

Trump should be seen as an effort by prophets and apostles associated with the NAR to battle the demonic spirits who controlled this nation's political and social life and to establish a stronghold for the Kingdom of God in the United States from which that dominion could spread and affect the whole world. As Wagner argues in his 2009 book, *Warfare Prayer: What the Bible Says about Spiritual Warfare*, he does not see "spiritual warfare as an end in itself" but as "a means toward the end of seeking and saving that which was lost," and proclaiming dominion over this world.[115]

Conclusion: An "Optimistic" Eschatological Vision

In this chapter, I wanted to introduce some of the significant constituent elements of the NAR that will come up later as we explore their justifications for supporting Trump. What we have discussed so far about the aims of the NAR—a reformation in how Christians organize church government by establishing various kinds of apostles in specific roles as leaders of the body of Christ, with a particular emphasis on the mandate for establishing dominion over the Seven Mountains, and engaging in specific kinds of spiritual warfare to that end—all play a certain role in how they described their support for Trump in 2016 through his presidency and into the 2020 election and advocated for other Christian to do the same. However, this is only part of explaining why and how they did so.

In conjunction with the NAR's particular form of dominionism, the progressivist vision of Kingdom-building that is actualized through a practice of intercessory prayer and spiritual warfare is central to the theological underpinnings of the NAR that sees the world as perpetually imperiled yet simultaneously on the verge of victorious salvation. As prophet Jonny Enlow says in *The Seven Mountain Prophecy: Unveiling the Coming Elijah Revolution* (2018):

> World systems are presently collapsing one by one and will continue to do so. Their "mountains" are failing, thus readying them to look to the only mountain of hope. This is not just a personal hope that individuals are looking for—i.e., the gospel of salvation—but a comprehensive hope that even entire nations can come under the rule and the glory of God.[116]

Dominion is possible in the defeat of the demonic forces aligned against America if Christians acted and prayed, informed by the insight provided by the Holy Spirit through His prophets and apostles. As such, avoiding the catastrophic consequences of the judgment of God on the nation was conditional on the action of God's people to overcome the schemes of the devil and those who either knowingly or unknowingly do his bidding.

This discourse makes the idea of a demonic conspiracy not simply ancillary to how NAR Christians think but a core theological element to their dominionism. To take control over the Seven Mountains Mandate, one engages in spiritual warfare guided by apostles and prophets against demonic entities and demonically influenced people and organizations who must be overcome so that God's Kingdom can be realized. It is to these millennialist and conspiratorial elements of NAR teachings that we next turn our attention.

2

Earthly Peril & Kingdom Promise

The fundamental mission of those associated with the New Apostolic Reformation is to restore the office of apostle to its full function while embracing the power of Spirit-filled and directed ministry to realize God's will on Earth as it is in Heaven through establishing dominion over the seven spheres of social and political life. From there, they would seek to eradicate social ills like poverty, sexual immorality, addiction, and crime through spiritual warfare and enactment of Kingdom principles in every aspect of public life. According to C. Peter Wagner and others who articulated this vision, it is nothing short of the fullest realization of what the Gospel means—bringing the good news not just of salvation but the good news of the Kingdom of God. As Wagner explains, "the dominion mandate is the Great Commission," the fullest expression of the command to "make disciples of all nations."[1]

To establish dominion fully and effectively, Christians, they argue, must make war on the various spiritual entities aligned against this endeavor who presently control aspects of society, even hold power over the Seven Mountains, and rule over entire cities and nations. Apostles act as generals in this war, leading God's people in battle against demonic spirits that seek to control and destroy humanity and inhibit the full realization of what God would have for society. Demons may exercise their authority over territories and can also manifest as and exercise control over vices like alcoholism, abortion, homosexuality, divorce, crime, poverty, and, significantly, any cultural or political resistance to what they regard as God's plan of salvation and restoration through dominion. These satanic forces must be defeated and removed from power, their territorial authority must be rescinded, and the people under their influence liberated if Christians have any chance of claiming that territory for God and exercising dominion over it. Those associated with the NAR understand dominionism and their practice of spiritual warfare cannot be separated. They must root out the demonic influences that obstruct and actively subvert that mission to take dominion over society's cultural and political elements.

Continuing from this point, the primary claim in this chapter is that the mission and mandate of the NAR rest upon a particular millennialist expectation that Christians will progressively conquer the world for God by removing the vestiges of satanic control over this nation and other nations until the Kingdom of God is realized and Jesus rules as Lord over all. However, connected to this narrative, particularly regarding supporting Trump, NAR prophets repeatedly state that the Devil could thwart such efforts should Christians falter in their adherence to prescribed strategies of prayer and other activities revealed through prophets. As we will see in the coming chapters, those associated with the NAR argued if they had not supported Trump in 2016, if they allowed "Fake News," the "Deep State," or any of the schemes of the Devil to prevail, those plans would be subverted, America would fall into ruin, thereby sabotaging America's prophetic role in establishing the Kingdom of God.[2] For these prophecy voters, voting and spiritual warfare went hand-in-hand as part of a strategy revealed by God through His prophets toward the goal of fulfilling the fullest sense of the Great Commission by resting America back to God through control, if we may put it this, control over the highest office in the land, the pinnacle of the government mountain, the presidency.

Connected to this particular expression of millennialism and apocalyptic warning standard in NAR discourse is the certainty that those opposed to Trump and Christian dominion were engaged in secret, nefarious, demonically inspired plans to subvert by any means at their disposal Trump's campaign in 2016 and his presidency through to his effort at reelection, to sabotage his administration to see God's plans for the nation fail, and to steal the election in 2020 to install an illegitimate regime that would seek to reverse any progress God intended for the nation. In the context of NAR support for Trump, apocalyptic warnings connected to a particular millennialist expectation as pertains to their understanding of the dominion mandate that incorporated spiritual warfare into its very political language that asserted conspiratorial narratives of demonic forces and political enemies that worked in the shadows against God's people and His anointed leader for the nation. Nevertheless, however specific the form of millennialism in the NAR is, and though it is distinct from what has been popular among the Religious Right in the United States, it is tied to a long history of apocalyptic narration of current events and millennial expectations in the American context that has shaped the political consciousness of American evangelicals through the twentieth century to the present.

Well before Donald Trump announced his intention to seek the Republican nomination and certainly before QAnon became a prominent part of his base of support through the 2020 election, politicians and other public figures have frequently used images of catastrophe to motivate their allies and supporters.[3] In 2016, political scientist Alison McQueen noted that then-presumptive Republican nominee Donald Trump often presented himself in a manner consistent with a "prophet of doom."[4] Trump's speeches frequently featured references to some dread event befalling America, usually at the hands of "illegals" or terrorists, should citizens fail to heed his call to vote for him so that he could save America from his opponents cast as destructive and anti-American themselves. McQueen notes that Trump "injects his own dangerous brand of megalomania into the country's apocalyptic tradition." Still, he repeats a broader narrative in asserting that some disaster or several disasters would befall America should his mission be impeded. McQueen writes, "it is easy and even comforting to think of apocalyptic rhetoric as marginal and extremist, as beyond the pale of mainstream politics," but continues to the contrary that "visions of tribulation and redemption also find their way into the mainstream of American politics." I also want for us to keep in mind, as McQueen notes in her book, "[t]he idea of the apocalypse is flexible, migratory, and unstable."[5] That is to say that apocalypticism shifts and moves over time, often incorporating contemporary events and anxieties into the frame of the narrative, something that Trump supporters associated with the NAR share with other Trump supporters. Indeed, in using conspiratorial and apocalyptic narratives to frame their political present, NAR Christians tap into a much longer-lived tradition in American politics.

My argument in this chapter is simple—there are particular expressions of apocalypticism, millennialism, and conspiracism that inform the discourse of the NAR even before the 2016 election, which shaped how they talked about Trump's candidacy, presidency, and attempted reelection. Many of the dominant narratives we will discuss in later chapters relative to the discourse in the NAR during the 2016 election, the Trump presidency, the 2020 election, and its immediate aftermath reflect the peculiarities of the theology that informs NAR positions on dominionism, eschatology, and spiritual warfare. However, as we will see continually in this chapter and in the ones that follow, many of the apocalyptic and conspiratorial elements in their narratives both predate the NAR and Trump and overlap significantly with those found elsewhere among Trump's base of support. In many cases, those who share little affinity with the theology of the NAR will nevertheless be as adamant about the existence of subversive forces attacking Trump, or the certain doom that would befall America should he be defeated or removed from office.

Millennialism, Apocalypticism, and Conspiracism in the NAR

Before we go too far into the specifics of the NAR's expressions of millennialism, apocalypticism, and conspiracism, we should clarify the main terms under consideration here. I briefly sketched out how a particular form of millennialism and conspiracism shaped NAR support for Trump in my article "Voting in The Kingdom: Prophecy Voters, the New Apostolic Reformation, and Christian Support for Trump" (2020). However, it is prudent here to elaborate upon what I described there. The first term, millennialism, presents a particular challenge in that even within the context of the history of Christianity in the United States, there are multiple millennialisms for one to consider. Indeed, dispensationalism and rapture theology have been the dominant millennialist expression for those writing about the Religious Right in America. However, Wagner and others associated with the NAR often contrasted their eschatology with the more familiar narrative popularized *Left Behind* series of books and films. To briefly summarize, the rapture of all true believing Christians will usher in a period of judgment on the Earth and everyone on it. At that time, the Antichrist will be revealed as a stabilizing force after the seemingly inexplicable disappearance of so many people around the world. As the next seven years progress, the judgments of God will grow more severe as the Antichrist becomes more violent and repressive. The events of this period end with Christ's physical return to destroy the armies of the

Antichrist and establish His kingdom, from which He will rule the nations of the Earth for literally 1,000 years.[6]

This form of millennialism rests on the eschatology developed by John Nelson Darby (1800–1882), referred to as dispensational premillennialism. As scholars of Darby and his eschatology have noted, this view was not developed in a vacuum. Still, it is important to note that it was Darby's formulation that became most influential on the likes of Tim LaHaye, who co-authored the *Left Behind* series, and Hal Lindsay, famous for his book *The Late Great Planet Earth* (1970), both of whom popularized in their respective times the premillennialist view. Religion scholar Amy Frykholm notes American Christians did not immediately accept Darby's views. Still, they had become popular through the efforts of C. I. Scofield (1843–1921), and then eventually among a boom of Bible schools emerging in the 1930s and 40s and became the staple view at places like Dallas Theological Seminary, where Hal Lindsay learned it.[7] Through these various avenues through Christian education and popular culture, dispensational premillennialism established itself as the dominant eschatological position among the American Religious Right.

Tristan Sturm and Jason Dittmer note in their introduction to *Mapping the End Times: American Evangelical Geopolitics and Apocalyptic Visions* (2010) that the majority of the most influential public faces of the "New Christian Right," including Jerry Falwell, James Dobson, Pat Robertson, and, of course, Tim Haye, all adhered the basic "dispensational premillennialist schema" laid out by Darby.[8] The premillennialist view is still common among many evangelical Christians, but its place in the discourse is not unchallenged even before the advent of the NAR. As sociologist of charismatic and Pentecostal movements Stephen Hunt notes, the dominionist theology of Rushdoony's Christian Reconstruction, for example, which held that Christians should transform their society, was at odds with premillennialism's assumption that Jesus would have to rescue the world from destruction rather than Christians gaining dominance and restoring godly order to the world.[9]

Like Rushdoony and his followers, the leading voices of the NAR strongly reject premillennialism and the doctrine of the rapture in favor of a triumphalist narrative of overcoming the world rather than leaving before the judgment of God is visited upon it. To demonstrate this rejection of the rapture doctrine and its accompanying doctrine of premillennialism, we can turn once again to Johnny Enlow in *The Seven Mountain Mantle*, where he argues that the expectation of a rapture of the church from the world is deeply flawed. He writes, "The rapture doctrine, as it is commonly expressed, is one of those sophisticated doctrines of doubt." He continues, "When we have little faith that God could reform and transform society using us, we embrace a theology of escapism."[10] I do not mean to say that they deny the return of Jesus but that the world will progress toward establishing the Kingdom until he returns. In the NPR interview from 2011, Wagner agrees and explicitly describes that his vision of the progressive establishment of the Kingdom of God leaves no room for a pre-tribulation rapture and, therefore, no room for the catastrophic millennialism of Darby, LaHaye, and Lindsay.[11]

So commonplace is the rejection of the rapture and the accompanying premillennialist expectations among the network of NAR affiliates that even in social media, it is common to find refutations. For example, in a Facebook post from October 2019, Lance Wallnau stated, "Forget 'rapture' as an escape. Try 'translation' as an act of defiance—by a remnant who refuse to succumb to the spirit of the age! Instead, we will bring Heaven's Kingdom to rule on Earth."[12] Here, Wallnau is retranslating the word rapture itself to translation, as in the sense of a generation of people transformed by the power of God to enact his will in this world. He writes, "Not a 'rapture' but a translation—like Enoch. The translation generation will make the Word flesh and 'translate' the message of the kingdom into the language of every sphere to AWAKEN every nation."[13] This statement may seem cryptic; however, what he means to do here is to restate the meaning of the rapture to shift the focus from leaving Earth before an outpouring of God's wrath to signifying that God will empower His people through "the flood" to establish His kingdom. Wallnau refutes the doctrine of the rapture and the catastrophic millennialism that accompanies it in favor of a narrative of progress in gaining dominion toward the eventual establishment of the Kingdom of God. However, in each moment, one is reminded by the prophetic voices of the movement that for this goal to be realized, one must behave as one empowered by the Holy Spirit.

Nevertheless, however triumphalist these narratives are at points, there is always a sense that Christians might fail. The battle, as it were, could go ill for the Armies of God. In his concluding chapter in *Dominion*, Wagner argues, "Satan has polluted the land and cursed it," making his defeat essential for establishing the Kingdom and ensuring that the powers of darkness do not "block the freedom of heaven flowing to earth."[14] In a sense, then, while the ultimate victory of God over the devil is assured, those called by God into his army must fight now to guarantee their victory in the present to fulfill the calling of the Gospel of the Kingdom of God. The success of this mission to establish dominion that leads to the realization of the Kingdom of God on Earth depends on the decisive action of God's people.

Though those associated with the NAR focus on triumph and dominionism and reject the escapism and pessimism of dispensationalist eschatology, they remain flexible regarding this eschatological view. André Gangé notes in his book on evangelical support for Trump that the NAR does not limit participation in the building of the Kingdom to those who agree with their millennialist position but invites pre-, post-, and amillennialists to "invest in the strategy of social transformation."[15] Though those associated with the NAR are indeed invested in their "victorious" eschatology, as Gangé describes it, they remain open to inviting participation in their dominionist project to those who share different eschatological perspectives, including rapture adherents with whom they so vehemently disagree.

Wagner himself stated plainly that, to some degree, these differences are not central to NAR in any case. "As I move among new apostolic leaders, I hear surprisingly little conversation relating to premillennialism or post-millennialism or a-millennialism, and even less about pre-tribulation or post-tribulation rapture," he argues in *Churchquake!* "These eschatological issues, once high on the agendas of many conservative church leaders, do not seem to be important today," he explains.[16] Wagner here gives us insight into the looseness with which NAR affiliates might hold others to their particular vision of future events regarding the End Times so long as those parties even marginally share their dominionist vision. For those associated with the NAR, fine points of theology will not prohibit cooperation in a common mission, in the case of supporting Trump, an effort to restore America to a closer covenant relationship with God.

How, then, should one describe the millennialism of the NAR? Catherine Wessinger defines millennialism as the "belief in an imminent transition to a collective salvation, in which the faithful will experience well-being and the unpleasant limitations of the human condition."[17] More applicable to the

NAR's millennialism is Wessinger's description of progressive millennialism in an essay titled "Millennialism With and Without the Mayhem" (1997). In this essay, Wessinger juxtaposes "catastrophic millennialism," a form of millennialism that expects the world to grow increasingly worse until a dramatic intervention by a divine agent, with what she describes as an optimistic form of millennialism that "entails a belief in progress."[18] W. Michael Ashcraft writes concerning this view that "[p]rogressive millennialism is an outlook that expects society on Earth to become increasingly purified or perfected."[19]

With reference to both Wessinger and Ashcraft's work, Daniel Wojcik proposes another category that I think applies particularly to the apocalypticism found among NAR networks. In what he calls "avertive millennialism," Wojcik describes this expression of millennialism as that which "shares features with progressive millennialism in the assertion that collective salvation and a golden age will be brought about gradually by human beings acting in cooperation with a divine authority or superhuman plan that will transform the world."[20] Wojcik argues that avertive millennialism accentuates a "nonfatalistic view of an apocalypse that can be avoided through human action."[21] As with the progressive millennialist view, not describe the world "as irredeemably evil or absolutely doomed," is very fitting to how Wagner defined his eschatology as optimistic, the avertive perspective captures the consistent warnings of NAR prophets, "characterized by a conditional attitude," as Wojcik puts it, in that the Kingdom of God may come, at least not soon, if the requirements for its manifestation fulfilled.[22]

Following this line of reasoning established in the contributions by Wessinger, Ashcraft, and Wojcik, I have argued that the NAR blends each of the elements of progressive and avertive millennialism into the view of Wagner and other NAR figures have described as optimistic and at times conditional.[23] Here, as with Christian Reconstructionists, those associated with the NAR do not disagree with the political and theological condemnations of homosexuality, divorce, and other perceived vices that one hears from Christian Right leaders like Jerry Falwell, Pat Robertson, or Tim LaHaye.[24] They do, however, reject that Christians should expect to be raptured before the judgment of God falls on those who commit such sins and abet those who do. In contrast, they expect to overcome their opponents to establish the Kingdom by gaining control over the most influential sections of society. However, though they do expect victory eventually, the avertive element enters the narrative through the warnings that should Christians neglect this mandate, ruin will befall their nation and the world. Such warnings were used quite frequently in the statements of NAR leaders like Lance Wallnau, for example, who argued that catastrophe would befall the United States and repression of Christians would ensue, which would have ripple effects throughout the world if Christians failed to support God's candidate and could result in Trump's defeat in the 2016 election.[25]

The term "apocalypticism" is also challenging and complicated. The prominent Christian thinker N.T. Wright, for example, noted the diversity of uses of the word "apocalypticism," arguing that the "word 'apocalyptic' has been pressed into service concerning at least three quite different sorts of things: an experience, a literary genre, and a worldview."[26] Moreover, as the scholar of apocalypticism Colin McAllister has noted, there is great difficulty in strictly defining what constitutes apocalyptic. In his introduction to *The Cambridge Companion to Apocalyptic Literature*, McAllister argues, "[o]ne common thread that weaves throughout [the] volume is the difficulty of defining and delimiting what properly constitutes 'apocalyptic' literature" across various groups and in different points in history.[27]

In the context of the NAR, however, I prefer to link the terms apocalyptic and millennialism as standing in relationship to one another. I understand their association similar to what religious studies scholar Tristan Sturm argues, in that he generally regards "apocalypticism" as referring to an "unveiling," more specifically to mean "the events before the ... Revelation—or the end of the world—and the Renewal is the Millennium."[28] That is to say, while there are diverse meanings to both the terms "apocalypticism" and "millennialism," they are often related in the imaginations of believers. I argue that those associated with the NAR see the rule and reign of Jesus as inevitable. Still, they relate this to certain apocalyptic narratives and contemporary prophetic revelations about how God is enacting this rule as they seek to apply their political activism and spiritual warfare practices to the shifting social and political landscape as guided by the prophets and apostles in the hopes of achieving the Kingdom in the present through dominion.

I, therefore, think it is best to think of apocalypticism in the NAR context as a particular narrative that serves a purpose as they continue to look to prophetic revelations concerning everything from specific targets for intercessory prayer to the kinds of political actions required in a given moment. I find the words of the distinguished historian of Christianity Bernard McGinn useful here to help describe how I understand apocalypticism in this context. He writes, "[a]pocalypticism was a way in which contemporary political and social events were given religious validation by incorporation into a transcendent scheme of meaning."[29] That is what I mean by focusing on the narrative function of apocalypticism in the NAR—it is a frame for their dominionism and how they understand its progress in a given political moment.

Although McGinn is concerned with the Middle Ages, the general framework fits well in the context of the NAR. We can take, for example, Johnny Enlow's statement in his 2009 book, *The Seven Mountain Mantle*, in which he claims that God is going to send His servants to "invade the seven mountains of society, and then He will intervene to cause current systems to begin failing."[30] The drama of political and cultural hegemony is a cosmic conflict between the forces of darkness and those who Enlow calls "the sons of light," echoing the long-used language of Jewish and Christian apocalyptic literature. Here, the idea of catastrophe can be described as something to be averted by a certain action, as with Wallnau's admonition for Christians to support Trump or one for which Christians should be prepared to respond appropriately to take advantage of the moment to bring about and witness the glory of God, as with Enlow's statement. In either case, the prophetic utterance proclaiming a coming catastrophe establishes the conditions for present and future actions that will, if prophetic prescriptions are followed correctly, bring them closer to establishing dominion and the world one step closer to the full realization of the Kingdom of God.

Accompanying what I describe as avertive, which is to say conditional, apocalyptic narratives wedded to the progressive millennialist expectations of the NAR are the repeated descriptions of demonic opposition to their efforts to establish dominion. Indeed, the notion of dominionism expressed in the Seven Mountains Mandate is meaningless without the existence of demonic resistance awaiting those who would wrest territorial control from Satan and his forces. Taking dominion is stated plainly as an act of warfare against dark powers. In her essay published in *Breaking Spiritual Strongholds in Your City*, Cindy Jacobs points out that demonic entities establish particular "strongholds" geographically as well as in other ways. She identifies what she calls "personal strongholds," or those things that Satan builds to influence one's personal life—"personal sin, thoughts, feelings, attitudes, and behavior patterns."[31]

Jacobs distinguishes a total of nine strongholds; however, there are two, in particular, to which we should pay attention for this point. She identifies what she calls "ideological strongholds," "occultic strongholds," and "social strongholds." She argues ideological strongholds are those ideologies like Marxism, humanism, Darwinism, and non-Christian religions, which she argues can "affect whole cultures," and by analogy, points to the atrocities of the Third Reich.[32] She argues, too, that Christians "need to understand that these ideological strongholds are inspired by the invisible forces and powers and darkness, which cause the creation of social structures and institutions to carry out their purposes." Consequently, she argues that these "strongholds must be attacked nonstop" to break the power of the demonic forces in charge of them.[33]

Jacobs then goes on to describe "the overt evil application of many ideological strongholds," which she calls "occultic strongholds."[34] Unlike the case of ideological strongholds that can be the result of, for lack of a better word, a permeation of ungodly and atheistic ideas into the fabric of society, occultic strongholds are driven by organized, purposeful, and persistent acts of witchcraft. Those who practice satanism and New Age religions "invite spirit guides to operate," which boosts the power of "territorial spirits that dwell over geographical regions." So empowered, these spirits, in turn, empower the workings of "witches, warlocks, and Satanists," who then do the bidding of the demons to "destroy the power of the church and the reign of God in that area."[35] Jacobs explains that God showed her the failing in her own heart—her personal stronghold, as it were—where she had sinned and directed her how to then appropriately pray to effectively thwart a related spiritual attack on her for her ministerial activities.[36] Once again, the demonic strongholds here are dealt with in prophetically insightful and targeted spiritual warfare; a significant part of that insight is understanding the network of demonic forces and human participants who attempt to keep control over territories and individual human lives.

In what she calls "social strongholds," Jacobs identifies "the oppression over a city in which social injustice, racism, and poverty—with their related problems—cause people to believe God does not care about their needs."[37] Here, she suggests not simply prayer, though she does not state that action is done without prayer but in compliment to particular social action. Quoting Romans 12, she says, "Be not overcome by evil, but overcome evil with good," by which she means that the way to "demolish this stronghold" is by social action—"giving to the poor, establishing homeless shelters, reconciling the races, and clothing those in need." She goes on to say that to engage this stronghold by "using the spiritual weapons of repentance and intercession," but also with "whatever social and political action" they can muster.[38]

In the last point, we see the progressive millennialist narrative coming into play in that one is admonished to elevate social harm through beneficent acts of charity and reconciliation. However, apropos our point here, this is not disconnected from the element of spiritual warfare that runs through the previous examples that specifically identify the negative effects of poverty, racism, and injustice from demonic activity. This demonic activity, too, is systemically implicated through various ideologies that Jacobs identifies by name—Marxism, humanism, and Darwinism—that are hostile to the Kingdom of God and are allegedly propagated by malicious actors seeking to gain power and are in turn used to empower the ruling demonic spirits that hold domain over a given territory. There is always a connection between social ills, political and social institutions acting poorly or being corrupt, and actions carried out by malicious human beings acting in league with demonic agents to destroy a society. And every effort to identify these wicked agents and overcome them is met with the command that God's people must act to elevate these harms by acting social and spiritual to overcome the power of the Devil and his angels.

Near the conclusion of the essay, Jacobs recites the frequently cited passage from 2 Chronicles 7:14: "If My people who are called by My name will humble themselves, and pray and seek My face, and turn from their wicked ways, then, I will hear from heaven, and will forgive their sin and heal their land."[39] She seems to affirm that God's will is to be done on Earth as it is in heaven. If catastrophe is to be averted, these strongholds must be destroyed, the secret plots uncovered, and the conspirators overcome so that spirit-filled, Prophetically guided Christians can bring about the restoration of the world to God's purpose in creating it. Necessarily connected, therefore, to the NAR's dominionism, with its hopeful millennialism, informed by avertive apocalyptic narratives, is an abiding sense of conspiracism.

We must note before going too far into the discussion of conspiracism in the NAR that conspiratorial narratives are not unusual in the contemporary political context. Religious studies scholars David Robertson, Egil Asprem, and Asbjørn Dyrendal write in their introduction to the *Handbook of Conspiracy Theory and Contemporary Religion* (2018), "Conspiracy theories are the defining issue of our age."[40] Historian Katheryn S. Olmsted argues that the "prominence of conspiracy theories in the 2016 U.S. presidential election has led some to believe that we are living in a new age of conspiracism." She quickly added, however, that "conspiracy theories are a normal feature of U.S. political history."[41] Though conspiracy theories may seem more mainstream recently, or in the light of their history, not that anomalous, the pejorative tone of the term remains strong in its popular usage. The term has long been used as a rhetorical device to stifle debate and to attack one's political enemies. As the social scientist Jovan Byford noted in *Conspiracy Theories: A Critical Introduction* (2015), "Conspiracy theory operates as a resource for delegitimization not only at an individual level, as a means of undermining the credibility of an individual author, academic, politician or activist but also on a collective level."[42] With this caveat in mind, he states in the conclusion of his book that conspiracy theories themselves should be taken seriously as "a historically rooted and continually evolving tradition of explanation."[43] In this sense, I see the discursive value of conspiratorial narrations as analogous to how to understand the rhetorical value of apocalypticism, that is, as a means of framing political and social experiences and aspirations.

The conversation among academics concerning conspiracy theories goes at least as far back as historian Richard Hofstadter's 1964 essay, "The Paranoid Style in American Politics." He defines the conspiratorial "paranoid style" as a misunderstanding of historical causality and a misinterpretation of the operation of political alliances and events that are far more complex than the conspiratorial narrative allows. The legal scholar Cass Sunstein writes that conspiracy thinking results from a "more general fact about human psychology, that most people do not like to believe that significant events were caused by bad (or good) luck."[44] That is, human beings simply need an explanation for events even if they cannot fully or rationally establish causality. Byford argues concerning the "anatomy" of conspiracy theories that they share common representations of conspirators as having "sinister plans and the means of mass manipulation." They also share, he writes, "Manichean moral dualism and the naïve optimism of the conspiracy theory," and a "whole suite of common motifs and tropes" that make them sound similar to one another.[45] However, Byford references the work of historian Geoffrey Cubitt to warn us against paring this down something like Hofstadter's "paranoid style," possessing a set of "immutable theoretical elements."[46] Again, for Byford, conspiracy theories are not simply the result of a defect in one's logic or some delusional paranoia but a continuing explanatory narrative tradition deployed and developed in new situations. He concludes that the "image of conspiracy theory" that emerges at the conclusion of his study is one of a "socially and historically bounded explanatory discourse, composed of a dynamic and evolving set of arguments, images, interpretations, and assumptions about causal relations in the [world]."[47]

There is much here that helps us understand, again, the discursive value of conspiratorial narratives in that they work to explain the otherwise inexplicably complex and bewildering events; however, I think the best summary of conspiratorial belief as it pertains to its function within the discourse of the NAR is that offered by political scientist and historian Michael Barkun in *A Culture of Conspiracy: Apocalyptic Visions in Contemporary America* (2003). Reflecting some of what Hofstadter also noticed, Barkun says that conspiracism "is, first and foremost, an explanation of politics" and further describes what he calls "conspiracy belief" as "the belief that an organization made up of individuals or groups was or is acting covertly to achieve some malevolent end."[48] Barkun argues further that the "conspiracist worldview implies a universe governed by design [rather] than by randomness" and identifies three general principles for conspiracy belief: "Nothing happens by accident"; "Nothing is as it seems"; "Everything is connected."[49] Conspiracy belief can then be said to be false, in a sense, and yet effective in constructing a cosmographic framework that is at once reassuring and frightening—"frightening because it magnifies the power of evil," yet simultaneously reassuring because it is assumed that events are "nonrandom."[50]

The conspiracists' world is indeed a frightening one in which the forces of good and evil struggle for the future of all humankind, but it also infuses one's actions with lasting significance and consequence. In this cosmology, one faces malicious adversaries organized in a malevolent cabal bent on humankind's enslavement or eradication, but these forces can be overcome. Evil is real, but good can triumph over it. In the context of the millennialism and apocalypticism of the NAR, woven as they are to the dominionist ambitions of the movement, narratives about evil cabals organized toward nefarious ends are vitally important for their understanding of the world. The very social imaginary of the NAR's optimistic eschatology incorporates the narrative that God's people are progressively overcoming Satan's dominion and, yet, that Satan and his servants and those whom he has deceived are not going to simply allow God's Kingdom to manifest. In reference to what he calls "5 steps to powerful Kingdom activism," Lance Wallnau makes this point while advertising his teaching series *Sheep Nations Rising* by noting that believers will have to continue to fight to overcome "big media" and the "desperate elites" who seek to "dethrone a President [Trump]." In this advertisement, Wallnau quotes Aragorn from the *Lord of the Rings*, "A day may come when the courage of men fails, when we forsake our friends and break all bonds of fellowship, but it is not this day … This day we fight!"[51] Conspiracism is a central feature of the NAR's formulation of spiritual warfare, which is a central element of their dominionist project, ultimately defining what the NAR represents.

Christ or Communism

In the context of the NAR, conspiratorial narratives, apocalypticism, and millennialism work together to form key discursive elements in the way they articulate their understanding of what it means to take dominion. Historian Matthew Avery Sutton argues in particular that apocalypticism was central to the development of early fundamentalism and for the history of post-Second War Evangelicalism.[52] In these expressions, one often sees familiar tropes appear from the past and other segments of Trump's Christian support base. One of the most enduring conspiratorial narratives for conservative American Christians is the notion that Christianity, and specifically Christianity in the United States, is locked in a desperate struggle against communism. The famous evangelist Billy Graham frequently claimed the Cold War was, in fact, a battle between two religions—communism and Christianity. As historian

Richard V. Pierard notes, as early as 1949, Graham's political views pervaded his sermons. "At that time," he argues, Graham "portrayed a world divided into two factions: Western culture, which had its foundations in the Bible and the great revivals, and communism, which had declared its opposition to all things religious."[53] Historian of Christianity Grant Whacker noted as well that Graham's pronounced anti-communism in the 1950s, in which he perceived communism as both a military threat and a spiritual one.[54] Wacker argues that Graham "preached frequently and forcefully about the peril of communist expansionism abroad and infiltration at home," and like many others of his day, "saw communism as both a military threat and a religious menace."[55] Wacker continues that in the 1950s and 60s, "Graham defined himself not only politically but also culturally and even theologically as a warrior against communism," which he was convinced was expanding abroad and infiltrating at home.[56]

To illustrate this point, we can reference an episode of Graham's radio program *The Hour of Decision* from 1963, titled "Why Communism Is Gaining Ground."[57] Graham argues that "communism is the greatest challenge that Christianity has ever faced." He goes on to explain that modern communism is an "animal without a soul," and that a communist is one that does not adhere to universal morality or "the Ten Commandments." Though it is bereft of any moral substance and is no way a "superior ideology," Graham argues that communism continues to gain ground because Americans have "lost their faith" and their fervor for "American ideals." Moreover, he argues that Americans "are in danger in losing faith in God."

Though Americans go to church, he contends, the average Christian has little understanding of their Christian faith and has "unwittingly" adopted the premises of communistic materialism. For this Graham blames subversion in college classrooms, where students are indoctrinated in the ideologies that critique the Christian faith. Remarking on this dire condition with ever-growing intensity, he exclaims that until the West "have a revival of spiritual faith [they] will continue to lose the Cold War." The apocalyptic warnings are indeed dire, and great doom would befall the nation should Americans not act to address these conspiracies against them.

In an address on that program from 1961 titled "How to Combat Communism," Graham noted that in the battle of the global Cold War that the forces of the West have not won a single victory, while communists advance everywhere. "In my opinion, from the human point of view things could not be worse," he argues. Since the Western world has abandoned its Christian foundations, Graham argues further, there is no ideology powerful enough to rebut communism's utopian promises and without a return to these biblical roots, there is not a chance of stopping the communist advance. This abandonment, he contends, happened first with "modernism," which he says "robbed Christianity of the powerful tenants that made it strong." A new god was made in this expression of humanism that permeated modernist theology and "moral absolutes were swept away" leaving the West without any moral foundation strong enough to combat communist totalitarianism. "A war of ideologies," between "the secular against the spiritual," is being fought throughout the world and in "the hearts of men."

The choice is stark—"Revolution and chaos or Christ and righteousness and freedom." Without a return to the true evangelical Christian faith as Graham understood it, the West and the world would be doomed to fall to communism which Graham defines as one of the "devices of Satan." "Many thoughtful students of the Bible believe we are living in the last events of history," he exclaims and argues that satanic power is being unleashed in a way that is unprecedented in world history and immediately references to the battle at Megiddo as described in Revelation to describe what is forthcoming for the "world that has rejected Christ." Expecting that he and his listeners may be living in the days prior to the judgment of God, he urges that the best defense one can mount against communism and in preparation for "the judgments of the future" is personal salvation which guarantees protection in Christ.

There are two interesting points here for us to consider. The first is the geopolitical importance in the battle against communism that is placed in a personalized orthodoxy in which a properly understood evangelical Protestant faith in Jesus is at once a guarantee for protection from the judgments of God in the last days and against the influence of communism; and simultaneously necessarily a strategy to return the nation to its Christian foundations as a guarantee for protection from the same. Secondly, there is the conviction that those who may disagree with Graham's propositions are either wittingly or unwittingly contributing to the downfall of the United States, the West, and the entire world. As they formulate "modernist" theologies, humanistic ethical rationales for dealing with political questions, and further secularize the nation, especially in the context of education, these political and theological heretics damn the nation for their lack of spiritual insight and action. Graham often warned that if these secularists and their ideas remain unchallenged, then the nation and the whole world are doomed to fall under the sway of demonically inspired communism.

This narrative did not die with the Cold War or cease after Billy Graham's passing in 2018. His son Franklin Graham, who supported Trump in the 2016 and 2020 elections, posted an open letter to the website for the Billy Graham Evangelistic Association on June 29, 2021, that argued, echoing some of his father's language, "we are being defeated from within—and no one had to fire a shot."[58] Here, the younger Graham remarks, as his father did decades ago, that "we must realize that the great enemy of the Church is communism" and that because of a weakening of Americans' commitment to the "Biblical principles" on which America was founded, America itself may succumb to communist propaganda. He also argues, like his father, that the main site of this indoctrination is in schools. "It takes a North Korean defector to point out a common thread in North Korea's education system and ours—communism," he argues.

Graham goes on to describe the experience of Yeonmi Park, a young North Korean defector who came with her family to live in the United States and attended Yale and claimed that she found that at Yale "the educational institution indoctrinated students with anti-American propaganda" on par with what she experienced in North Korean schools. In apocalyptic tones that are nearly identical in phraseology to statements of the elder Graham in the 1960s, Franklin Graham states: "The United States has been a guardian of liberty for the world for many years—a place where rights like freedom of religion and speech were protected. Today, however, a new tyranny is at work to erode these freedoms, rewrite our history, and take this nation in the opposite direction." Just as his father did, he claims that the only way to resist this internal subversion of the supposed founding values and rescue the United States from communist dominion is to turn the nation's heart to Jesus.

Wallnau's dominionist eschatology and Franklin and Billy Graham's premillennialism are not compatible with one another to be sure. Further, as they are both Baptists, it is fair to say that neither of the Grahams ever expressed any inclination to charismatic expressions of Christianity and certainly would not agree with Wagner or Wallnau on the role of apostles in the modern church. However, they agree on the spiritual and political danger to the individual, the nation, and the world presented by communism. In a post on YouTube from July 9, 2020, Wallnau mixes the narrative of a "one-world government" with the idea that communists infiltrated American institutions, reducing every political enemy, including Black Lives Matter, to Marxist infiltration.[59]

In this address titled "The Crimes of Our Educators: Brainwashing America's Kids into Communists," Wallnau, as Billy Graham had done decades before, defines communism as a "counterfeit" of what Christ offers. From his website, where the video is linked, he summarizes the points made in the video:

> These kids have been trained in the schools. What you've got now is the fruit of the American academic system, the universities, which are manifesting now. It doesn't matter if it's the elite schools of Harvard, Yale, or Duke, our young people's minds have already been infiltrated in left-wing ideology, like a cult. All of them talking about social justice, cultural Marxism, and intersectionality. They're being turned into weaponized machines by socialist teachers. Schools are intimidating parents, and indoctrinate kids in elementary school, high school, and junior high with a curriculum of common core brainwashing.[60]

Wallnau's address here is contextualized at the beginning of the video as describing the global struggle against communist ideology: "There's a game going on and the only thing standing in their way is Donald Trump."

With the prospect of losing the Senate and the Oval Office, Wallnau explains that as God is attempting to manifest His will on Earth, those spiritually aware Christians need to "contend with hell" to make sure it does not get its way. For Wallnau, this corruption is the fruit of the American education system, which has already been infiltrated by harmful dogmas "like a cult." These ideologies are "social justice," "cultural Marxism," "intersectionality," and, he dismissively says, "blah, blah, blah." What is at stake for Wallnau in the 2020 election: control over the government mountain, and standing in the way is the media, which he refers to as a "false prophet," and the fact that schools have indoctrinated children with Marxism and weaponized them against America. Wallnau exclaims that with the "globalists'" plans afoot across the planet, Donald Trump is the only thing standing in their way, and states in a prayerful sense, "And in Jesus' name he will stay in their way," of course, here, prophetically announcing the necessary and hoped-for outcome for the 2020 election.

Wallnau's address was posted late in the Trump administration's term, it is consistent with narratives from before the 2016 election, and as we have seen, far earlier than that. In many ways, Wallnau was retelling the tales of communist subversion that Billy Graham preached about with a similar sounding remedy in Jesus. Of course, apocalyptic narratives reflect their time as well as the particular theology of their teller. Wallnau and those associated with the NAR were not looking necessarily for the end of days but a way to take dominion. They were not looking only for spiritual revival but a political barrier to the opposition's advance in the form of Donald Trump. In any case, there is nexus of conspiratorial and apocalyptic narratives about communist subversion that imperils the nation, and indeed the world, that permeates the broader discourse of Trump's evangelical base regardless of their position inside or outside the networks of the NAR, one that draws on much older and persistent tropes among America's Religious Right.

The Judgment of God on a Wayward Nation

The avertive element in the apocalyptic narratives of the NAR is certainly present in the way those associated with the movement express conspiratorial narratives of Marxist subversion. If this subversion is not rooted out and stopped, they argue, America will fall, eaten away from within by its ideological and even spiritual enemies. However, this is only one plot element within a broader apocalyptic narrative scope. And just as we saw with the trope of communist subversion continued from the 1960s, the NAR has also adopted components from a long history of apocalyptic references to the United States among Christians that go back much further than the mid-twentieth century. As Wojcik notes, "Eschatological beliefs pervade the writings of the Puritans, many of whom maintained that they had been elected by God to fulfill a divinely determined historical plan."[61] Along with this notion that they had a special place in God's plan for the entire world was the caveat that things could go ill if they rejected God's laws and neglected to maintain the covenant.

One can see this basic narrative in John Winthrop's words from what has been called the sermon on the Arabella in 1630, which he closes with the admonition referencing Deuteronomy 30, and warns of the judgment of God should the people abandon His covenant with them.[62] If God's people in this new society keep faith with God, they will prosper; however, if they break his laws and follow after other gods, judgment will follow. This narrative persists today, and has appeared in key moments in American history.

There is perhaps no more poignant example of the persistence of this narrative than the statements from Jerry Falwell and Pat Robertson on *The 700 Club* the day after 9/11. To explain the devastation America suffered the day before, Falwell exclaimed that God had removed his protection because the federal courts had removed God from "the public square" and "from schools." Falwell went on to say that abortion, too, had made God "mad" and that "pagans and the abortionists and the feminists and the gays and the lesbians who are actively trying to make that an alternative lifestyle, the ACLU, People for the American Way—all of them who have tried to secularize America," were to blame for the attack. "I point the finger in their face and say, 'you helped this happen,'" he stated. Robertson replied, "Well, I totally concur."[63] Though Robertson and Falwell attempted to retract their statements, the point, of course, is that America had enjoyed the special favor and protection until it violated the conditions of that favor, and then God imposed judgment.[64]

Those associated with the NAR often evoke the image of America as having a special place in God's plan for the world and anticipate His divine wrath for America's going astray. For example, in a 2010 volume compiled by Ché Ahn, Lou Engle echoes the condemnation we just read from Jerry Falwell concerning America's tolerance of abortion. He argues, "God will not have fellowship with a government that practices iniquity by passing laws legalizing the shedding of innocent blood through abortion."[65] To support this claim, Engle references Psalm 94:20–21, a passage that specifically refers to God as the "God of vengeance" and as a protector of the righteous.[66] In June of 2012, Lance Wallnau affirmed this belief in a message posted on his website, using the wars between the Philistines and Israel during the days of King Saul to make a point about anointing and authority relative to the church in America. He argues that just as David, who possessed a special calling from God, was given authority by King Saul to do battle against Goliath, so too the church "must be like David and merge our bridal love of spiritual intimacy and passion for God's presence with a warrior's resolve to advance against an intimidating foe and formidable heights."[67] He argues further, "Hell will not yield, and America will not be saved because of our prayers alone. The strong man will only budge when one mightier than him comes upon him—in his house ... THEN those prayers for America, stored up in the heavens like latent nuclear power, will be unleashed."

In Wallnau's narrative, the chosen people of God battle against strong forces of evil for the sake of the nation's survival, and they could lose if not for the supernatural power given to them by God. He is confident that victory is assured, but only insofar that God's people act as the Holy Spirit empowers them. "The only ones truly able to resist are those who are full of the Spirit of God," he argues. He goes on to say, "Those who confront Baal are those who never bowed the knee." Interestingly, in a post from October of that year, Wallnau stated, "if we let the lights of Christianity get blown out, our children will be slaves of the nations [sic] debt in the divided States of America."[68] These avertive or conditional statements are actually quite common in Wallnau's discourse, especially as they relate to the fate of the United States and the battle to save it.

Wallnau, however, was not alone in making a comparison between God's judgments on Israel and the present condition of America. Once again, echoing much of what we heard from Robertson and Falwell, prophet Dutch Sheets posted a letter on the Elijah's List website in 2010 stating that God's judgment would fall on America unless there were a significant change. "If God brought corrective but serious judgment to Israel, we are horribly deceived if we think it will not happen to us. If something doesn't happen to lessen this judgment—and it can be lessened—we are headed for very difficult times," he stated. "Generally speaking, we are a narcissistic, self-loving nation that has accepted a culture of death, perversion, drugs and violence, and more," he argues. "We have murdered 51 million babies in the womb, and to satisfy the cry for a toleration of immorality and perversion, we are ready to throw away 6,000 years of honoring God's definition of marriage and family."[69]

With the corporate and individual sins of the people of the nation cataloged briefly in his letter, Sheets states, "America is in a moral and spiritual crisis of such magnitude that it is almost unbelievable." And yet, in keeping with the pattern of avertive apocalyptic narratives in the NAR, he argues that "God desires to bring a Third Great Awakening to America," which can happen if the church acts in prayer and evangelism, if people are saved and, crucially, referencing the prophet Joel, if the people of the nation repent and return to God. As we will see in the coming chapters, this is a narrative that continues through Trump's administration and through to after the 2020 election as the prophets urge God's people to support his candidacy and presidency.

The narrative of the wayward nation coming to judgment from God for its transgressions is a common enough story for conservative Christians and among the network of apostles and prophets of the NAR. However, it is a narrative that also functions to unite Christians who share neither a similar eschatology and ecclesiology nor a similar position regarding the gifts of the Holy Spirit. One site where varying opinions on theological matters converged before the 2016 election over the need to rescue the nation by returning to God in repentance was a book by a Messianic Rabbi who figures significantly in the networks of NAR support for Trump, Jonathan Cahn.

In *The Harbinger: The Ancient Mystery That Holds the Secret of America's Future* (2011), Cahn, as the epigraph to the book, writes "in the form of a story" but claims that "what is contained within the story is real." In twenty-two chapters, following a form that resembles Socratic dialogues, an unnamed character converses with a mysterious stranger who promises to explain an "ancient mystery" concerning America's future, a "mystery behind what is happening in the twenty-first century from politics to the economy to foreign affairs," as revealed in the prophecies given to ancient Israel.[70]

In the book, Cahn's prophet figure explains, "On the altars of Baal and Molech, their newfound gods," the Children of Israel killed their own children—a clear reference to abortion. The stranger goes on to explain that Israel ignored the warnings of the prophets to return to the God of their fathers and attacked the prophets that God sent to them. The Israelites "rejected the call and declared war on those who remained faithful" and further "branded them as troublemakers, irritants, and dangerous, and, finally, enemies of the state." And as the warnings from God through His prophets became "louder and the warnings more severe," God's chosen nation still turned away from Him until he finally the nation "would enter a new stage ... God would remove the hedge."[71] If there were any doubt about the way in which Cahn wishes to juxtaposition America as God's new Israel—a nation founded by Him with divine favor conditional upon an original covenant, the stranger says plainly, "The same nation that was formed after the pattern of Israel now follows after the pattern of its moral descent, its spiritual departure from God."[72] And as it was with ancient Israel, God chastises His chosen.

From this point forward in the narrative, the stranger discloses several "Harbingers," or foretelling events that signal an ever more severe reproof of America's Godlessness in an effort to get her to return to God in repentance, just as it was with ancient Israel. The first is what the title of chapter 4 calls "The Breach."[73] Once again, there are echoes of the response to 9/11 from Falwell and Robertson in Chan's narrative. The "evil men" that had been "restrained" by the Hand of God were finally able to penetrate America's defenses and strike deep into its sense of security.[74] Subsequent warnings would follow; other "harbingers" that would warn America to return to full covenant with God. "So it was given to ancient Israel, and it's *about* ancient Israel, but now it's *reappearing* as a sign of warning to America," as Cahn's inquisitive character in dialogue states.[75]

The pattern of God's judgment on Israel to compel her to return to God is repeated exactly for the new Israel, America, which has also turned from her God and followed after foreign gods and given herself over to abominations— abortion, homosexuality, humanism, and various other corrupting vices. But what is most significant to note here is that the destruction is not devoid of meaning, "It means there is a purpose behind that first calamity," as the stranger states. "The purpose of the seemingly incomprehensible tragedy of 9/11," which is compared to the first Assyrian invasion of Israel, "was *remedial*—to correct, to wake up the nation, to turn it back to God, a purpose of redemption."[76] All the disasters from 2001, through the financial collapse of 2008, the "collapse of Fannie Mae and Freddie Mac," the "collapse of Lehman Brothers," and other catastrophes yet to come all are part of a pattern of judgment for reasons of reproof and correction for a wayward nation that may yet still be a vessel for God's will.[77] "The progression of judgment is only a reaction to the progression of a nation's apostasy, the progressive severing of its connection to God and the biblical foundation on which it was established."[78] The calamities may serve as a warning and instruction, and further calamities may be avoided. As the stranger says, "So too redemption comes not only apart from calamity ... but also through it."⁷⁹ More harsh judgment may be avoided if the warnings are heeded, and America returns to her God and to the founding biblical principles on which it was founded.

The promise of future financial ruin resulting from the nation not returning to God is a major theme in the latter part of the book. It is significant, therefore, that when Lance Wallnau recounts his first visit with Trump in 2015 at Trump Tower, along with other religious leaders, he makes specific reference to Cahn's book stating the impending financial collapse of the United States saying that "[h]ere is the real 'Harbinger' Jonathan Cahn is talking about … We have an economy going over a cliff and drunken Liberals scheming like Socialists behind the wheel," and suggesting Trump is a "prophetic businessman."⁸⁰ What is implicit in Cahn's narrative is more explicit in Wallnau's reference: the schemes of liberals, socialists, abortionists, and secularists are bringing the United States to judgment, much like what Robertson and Falwell had asserted days after 9/11. It is significant to note that Cahn's book was a New York Times Best Seller and was praised by those who would become staunch Trump supporters, like Pat Robertson and former Arkansas Governor Mike Huckabee, who said it was "soul-stirring and stunning" while introducing Cahn to an audience gathered to hear Cahn speak at Capitol Hill in 2014.⁸¹ In his talk, after being introduced by the former governor, Cahn recalls the words of George Washington to echo what he regarded as Washington's "prophetic warning" that secularism and abortion will alienate America from "the smiles of heaven."

Conclusion: Trump's Anointing and Mission

In the introduction to *The Apocalyptic Complex: Perspectives, Histories, Persistence* (2018), religion scholar Matthias Riedel and the scholar of religious literature David Marno write, "The last three decades have been particularly rich in literature reflecting on the apocalyptic. The turn of the millennium, the attack against the Twin Towers of the World Trade Center, and the ensuing cultural and military clash between East and West were all perceived as potentially apocalyptic events."⁸² Even before Trump announced his candidacy for the Republican nomination for the 2016 election, those associated with the NAR were adapting more broadly appealing narratives of conspiracy and judgment, weaving into their narratives the politics of the day. Authors less associated with the Christian Right and even less connected to the NAR, like Jerome Corsi, were capitalizing on a flurry of conspiratorial narratives regarding the Obama administration at this time as well.

In 2008 Corsi published a New York Times Best Seller, *Obamanation: Leftist Politics and the Cult of Personality*, the main claim of which was a warning of leftist subversion; claims that Wallnau echoed in his messages about Obama and his allies.[83] Then, in 2011, Corsi wrote *Where's the Birth Certificate? The Case Barak Obama Is Not Eligible to Be President*,[84] a text that is partly responsible for the popularity of the "birther" conspiracy that Trump repeated on several occasions from 2012 through the 2016 campaign.[85] The conspiratorial narratives about the "Deep State" and socialists seeking to destroy America from Trump allies like Jason Chaffetz, George Papadopoulos, and Corey Lewandowski persisted throughout Trump's presidency. Such narratives, too, found their way into the statements and writings of those associated with the NAR, blended with their particular understanding of the spiritual nature of the conflict that God empowered Trump to wage and their role in that war by supporting him politically and through prayer.

Though we should not confuse people like Corsi, Landowski, or Chaffetz with the prophets and apostles of the NAR, the language they use to describe former President Obama, the Democratic Party, liberals and leftists in general, and Trump's war on the "Deep Sate" is shared by the most prominent figures of the NAR. Despite what they do not share theologically, they could all agree that Trump was the best person to combat the corrupting influence of socialists who were ruining America. As Wallnau puts it in his book, *God's Chaos Candidate* (2016), "National suicide is the path that America is on and the 2016 election will determine if that future can be altered," and continues by exclaiming, "I believe it's the wrecking ball—Donald J. Trump—that has been sent to stop the momentum of this self-destruction."[86] The ultimate enemy in this political struggle, however, is evil itself. Wallnau argues, "We are up against a malevolent and demonic agenda aimed to destroy the global force for kingdom expansion that is America."[87] Voting for Trump was not merely a political act. It was spiritual warfare.

For those associated with the NAR, conspiratorial narratives set within their "optimistic" millennialism, expressed in avertive apocalyptic narratives describing the people of God waging war to take dominion from Satan and his allies, established not only a theological framework for political events but an activist vision and directive to engage in the political process as spiritual warriors guided by prophetic insight. Long-standing tropes of communist subversion of American and the Christian faith and the idea that God would judge America, the New Israel, for abandoning her covenant with Him blended with the ideas of dominion so central to the NAR's sense of a dominion mandate encouraged support for Trump as God's chosen leader to spearhead the fight. Voting in the 2016 election was for prophecy voters a means to wage spiritual, political, and cultural war on the various cabals that aligned themselves with a satanic conspiracy to destroy America who attempted to resist the fullest realization of the Gospel in the form of Christian dominion over all seven spheres of American political, cultural, and social life.

3

"God's Chaos Candidate"—Prophecy & Trump's 2016 Campaign

One of the most intriguing aspects of prophecy voters' support for Trump in the 2016 election was the alleged prophecies that foretold God would choose him to become President of the United States. There were many such prophecies leading up to the 2016 election, and a few were given much earlier than that, and we will discuss some of them in this chapter. However, we should try to understand this phenomenon not simply as an oddity or spectacle but as a further expression of the avertive apocalyptic narratives and "optimistic" millennialism, blended with conspiratorial tropes, that express the dominionist ambitions of the movement. I argue that we should read the Trump prophecies as having a specific theological perspective that expresses the desires and wishes of the producers and consumers of the media that affected their support for Trump. This reliance on prophecies is why I call these Christians prophecy voters. The prophetic narratives motivated this support tied as they were to other concerns, including issues like ending abortion and opposition to gay marriage, but also to claims that the political domain was a stage for the cosmic battle between the forces of good and evil in a struggle for dominion.

In *American Possessions: Fighting Demons in the Contemporary United States* (2015), religious studies scholar Sean McCloud notes that "Third Wave practices such as spiritual mapping" are ways of seeing the world differently.[1] McCloud quotes C. Peter Wagner to point out that for believers, spiritual warfare practices present "the world around us as it really is, not as it appears to be"; and "that reality is more than appears on the surface."[2] We could then say that a crucial claim made by those associated with the NAR, especially as it relates to spiritual warfare, is one of possessing insight into an otherwise invisible dimension that explains the source of all fears. For these Christians, prophetic messages foretell calamities ranging from economic recessions to conspiratorial narratives about socialist subversion and demonic cults while offering an optimistic perspective and even strategies for overcoming fear and challenges in the knowledge that God is in control and has a plan and remedy is not only possible but inevitable through the Holy Spirit.

This aspect of NAR Christian perspectives is certainly more broadly shared among charismatic Christians and played a role in the support that Trump received from them. Daniel Silliman notes in *Reading Evangelicals: How Christian Fiction Shaped a Culture and a Faith* (2021) that Trump had "won the imagination of vast numbers of American evangelicals" whose imagination had been "shaped and informed and fostered" by the books they read. "Trump spoke," he argues, "to those hopes and fears" that Christian readers found in the pages of works like the *Left Behind* series and the horror novels by Frank Peretti. "The books imagined conspiracies destroying small-town America, aided by deceptive neighbors and invisible, invading forces." When Trump promised to "Drain the Swamp" and to "Lock Her Up," it seemed that he was as aware as they were of what motivated and frightened them.[3]

I agree with Silliman that Christian fiction was not the only motivating factor for Trump's evangelical Christian base.[4] However, we cannot overlook how the presence of imagined enemies that threatened to destroy Christianity and America added to Trump's appeal to that demographic. Moreover, as it concerns those associated with the NAR, various prophecies addressed these anxieties. They foretold that God chose Trump to reverse the fortunes of Christians in America and for America itself. For those associated with the NAR, such a view was perfectly in line with their theological perspectives. As André Gangé notes, Wagner regarded Frank Peretti's novels as the best illustration of actual spiritual warfare.[5] Gangé goes on to explain that Peretti meant to promote these ideas about spiritual warfare and how he saw the world through his novels and that though the novels were fiction, the "demonology" presented in them "is not fictional."[6]

Suppose we want to understand the dynamics behind the Trump prophecies that inspired so much support from those associated with the NAR. In that case, we should approach prophecy in the NAR, especially as it relates to Trump, as a project of imaginative world-building. By world-building, I mean an imaginative practice whereby the author constructs a believable space wherein the story's drama takes place and invites the reader to immerse themselves in it. Professor of theology and religious studies Mark Godin argues that "one important aspect of world-building for both fantasy worlds and institutions is the way that boundaries are imagined, not only for the purpose of designating identity and belonging but also for presenting possibilities for crossing those boundaries and entering these worlds."[7] His focus is on works of literature like Tolkien's *Lord of the Rings* as a case study of theological aspects in fictional world-building, but I think the point still works for the Trump prophecies. Though the authors and readers of these prophecies do not regard them as fictional, we should remember that even in his overtly fictional novels, Peretti did not think of demons and spiritual warfare as fictional. To them, demons are real and an integral part of their religious cosmology. In the imaginative deployment of narratives of demonic conspiracy, authors of the prophecies concerning Trump's candidacy and presidency framed the political, social, and cultural fabric of their reality as a cosmic battle for the future of the nation and the world, thereby imbuing the 2016 election with soteriological meaning as well as eschatological importance.

Prophesying Victory

In the months before the 2016 election, especially after Trump solidified his hold on the Republican nomination, the prophets seemed confident that Trump would be victorious and that his victory would translate into revival and blessings in America. On October 26, 2016, prophet Kat Kerr wrote on the website Elijah List that she had a prophetic word concerning the election. She claimed, "we are in the kingdom age," wherein "the hand of our government will be extended to the believer."[8] She explains that "God himself has told me Trump will sit in the White House," though many "may not like him" this is irrelevant. Her conviction resulting from her vision is that "God Likes him." Concerning criticism of Trump's brashness and lax morals, Kerr explains that Trump had become born again only a few months prior and that Christians should be more patient with him because "he's a baby Christian."

Kerr explains the difference in Christians' views on Trump's behavior with a distinction between those who are "operating in the flesh" or those who are without prophetic and spiritual insight, who cannot see that despite his flaws, Trump has been chosen, and those like herself who operate "in the Spirit," who rightly discern that God is bringing "forced change" in taking on "demonic" forces so that "we can rule in reign with Christ in this time." She further exhorts the audience to reject the seemingly logical positions regarding the presidential election, asking them to "throw their mind on a shelf somewhere" and to "put on the crown." However, she asserts, we cannot "wear that crown if we do not have the right person in here on Pennsylvania Avenue." Kerr goes on to say that Trump would win in a landslide despite what the "liberal media" is saying, whom she claims is "not on God's side" and does not "want God in our government, they do not want God in our country." God's plan is for "twenty-four years of freedom," which she describes as different from "liberal freedom," which means for her removing Christianity and "the truth about the history of our country." The freedom offered by the political opposition, claims Kerr, offers "no freedom to operate for Christ, no freedom to build," and, with explicit reference to Wagner's great wealth transfer, "no freedom to handle the wealth of the wicked."

Kerr's message is clear, "God has an agenda," and He "is voting this time." She explains that there is a clear choice in this election—a "platform" of "light and one of darkness, one of life one of death." Her "revelation report" repeats much about what we know about the NAR concerning their perspective on the current relevance of prophecy for an ever-evolving plan of God, the reliance on references to spiritual warfare in relation to what moves events in politics, and, of course, an avertive apocalypticism that promises catastrophe if Christians make the wrong political choice, despite the optimistic assertion that God will place Trump in the White House. So optimistic is she that she states that she "would not want to leave this Earth right now" in anticipation of what is about to happen with the election and where that will take the nation. She closes with another repeated element in NAR discourse about the United States, comparing it to Israel as both nations established by God.

America, Kerr claims, "was birthed in the heart of God," which is revealed in the "word Jerusalem," and spells it out, "J-E-R-U-S-A-L-E-M," making a note of the letters U, S, and A in the spelling. There is prophetic significance for her in the arraignment of the letters themselves telling her, and that God's destiny for America in relation to the election, further affirming her view that, as nothing is random, God is directing the events of the 2016 election for the benefit of God's people. He was going to save America. To be part of what God is doing, to be aligned with His will and purpose in this election, Kerr exhorts the audience to "get on the Trump Train" and to "get out and vote."

After Trump won the election, prophets associated with the NAR made connections to Trump's unexpected victory to earlier prophecies. For example, on November 24, 2016, a video that contained audio and transcription of a prophetic word from prophet Kim Clement alleging he had prophesied Trump's victory in 2007 was posted on YouTube and soon gained traction within charismatic and NAR networks.[9] "Trump shall become a trumpet, says the Lord. Trump shall become a trumpet. I will raise up the trump to become the trumpet," Clement says in the recording. It is difficult for one to be sure if this specifically refers to the word "trump" refers to Donald Trump because, in the same prophetic utterance, Clement goes on to state that "Bill Gates will open up the gate of a financial realm for the church, says the Lord." Of course, the latter did not happen. In other words, the prophetic utterance here may be an example of homiletical wordplay that is read selectively and retroactively as a Trump prophecy.

Nevertheless, the resurfacing of Clement's prophecy itself seemed to speak in similar terms as later prophecies. The video itself is also heavily edited to make the rest of the revelation seem to infer that Clement was talking about Donald Trump. In the clip, he speaks about the "trump who will become a trumpet" and who is indeed destined for the "highest office in the land," who Clement goes on to describe as a "praying president, but not a religious one," and person of "hot blood" and bring the "walls of protection around this country" and change the "economy." As with other Trump prophecies, too, Clement goes on just before the video cuts off to say that this president will serve "two terms." Of course, this portion of the prophecy did not happen as Trump lost his bid for reelection, but in 2016 it seemed a real enough possibility.

There were differing opinions among Christians about such alleged prophecies concerning Trump. In November of 2021, *Christianity Today* ran a story that specifically referenced Clement's prophecy and its use before the election, asking, "Are evangelicals so obsessed with Trump that they've crossed the line into civic idolatry?"[10] James A. Beverley, professor of Christian thought and ethics at Tyndale Seminary in Toronto, wrote in *Faith Today* in 2017 that such prophecies should be held to the highest scrutiny, even for those who believe in the gift of prophecy. He refers to Kerr's prophecy discussed moments ago and the alleged prophecy by Clement from 2007, along with those of Lance Wallnau and Mark Taylor, both of whom we will discuss later. Beverley's main point is that there is something suspicious and dangerous about these prophecies, warning of such utterances distracting from scripture and that such prophecies often get read selectively after the fact to fit a particular narrative.[11] Pointing to Clement's prophecy, Beverly states that the context for the prophecy seemed to be predicting the outcome of the 2008 election, not 2016. However, for some Christians, Clement's prophecy was the earliest word from God on Trump's victory in 2016.

Among those who were attentive to these prophecies was Stephen Strang, CEO and founder of Charisma Media, publisher of *Charisma Magazine* along with the popular books by Messianic Rabbi Jonathan Cahn, *The Harbinger* (2012) and *The Paradigm* (2017), which we will discuss later in this chapter. In 2019 Strang interviewed *American Adversaries Radio* host Christopher Hart and discussed prophecies concerning Trump delivered by Clement and others, and indeed validated that Clement gave the earliest of the Trump prophecies.[12] Later, Strang remained so convinced of the prophecy's predictions concerning Trump, denied that Biden won in 2020, and claimed that the election was "stolen" in part on the power of Clement's prophecy.[13] Elsewhere, Strang continued to speak about the validity of these predictions, and in particular, the place of Clement's prophecy. In his 2017 book *God and Donald Trump*, he wrote that the string of prophecies pointing to Trump's 2016 election went "as far back as 2007" with Clement's foretelling of Trump winning the White House placed there by God.[14]

Though Clement's prophesy was regarded by many as the first Trump prophecy, other prophecies seemed to affirm Clement's alleged 2007 prediction. With the advantage of hindsight, Strang goes on in *God and Donald Trump* to discuss other prophecies concerning Trump. He mentions a prophetic word from Chuck Pierce, whom Strang describes as a prophet whom he respects, as having said in 2008, "America must learn to play the Trump card."[15] Strang goes on to explain that three months later, as Pierce was driving to speak at a church in Las Vegas that he passed by Trump's hotel and was struck with another revelation. "When I drove by the Trump hotel," as Strang quotes Pierce, "I knew exactly what God was saying—that it would take someone like Donald Trump, who would not have the political background of either party; and he would be willing to address the structure that was presently taking America in the wrong direction."[16]

On October 12, 2017, Strang posted the interview with prophet Chuck Pierce that was transcribed in his book.[17] In the interview, Pierce claimed that on May 31, 2008, God "took him up" and showed him "every state in the union," and which time he claims God told him about the "trump card." Strang notes that Frank Amedia, an Ohio pastor, prophet, and founder of the prayer group POTUS Shield, and Mark Taylor had already gone "on the record" to directly say that God was going to put Trump in the White House and asked Pierce if he had also said that point directly before the election itself. Pierce stated that he was averse to saying, "something other than what the Lord was saying to [him]," but that he did keep repeating the phrase that Christians should "play the trump card." He claims that when he "got flak" about his claims, especially after the election, he "would have to say that he did not jump on any bandwagon," and that God had revealed this to him in 2008.

Pierce explains that through Obama's two terms, rather than "getting bogged down" in American issues, God directed him to pray for Israel and Netanyahu. He claims that God then revealed to him that Obama "was trying to take him [Netanyahu] out," but if Netanyahu could stay in office that "America would be ok." At that time, Pierce claims to have prophesied that Netanyahu would win his election in 2015 and that this victory signified for him that Trump would win as well because "it was the God of Israel backing Trump." What seemed like two unrelated political events were prophetically aligned events that signified to the spiritually aware that God was behind Trump in 2016.

Pierce goes on to explain that what was happening with the election of Trump was America averting a crisis in that the nation was straying from the "God of Israel," thereby "negating our relationship with the God of Israel." In this way, Peirce regarded the prophecies revealing that God wanted them to support Israel via supporting Netanyahu and that if America could see Trump elected, who also supported Israel, America could "prolong [its] status in the world." Pierce was convinced that God had backed Trump as a "Cyrus" and a "Jehu" to bring about a drastic reversal of the nation's course, echoing a common phrase for Trump among NAR-affiliated Christians. Here the "covenant alignment" of the United States was connected to support for Israel, and that support was secured in Trump's election. On these grounds, Peirce argues that one must "look past [Trump's] unrighteous moves in the past to see how God has righteously chosen him to affect the way that this nation goes forward."

Strang is clear both in his book and in the interview with Pierce that his decision to support Trump came only after Ted Cruz dropped out of the race. He is equally clear that this support had a great deal to do with Trump's policy positions and his own aversion to Hillary Clinton as the alternative. However, in the conclusion of *God and Donald Trump*, he writes that he also trusted the word of the prophets Mark Taylor, Frank Amedia, Lance Wallnau, Chuck Pierce, "and others who prophesied that Trump would be the next president."[18] He goes on to explain that he knows and trusts each of these men, and, though he is not a prophet, that he is "convinced that God has a plan for America" and that he is "equally convinced that, for this moment in our history, He has lifted up one of the most unlikely leaders anyone could imagine to guide this nation." The issues mattered to Strang, but the trusted prophets associated with the NAR helped confirm for him that Trump was the right man at the right time and chosen by God to lead the nation.

"The Trump Prophecies"

Many of the prophecies concerning the 2016 election came quite close to the time of the election, as with the word from Kat Kerr, or contained vague references that only seem to be talking about Trump in retrospect, like what we saw in the reflections on the prophecies by Kim Clement and Chuck Pierce. However, Mark Taylor's word of prophecy specifically references Donald Trump and predates Trump's actual run for the Republican nomination, dating back as far as 2011 when he claims that God told him that Trump would become president.[19] Taylor explains that he was extremely ill after retiring as a firefighter, was suffering from depression and other ailments, and was attending an apostolic church at the time.[20] As he recounts the events, he was watching television and saw Trump appear on a program. One evening, while feeling particularly ill, He writes, "something deep in my spirit immediately snapped into awareness ... like an invisible sergeant within the Army of the Lord calling me to attention."[21] Taylor goes on to explain that he was "allowed in the Spirit to weave together the connecting threads between the man on the screen and the enigmatic message blaring within me like a siren louder than anything I'd known in my career as a fireman," which was the Lord speaking to him and say, "*You are hearing the voice of a president.*"[22]

Taylor's story first appeared to the broader public in his 2017 book titled *The Trump Prophecies: The Astonishing True Story of the Man Who Saw Tomorrow ... And What He Says Is Coming Next*, which was revised, updated, and expanded in 2019, but he and others claim he had these prophecies well in advance of the book's publication. In the aftermath of the 2016 election, Taylor became a common name among those who were fascinated by his incredible predictions. He was even featured on a December 2017 broadcast for a Christian Broadcasting News (CBN) story titled "He Predicted Trump Would Be President 6 Years Ago; Here's Why This Prophet Says Trump Is in for Two Terms."[23] Supportive Christian media outlets, like CBN and *Sid Roth's It's Supernatural!*, relayed the Trump Prophecies message to their audiences after the election, framing Trump's 2016 victory as an affirmation that God was actively engaged in these events.[24]

What Taylor titled the "Commander in Chief" prophecy was allegedly given in 2011 as recorded in the book and on his website, and as he recounted in the CBN interview. The prophecy as posted on Taylor's website, which is dated November 11, 2017, states, "The Spirit of God says, 'I have chosen this man, Donald Trump, for such a time as this. For as Benjamin Netanyahu is to Israel, so shall this man be to the United States of America!'" This resembles both the general claim that America is like Israel, common in American evangelical discourse, and Chuck Pierce's prophecy about the connection between Netanyahu's victory in the 2015 election and Trump's victory in the American election of 2016. This commonality points again to a broader discourse about the special relationship that both nations share with God in NAR discourse. The prophecy reads in part:

> The enemy will say Israel, Israel, what about Israel? For Israel will be protected by America once again. The Spirit of God says yes! America will once again stand hand and hand with Israel, and the two shall be as one. For the ties between Israel and America will be stronger than ever, and Israel will

flourish like never before. The Spirit of God says, I will protect America and Israel, for this next president will be a man of his word. When he speaks the world will listen and know that there is something greater in him than all the others before him.[25]

Through Trump, God will bless both nations with security and financial prosperity.

Near the beginning of the prophecy, Taylor states that God will favor US currency in the world, and then discusses something quite close to Wagner's notion of the great wealth transfer, but on a national scale. That section states that the "enemy" will worry that Trump, being aware of their "tricks," will put a stop to their theft, "robbing America for decades." God promises in the prophecy to take that stolen wealth and return it to the nation, "For I will use this man to reap the harvest that the United States has sown for and plunder from the enemy what he has stolen and return it 7-fold back to the United States." Further, the prophecy states, "The Spirit says, when the financial harvest begins, so shall it parallel in the spiritual for America." In keeping with the general "prosperity gospel" inclinations of the NAR, Taylor's prophecy sees a connection between spiritual maturity and blessing with financial affluence.

This first prophecy also discusses the opposition that Trump would face in the election to come. This section of the prophecy states that the opposition "will spend billions to keep this president [Obama] in, but that such efforts would be futile, like "flushing money down the toilet." Because this wealth "comes from and … is being used by evil forces," God assures that it will be to no avail, "for this next election will be a clean sweep for the man I [God] have chosen." Speaking of Trump in this 2011 prophecy, Taylor claims that God told him that the enemy would say many unflattering things about him, "but it will not affect him, and they shall say it rolls off of him like the duck, for as the feathers of a duck protect it, so shall my feathers protect this next president."

There are many things to note here. Even if this were referring to the 2016 election, spending from both candidates in 2016 was lower than in previous elections.[26] However, more to the point, the prophecy, as allegedly given in 2011, describes what was expected for the 2012 election, not 2016. This discrepancy is something that Taylor addresses in the book and in the CBN interview. He explains in the book that, of course, Barak Obama won a second term and that he "thought for a while that [he] had gotten it all wrong," but that he nevertheless "truly believed that the Holy Spirit had guided [him] that day," so he continued to "believe the message had some kind of relevance to God's people in some way," even if the message was not what he thought it was.[27] Later, Taylor and his supporters clarified that he was not wrong about the content of the prophecy, only the timing and the year in which Trump would win the presidency.

Taylor's prophecy states further, "They," the opposition, "will say things about this man (the enemy), but it will not affect him, and they shall say it rolls off of him like the duck, for as the feathers of a duck protect it, so shall my feathers protect this next president." It is difficult to agree that this was Trump's temperament in the 2016 campaign or since regarding criticism, but the final line proved most difficult to place even after the 2016 election. It reads, "Even mainstream news media will be captivated by this man and the abilities that I have gifted him with, and they will even begin to agree with him, says the Spirit of God." Taylor agrees in the CBN interview that this was "the only line of prophecy that has not come to pass yet," but is confident that it might still happen. He rhetorically asks, considering that so much of the prophecy had come true in his estimation, "We have to ask ourselves, what's fixin' to happen to make the mainstream news media to start to agree with him." The interviewer then asks, "What is fixing to happen?" Taylor responds, "God's going to clean out the news media." According to Taylor, God is sending his "millionaires and billionaires" to "buy 'em out" the media because "there's no spirit of truth in 'em." The interview goes on to state that the "Army of God will have victory after victory."

Though there are obvious inconsistencies with the 2011 prophecy, that is not the point. The prophecy, especially as it, and the accompanying prophecies in Taylor's book and the supportive Christian media describe the political landscape in terms of spiritual warfare with consequences that reflect both the optimistic millennialism of the NAR's conception of what it means to establish dominion and how Trump's election in 2016 was a key moment in accomplishing that mission. The CBN interview framed Taylor's prophecy as having pointed out that God was using Trump to "stop an anti-Christian agenda that was taking hold of America." Taylor says in the interview, "The Most High God is denying the enemy's timeline, and it's through Donald Trump that a lot of this is being denied right now."

In keeping with the aversion to dispensationalist pessimism regarding the end times, Taylor remarks in the book that far from things coming to judgment, God is demonstrating that he is rescuing America and that Trump is an instrument to that end. "Systems of power in this country are about to fall under judgment," he claims.[28] However, he is clear that this does not mean that all of America is about to be judged or destroyed. He thinks that judgment is specifically reserved for the church and for the government, particularly because they had failed to end abortion in the United States.[29]

As for America in general, Taylor brings the reader's attention to his prophecy titled "America, America," which he says he received in October of 2015.[30] In this prophecy, he says the Spirit of God proclaims America's special relationship with Him—"America, America, oh how I love these! America, America, oh how I have chosen thee." The prophecy goes on to state that God is going to heal the nation because of the "cries of [His] people" by enabling the "Army of God" to "take hold of [their] ground" and make America "the great light" again. Taylor also claims that God said that he has "chosen this man Donald Trump and anointed him as President for such a time as this," and continues, "For even his name, Donald—meaning world leader (spiritual connotation; faithful); Trump—meaning to get the better of, or to outrank or defeat someone or something often in a highly public way." Through this "faithful world leader, and together with [God's] Army," the prophecy states, "all of America's enemies" will be defeated "in the spiritual and in the natural."

For Taylor, the Trump Prophecies collectively not only explain the election of Trump but place that election in a broader narrative in which America and the church are victorious over its enemies; both the demonic, "spiritual" forces and the "natural," or political, human forces that are under the sway of the satanic opposition. In a prophecy titled "The Fourth Reich, ISIS," for example, Taylor writes that the Spirit of the Lord proclaims that America and Russia will ally themselves against ISIS, "and with one stone they shall slay it and all those that are behind it."[31] Echoing much of what became more common discourse in the years after 2016 and after the election about the so-called "Deep State," the prophecy continues: "For it is not just ISIS they will fight, but the Elite, the Globalists, and the Illuminati who will be exposed by My [God's] light."[32]

In these narratives, Donald Trump's unlikely, and for some, surprising victory in 2016 was ordained by God. What seemed to be inexplicable to the professional observers was for Taylor and his readers as prophecy fulfilled, which in turn affirmed that God was indeed the final arbiter of the affairs of nations. However, the war for America was far from over. Spiritual warfare was established as both the means of victory in 2016 and the means by which God's army will work with Trump to secure God's blessing and special purpose for America going forward from 2016. Using the rather ubiquitous conspiratorial narratives of human-led subversion and demonic forces inspiring them, Taylor assures the reader that the enemy will not simply surrender in the face of their recent defeat at the polls.

Taylor uses military imagery consistently and references D-Day throughout the book. In the first line of the final chapter titled "Taking Ground," Taylor writes, "God has given me the word that likens modern-day America to the hub of D-Day activity."[33] Using the language of dominionism and spiritual warfare common among NAR networks, Taylor states that the "most important message" he can impart is that Christians should "Take ground and hold it at all costs." He continues, "The Church has a terrible habit of taking ground and then backing off when pressure subsides. This leaves territory unclaimed and vulnerable to further invasion and habitation."[34] By use of "spiritual warfare," referencing the passage from Ephesians 6: 11–13, the "Army of God" continues this struggle to "take ground" and make constant war against "the enemy," which, again, includes the demonic spirits attempting to subvert God's plan for Trump, the Church, and America, and human-led organizations like "the Illuminati" and "the Cabal."[35]

It is perhaps sufficient to recognize that Taylor's prophecies received attention from *CBN* and other Christian outlets to demonstrate the popularity of his prophecies, but we should also take note of their significance to the broader network of apostles and prophets associated with the NAR. Taylor's book was published by Defender Publishing, which is managed by Thomas R. Horn, who also is the CEO of SkyWatch TV, both of which are Christian media outlets. Horn's bio on the website for SkyWatch describes him as an entrepreneur in the field of Christian media, publishing stories on "cutting-edge stories covering religion, prophecy, discovery, and the supernatural."[36] Horn has also contributed allegations of plots to subvert Trump's presidency in a book titled *Saboteurs* (2017), which connects everything from Wikileaks to "satanism in the US Capital" to "Deep State Occultists" allegedly "manipulating American

Society" and included a contribution from the Fox News commentator and SkyWatch regular, Lt. Colonel Robert Maginnis,[37] Donna Howell, managing editor at Defender Publishing, also contributed to some of the additions to the 2019 expanded version of *The Trump Prophecies*. She also wrote the introduction for the 2019 edition, wherein she thanks Thomas Horn for asking Taylor to write the book and states, "I truly believe its readers will be inspired toward a united Kingdom goal as a result."[38]

In *The Trump Prophecies*, Taylor places a high value on prayer and describes the intercessory prayer chain that began as a result of him initially sharing this word from God, including leaders of the charismatic movement like Dutch Sheets, Rick Joyner, and Stephen Strang, among others.[39] In the CBN interview discussing the "Trump Prophecies," Mary Colbert, the wife of Taylor's physician who attended to him at the time of the 2011 prophecy, describes her reaction to the prophecy. She describes being moved to get a "prayer chain" focused on the details of the prophecy to see its fulfillment and stated that when she and her husband heard the prophecy from Taylor that she "saw the Father's rhythm" in it and recognized it as a "word from God." She focused on getting the prophecy into the hands of major church leaders and "influencers," beginning on Labor Day because, as she describes it, "the Lord instructed [her] to do it Labor Day" as it was "going to be a labor of love." Mark Taylor, Mary Colbert, and her husband, Dr. John Colbert, appeared on long-time televangelist Jim Bakker's program in 2016, where Jim Bakker called Taylor a "prophet" moments after holding up one of Jonathan Cahn's books to call attention to the need to raise funds for the show to stay on the air, offering "a baker's dozen" for $150.00.[40]

Whatever criticism Taylor's prophecies received from the general public and from Christians who did not think he was a prophet, there was a segment of Christians, most of whom were charismatic in orientation, some deeply connected to NAR, who saw the "Trump Prophecies" as the very word of God for His people in the 2016 election and Taylor's directives from God as a means to further the mission of building the Kingdom in the years to come during Trump's presidency. Taylor was then a fixture among the most respected prophets in the network of prophets and apostles alongside Cahn, Sheets, Joyner, and others.

God's Wrecking Ball

In the prophecies concerning the 2016 election, Trump is described as a remedy for the harm that has been done by subversive and anti-Christian forces in the United States and is empowered by the Spirit of God to lead the United States toward right relationship with Him and free America's government to follow God's directives for the nation closely. As a result, America will again be aligned with God's covenant purpose for the United States and prosper. This narrative is ultimately a message of hope and optimism, not of judgment on the nation. However, the always-present warnings insist that things could go very differently should Christians neglect their spiritual and civic duties.

The prophecies by Clement, Taylor, and others certainly drew attention, especially after the election's results were known. However, there was one prophecy that seemed to define the terms of what the election meant more than the others. While some Christian leaders looked at Trump's behavior as disqualifying and regarded his past with suspicion, Lance Wallnau saw his bellicosity and rashness as positive attributes fitting for a leader at this moment in America's history. In an interview on the *Charisma Podcast Network* on May 6, 2016, he claimed that God told him that Trump was a "wrecking ball to the spirit of political correctness."[41] Wallnau argues elsewhere that prior to his first meeting with Donald Trump in Trump Tower in 2015, he "heard the Lord" say to him, "Donald Trump is a wrecking ball to the spirit of political correctness."[42] He stated further in the interview that in an era in which gay rights were acceptable, and amid "Kaitlyn Jenner" and "safe spaces," Christians had been losing the debate in the culture wars. However, now, Trump had come to "change the discourse." "We have not had the same political sensitivity since then," Wallnau stated regarding Trump's 2015 announcement that he would run for office, "because Trump has been the wrecking ball." In his estimation, the norms of the existing debate were shattered because that was Trump's gift from God—to be the "chaos candidate."

Wallnau published a book in September 2016 titled *God's Chaos Candidate*. Discussing the book and what he called the "Cyrus connection" for a special report on *CBN*, Wallnau said Trump had "a Cyrus anointing" and that as America is facing an uncertain and chaotic future, but with Trump, "we have a

Cyrus to navigate through the storm."[43] The book itself restates that point. He claims that he wrote the book because he believed that "Trump has the Isaiah 45 Cyrus anointing," and his conviction that there was "unprecedented warfare over this election because of what is at stake."[44] Wallnau grounds his claims in the conviction that America has a particular role in God's prophetic plan for the world and that the 2016 election was a pivotal point in that destiny. That election was an opportunity for God's people to strike a blow for the Kingdom of God against the satanic forces aligned against Trump and America.

The assertion that demonic and secretive forces are at work counter to the benefit of America, as is the case with these prophetic narratives, is central to Wallnau's political cosmology, and it is set within his progressive millennialist views tempered with repeated apocalyptic warnings. "We are up against a malevolent and demonic agenda aimed to destroy the global force for kingdom expansion that is America," Wallnau writes.[45] He explains that there is a "shadow cabinet … behind the scenes coordinating uprisings and media coverage," and that behind that is a "spirit" which he defined as a "powerful resurgence of a lawless spirit that is rooted in the radicals of the 1960s."[46] As is common in these prophecies, politically leftist organizations are not simply political adversaries who differ from the author on ideological grounds but are alleged to be in league with demonic powers, teaching the "doctrines of demons" that have emerged from "the myriad of well-funded single-issue activists on the Left." The falsifications of truth pushed by university professors, here echoing much of what Billy Graham warned about in the 1960s, and the "counterfeit evangelism" of the Left are to him the promise from Jesus that there would be "tares" among the wheat, "people the devil plants … to thwart the harvest of God."[47]

Wallnau is explicit in the book regarding his conviction that the "old design, sourced in Marxist-Leninist doctrine" is at work in 2016, that the "same spiritual and ideological battle has resumed today in hyper drive and goes deeper than the labels we now have of 'liberal,' 'conservative,' 'democrat,' or 'republican.'"[48] Furthermore, in this seemingly nonpartisan construction, one that is often repeated by other prophets describing the 2016 and 2020 elections, Wallnau solidifies a binary choice between Trump and God's adversaries. Political choices are thereby inscribed onto a metaphysical terrain of right versus wrong, good versus evil, God versus Satan. To choose Trump in the 2016 election is to align oneself with God's plan. Voting is, in this sense, an expression of spiritual warfare and a recognition of the validity of the prophetic word. To defeat the "Leftists" who propagate destructive and demonic ideas at the ballot is to strike a blow against Satan's plans and a step toward claiming dominion over America.

As we have seen thus far in the prophecies concerning Trump, the basic conclusion is that God has a divine plan for America to usher in the future Kingdom of God. However, consistent with this affirmation of the coming Kingdom is the warning that this plan could be disrupted if Trump is defeated. Wallnau writes concerning court appointments that the victor of the 2016 election would make, "Imagine the impact on religious liberty and free speech when courts with a liberal majority hear cases by the 'Human Rights Campaign'—America's largest civil rights organization advancing lesbian, gay, bisexual and transgender equality."[49] In addition to these domestic concerns, Wallnau sees a greater drama unfolding. The 2016 election is, for him, nothing short of a cosmic battle for the future of all nations. In keeping with what we might see as prophetically authorized American exceptionalism, Wallnau argues:

> The United States has held the door of democracy open. Satan intends to shut it. By now I hope you can see that this is far beyond a battle of politics. It's not a matter of party versus party, Republican against Democrat. We are up against a malevolent and demonic agenda aimed to destroy the global for kingdom expansion that is America.[50]

He continues concerning the need for the church to engage in more concerted efforts at spiritual discernment and the rejection of "the political correctness of Babylon" because, he says, "Satan, well aware of America's unique assignment to globally advance the discipleship of nations, recognizes the influence of what we export."[51] With this in mind, he urges the reader to take up their calling in God's plan and to "have strategic intercessory impact in the unseen realm and impact the course of world history."[52] "The next season in America will be a time of both grace and spiritual warfare," he argues. Though he does expect troubling times ahead for the country, for which Trump is uniquely suited to lead the country through, he believes "God will use the pressure of circumstance to forge something new for the United States."[53]

In an interview on the *Charisma Podcast Network* on May 6, 2016, Wallnau claims to have received a "second hearing from God." He said that the Lord told him to turn to Isaiah 45:1 to "find out who this man [Trump] is." The passage in the King James version, Wallnau's chosen version here, states: "Thus saith the LORD to his anointed, to Cyrus, whose right hand I have holden, to subdue nations before him; and I will loose the loins of kings, to open before him the two leaved gates; and the gates shall not be shut." For Wallnau, this passage was significant because I matched Isaiah 45 in his realization that Trump could be the 45th President of the United States if elected. The number of the scripture reference itself held prophetic meaning for him and confirmed further that God had indeed chosen a new Cyrus to reform and revitalize America, consecrating it back to God as His chosen vessel for establishing the Kingdom.

There were more seemingly practical concerns to Wallnau's support as well. Trump's role in God's plan, according to Wallnau, is to prepare America for "the chaos that is coming" that Wallnau describes in the interview as part of the immanent "unraveling" of America. Furthermore, Trump was the perfect candidate to confront the Clinton "machine" that Wallnau describes as "taking America socially, spiritually, and economically" into disaster. "National suicide is the path that America is on," he argues in the book, "and the 2016 election will determine if that future can be altered." The prophetic word was for Wallnau deeply related to concerns about America's decline that were shared more broadly by Trump's Christian supporters. But for Wallnau and for other NAR-affiliated leaders, the prophetic word confirms the practical choice. Wallnau states, "I believe it's the wrecking ball—Donald J. Trump—That has been sent to stop the momentum of self-destruction," because Trump has the "Cyrus anointing is to build and restore."[54]

Jehu versus Jezebel

The narrative of Trump carrying a Cyrus anointing from God for the furtherance of God's purposes, of course, comes from the Book of Isaiah in what Christians call the Old Testament, and, more specifically, refers to King Cyrus's repatriation of Jews back in the land of Israel and his aid in rebuilding the temple in Jerusalem. The historical complexities of why Cyrus did this are beside the point for the NAR Christians. For them, especially for Lance Wallnau, Cyrus was an example of God's work in the world through fallible human agents. So strong is God's hand in the world that the Spirit of God can move even an unbelieving gentile to do the work of the Kingdom. This trope became especially powerful in relation to Trump precisely because his Christian bona fides were suspect. However, the reference to Cyrus was not the only biblical type used to qualify Trump in the 2016 election. Another biblical figure was used to inform the narrative of the election in a book published in 2017 by Jonathan Cahn titled *The Paradigm: The Ancient Blueprint That Holds the Mystery of Our Times*.

The line between fiction and prophecy in Cahn's previous book, *The Harbinger*, was thin indeed, as the back of the paperback describes it as "[w]ritten in a riveting narrative style," a claim repeated and embellished on the website for the book and DVD set, but also claims to have revealed prophecies critical to the future of America.[55] In this new book, however, the narrative style of characters interacting in the text is exchanged for a more expository structure. It was published by Frontline, one of the properties of the Charisma House Book Group, one of the outlets of Charisma Media. The website for Charisma House advertises *The Paradigm* as having revealed "the Ancient Reason Trump Won." It goes on to say about Cahn's message in the book, "In 'The Paradigm,' Cahn writes that the 2016 presidential race between Donald Trump and Hillary Clinton was the most unpredictable election in American history, yet signs pointed to it in an ancient paradigm."[56] Though the book was released after the election, the website quotes Cahn as saying concerning Trump's victory that it "was against all odds, yet at the same time, it was foretold in the paradigm. Can God use those who do not know Him to accomplish His purposes? He can, and He does it all the time."

Cahn claims that his book's narrative is "not political but spiritual and prophetic"; however, we should understand two points in that regard.[57] Firstly, there is no way to disconnect the political events and issues surrounding the 2016 election from the prophetic discourse in the book except through an arbitrary distinction. Throughout the book, Cahn goes into detail explaining how political events in the United States and the people involved are linked to the biblical paradigm he argues is related to past, current, and future events.

Perhaps the claim that his narrative is not political is to evade any accusations of defamation. Christian apologist John Patrick Holding writes on the website for The Christian Research Institute writes that Cahn's comparison in the book between Bill Clinton and Ahab, Hillary Clinton and Jezebel, and Obama as Ahab's son was "much like that of an examination of an impressionist painting; the parallels look convincing from a distance, but as the observer gets closer, the parallels dissipate into a vague mist."[58] Holding further argues that Cahn manipulates facts to make the timelines match and frequently engages in "semantic equivocation and manipulation."

The point for me is that perhaps the caveat placed there in the preface, which he states he does not usually write in his books but "must do here," is to avoid possible legal issues with the claims in the book.[59] I cannot confirm this is the case, but it could be why Cahn makes such an arbitrary distinction between political events and his prophetic insight in the case of this book.

After the preface, the book presents a series of rhetorical questions about whether there can be a "master blueprint" that explains the events in the "modern world" and if this "blueprint" can "foretell the rise and fall of modern leaders and governments," the answer to which is of course yes.[60] Cahn clearly regards as "the master blueprint" and "the template" for coming and past events that is "objective and fixed."[61] In an interview in January of 2018 with Marilyn Hickey, a prominent evangelist and healer, Cahn is clear that he had this blueprint for what had gone on in the election, the broader history of the United States, and what is coming for America.[62] In the interview, Cahn claims to have received this information via inspiration or that he had, in a sense, "downloaded" it and confirmed the information via the "Internet." In the text itself, Cahn claims that "[i]f *The Harbinger* opened up prophetic revelations and warnings in the forms of specific objects and actions, in *The Paradigm*, it is the age itself that constitutes the prophetic revelation and the times in which we live."[63]

From there, Cahn describes the basic "paradigms" established in the Bible concerning Israel that he thinks establish a pattern for America. Though his historical precision is lacking, and a number of historical details are omitted, the presentation of these parallels is quite complicated. The basic point is that for Cahn Israel and America are linked. He explains that Israel is "the exemplar nation," and that "every nation and culture of Western civilization is in some way connected to the civilization of Israel," but that "American civilization is especially connected, as it was founded by Puritans to be an Israel of the New World."[64] The rest of the book then details the parallels in general at first and then makes particular comments on the social and political environment of the United States. In the first mentioned paradigm, "metamorphosis," for example, Cahn describes Israel as having been "established" as a nation dedicated to God and founded on a certain "biblical morality," but that it had come to fall away from that morality little by little.[65] "As Israel's apostasy progressed," he argues, "the worship of Baal grew less and less subtle and more and more braze."[66] Along with this drawing away from God and the moral foundations of the nation came a coarsening of the manners and conduct of the society.

Key among the indicators of this process of withdrawal from God and His law was, for Cahn, the abandonment of specific gender roles and the sanctity of marriage. The "sacred vessel of marriage" was abandoned, the "culture became more sexualized," and "Baal's war against God's order" progressed to the point where nothing was regarded as sacred, not even "the nature and distinctions of male and female—gender."[67] In Cahn's narrative, as Israel metamorphosed into something other than its original state, founded on biblical morality and God's word, the marriage covenant was profaned, and sexuality became even more permissive, to the point of even including homosexuality.[68]

In the first phase of the metamorphosis of the society, the "attack" was about "sexuality [became] divorced from marriage," and in the second phase, "it was removed from gender, biology, and nature." The decline of Israel, however, continued to reach new depths of depravity as they became more and more accustomed to the rights and rituals of Ball worship, writes Cahn. "Baal demanded sacrifices more precious and costly than grain and livestock," he writes. "If the worshippers would offer up their own children, then he would bless them with increase and prosperity," and so they did. Cahn writes, "That was the price of the new morality—their children."[69] This is the ultimate level of depravity that the nation undergoes to then be fully divorced from the ways of God. "The nation, culture, and civilization that had been established on the Word of God and dedicated to the ways of God will begin to depart from the God of its foundation," Cahn writes, and the "departure will begin subtly at first, but as time goes on, it will become more and more blatant and brazen."[70]

Quite obviously, this narrative about Israel is meant to be a representation of America from the middle of the twentieth century to the present. He argues that as America was "dedicated from its inception to the will and purposes of God," it has since fallen away, mainly since the early 1960s. At this time, he claims, "America's departure from God became increasingly apparent as it began driving God out of its public square, out of its educational system, out of its government, out of its culture."[71] What has filled the place of God, according to Cahn, is the worship of Baal. Though he admits that few modern people would consider themselves "servants of idols," Cahn claims that "when a civilization that has once known the ways of God turns away from those ways, it inevitably turns to Baal."[72] What then follows is the "coarsening of culture," the proliferation of pornography and sexual immorality, the "celebration" and mainstreaming of homosexuality, and the "killing of unborn children," which he equates to Ball worship in the performance of human sacrifices.[73]

The picture that is painted here of America via a narrative of Israel's biblical past is one of a nation gone astray in all the worst possible ways in his estimation. It is interesting that slavery, Native American genocide, and poverty do not make the list of grievances, but is significant that the narrative pattern discussed in Chapter 2 about a Godly nation gone astray from God's plan and will for it, as well as the linkages between America and Israel for the foundation of the claims in Cahn's prophetic narrative. And in keeping with the avertive tone of the prophecies discussed so far, Cahn sees these general parallels as significant for understanding the 2016 election as a particular victory for God's people in the defeat of malevolent forces.

In the chapters following the discussion of the apostasy of Israel and of America, Cahn goes on to describe the biblical types that figure into the ancient pattern in the modern world. In Chapter 4, Cahn identifies King Ahab as having "epitomized the nation's fall," and, after generations of apostasy, having weakened its belief in "absolutes and the altering and redefining of values," Ahab "became an agent of a form of moral relativism."[74] "The Paradigm of the King," as Cahn describes it was then fulfilled by Bill Clinton in that, according to Cahn, Clinton had capitalized in 1991 on the ongoing vernacular of the "culture wars" to gain political office.[75] Cahn further argues, "As with Ahab, Clinton would be linked to a culture war throughout his days in power, and was, as Ahab before him, "a man of moral weakness."[76] Not only is President

Clinton compared to King Ahab in his morality but also in his rule. "As it was with King Ahab, President Clinton was especially connected to the blood of the innocent," Cahn writes.[77] Clinton and Ahab, perhaps because of their moral weakness, perhaps because of their ambition, accelerated the degeneracy of their respective nations, and though they are not the primary cause or the catalyst for the events that come after, they nevertheless "opened the door" to even greater degeneracy and social decay.[78]

The figure of Ahab in this narrative is not the only type mapped onto the United States' recent political history. Jezebel, "a stranger to the land of Israel, a Canaanite," and a devotee to Astarte, is connected in Cahn's narrative to Hillary Clinton.[79] "If Bill Clinton is he Ahab of the modern apostasy, the modern antitype to the ancient queen [Jezebel] must be Hillary Clinton," he argues.[80] Just as Jezebel "left the cosmopolitan world of her homeland to join her husband in a decidedly anti-cosmopolitan culture," he writes, so too Hillary Rodham "left a cosmopolitan culture" of Chicago and the East Coast "to be with Bill Clinton."[81] In both cases, this was a political alliance more than a marriage, as Cahn describes it and allowed both Jezebel and Hillary Clinton's "restrictive and adversarial" attitudes toward "the conservative values of her land and particularly the religious conservative values" to be manifest in that she attempts to change those values. "The first lady and queen will seek to change the nation to adapt to her ways and values" and act as "an activist, an agent for societal and cultural change."[82] Together, Ahab/Bill Clinton and Jezebel/Hillary Clinton are able to take their respective nations deeper into the "metamorphosis" from a nation of biblical values dedicated to God to one mired in sexual depravity, gender confusion, and Baal worship in the form of child sacrifice, or abortion, in modern terms. "As with the reign of Ahab and Jezebel, the age of the Clintons was unlike any other America had ever seen," Cahn writes.[83] The Clinton administration was different in that the First Lady did not play a supporting role but was given extraordinary authority. Hillary Clinton is said to have goaded President Clinton would expand access to abortion and Clinton would become "the first president in American history to dedicate an entire month to the celebration of homosexuality."[84]

In Cahn's narrative, all these events overlap the two nations in their respective periods of decline as they move away from the founding ideals and purpose. Tying much of what was discussed in *The Harbinger*, Cahn describes the parallels with a "nemesis" stirred up against Israel in Ben-Hadad, who, in Cahn's words, "would go on to threaten and endanger the nation's security," and present a "paradigm of the of the nemesis, the invader," whom he likens to Osama bin-Laden.[85] And just as it was with Ahab, it was Clinton's carelessness that leads to this enemy who devised plots against America to strike at will.[86] Offering further parallels for Jezebel and Hillary Clinton post the Clinton Administration's second term, Cahn refers to here as a "shadow Queen" who rules through other means—in a "new role and position of power."[87] This continues through the period Cahn refers to as the "paradigm of the heir"—for Jezebel and Ahab, it was their son Joram, but for The Clintons it was Obama.[88]

In this narrative, Cahn describes Obama as continuing the moral degradation as, according to the pattern, the "heir will continue in the king's policies concerning sexual immorality and the bending of gender."[89] This figure, whether Joram or Obama, will continue the "practice of sacrificing children" in the "continuance of Baal worship." In this role, Obama serves "as another link in the chain of the nation's apostasy from God," and "[u]nder his reign it will be further alienated from the biblical foundation on which it was laid."[90] Cahn concludes concerning Obama's two terms that he left "American less Christian than when he found it—culturally, morally, and statistically."[91]

After this period, Cahn writes, Joram/Obama's reign ends, leaving the figure of the queen/Hillary Clinton and the figure of King Joram/Obama, as the remaining "focal points in the conflict of cultures, values, and parties that saturated the election of 2016."[92] Cahn goes so far as to describe the Democratic National Convention that nominated Hillary Clinton as the Democratic candidate as "the most brazenly anti-biblical convention in the history of the Democratic Party."[93] Citing much of what he already objected to about the Clinton and Obama administrations, Cahn describes the Democratic Party Platform for 2016 as having established Hillary Clinton's main agenda issue as her priority and stated that "the practice of killing unborn children was to her the cause above all causes."[94] However, though the situation seemed dire, America would go further in the direction of apostasy from God's calling. There emerges another figure in the broader paradigm Israel established, whom Cahn calls the "warrior."

This figure for Israel was Jehu, whom Cahn describes as not being a "gentle man," a "rough and coarse man," a man without authority in matters "politics or civil government," but who was "ruthless and brutal," a "confrontational" man who did not demonstrate "the qualities one might have expected from a Godly man."[95] "The Paradigm of the Warrior," writes Cahn, manifests "suddenly" at the end of King Joram's reign and takes "Israel and its leaders by surprise." "For the manifestations of the paradigm to continue, it would mean that as the Obama years approach their end, an unlikely figure will take the government and nations by surprise," writes Cahn. In the case of ancient Israel, it was Jehu, the figure of the brash warrior. In the context of the 2016 US election, it was Donald Trump.[96]

Listing several points that he regards as parallels for Jehu and Trump, Cahn says this figure is "controversial," will "appear as a threat to the status quo," will be a "destabilizing force" who comes "to the national stage as an outsider"; furthermore, this man is a "warrior" who can at times be "brutal."[97] It is interesting that Cahn overlooks the several deferments that Trump took when he did have the opportunity to serve in the military and instead emphasizes his schooling at the New York Military Academy and describes his demeanor as "combative," also stating that Trump often speaks "in terms of battle, winning and losing, victory or defeat."[98] In the presidential race, Jehu/Trump is in a battle for the throne against Jezebel/Hillary Clinton, apropos the ancient paradigm in the book of Second Kings. However, as Cahn points out, the victory on election night was not the only or last battle to be fought to restore the nation.[99] The "Warrior King" now enters "the nation's capital with an agenda to purge the nation's leadership of corruption," Cahn writes, and "will seek to remove from government those stand against the ways of God." In completing this sentiment, Cahn writes that the "specific mission" of Jehu/Trump is to "drain the swamp."[100]

Cahn comments that Trump, like Jehu, is a complicated figure who will not fully become personally devout or godly.[101] However, that personal failing or lack of demeanor does not diminish his role in God's plan. Cahn notes, "The hope for the days in which the warrior reigns will be that they will not only slow the nation's descent but also that they will provide a chance for a massive spiritual and cultural returning to God." He adds, "Apart from such a return the nation's overall course of apostasy and descent will continue." For Cahn, Trump's electoral victory had "averted the sealing of America's apostasy" and created an opportunity for national revival. Cahn argues that now there is a "wide-open door for evangelical leaders and believers to impact the nation."[102] With Trump's victory, this new Jehu came unexpectedly to power over the nation, disaster had been averted, and that is what matters. However, now the work to restore America truly begins as Christians are encouraged to operate with the knowledge that their "Judeo-Christian faith" must operate as a "countercultural" phenomenon, and God's people "must increasingly become a revolutionary people, a prophetic people."

Conclusion: Cyrus Wins

Sociologist Rebecca Barret-Fox addresses the Trump as Cyrus phenomenon, arguing the "feelings of entitlement, fear, resentment, and the desire to dominate as they construct a vision of America as a fallen nation that has succumbed to the various forms of wickedness, encouraged by liberal politics" shaped and defined these narratives.[103] I would argue that the Trump prophecies narratively constructed the election as a part of an ongoing dualistic spiritual battle between the forces of darkness typified by Hillary Clinton and her supporters on one side, and Trump as God's anointed leader and his supporters on the other, offering a specific course of action. Within this discursive paradigm, the prophets associated with the NAR constructed a world of order and optimistic meaning, even if they could not simply wait for God to act on their behalf and had to fight for that future. The evidence of the truth of this construction was that God's "chaos candidate" did win. Trump's unlikely victory in 2016 shocked most observers, but the surprise of the election's outcome affirms the convictions of the prophets and those who listened to them that God was at work in the world and on behalf of the country. What else could explain such an unlikely outcome?

Cahn closes *The Paradigm* with several bullet points concerning the meaning of what it reveals. Among these are that "God is real," that God is "actively" and "dynamical" involved in the affairs of the world and the nation, just as He was with ancient Israel, "God hears the prayers of His people and moves on their behalf," and, finally, that "[w]e are living in biblical times."[104] For Kat Kerr, Lance Wallnau, Jonathan Cahn, and others, Trump's victory over Clinton in 2016 was a demonstration of prophecy given and fulfilled. The modern worshipers of Baal and the demonic spirits behind sexual immorality, homosexuality, changing gender dynamics, and abortion would now have to contend with God's anointed leader in the White House.

That said, as firmly as the prophets and apostles celebrated their victory and believed in a bright future in America, Wallnau, Cahn, and others were also determined to point out that this was only the beginning. The entrenched interests and secret cabals, the alleged 'Deep State', demonic principalities exercising dominion over the Seven Mountains, including government, would not so easily surrender dominion even in the face of a Jehu or a Cyrus, or even the newly encouraged prophets and prayer warriors of the NAR. During Trump's presidency, and especially in the months after his electoral defeat in 2020, as Lance Wallnau described the situation in January of 2021, the prophecy voters were "in the spiritual fight of our lifetime."[105]

4

Cyrus versus the Deep State

On January 21, 2013, Jonathan Cahn spoke at The Presidential Inaugural Prayer Breakfast, which describes itself as an interdenominational, bipartisan event held on the morning of Inauguration Day, delivering a sermon that very much reiterates what he wrote in *The Harbinger*.[1] He mentions the book by name in the address after he warns the audience that what he has to say will not be "politically correct." He then goes on to say that the same "harbingers" are present as he noted in the book, and for the same reasons he wrote about—America, like Israel before it, has abandoned God and His precepts in favor of wickedness. Recalling what he describes as America's true founding identity as John Winthrop's "city on a hill," Cahn explains that as Israel was "consecrated" to God and His word so was America. More recently, he notes, it has, especially under Obama's watch, become a place where sexual immorality and perversions of all kinds are tolerated and even celebrated; a place where God's precepts are mocked and those who hold to His word are "vilified" and "banned" from the public square. Most significantly for Cahn, America has continued forty years after Roe v. Wade to maintain the legality of "killing the unborn." Because of these sins and abominations, America is no longer the light to the nations it once was, he argues.

Cahn maintains that Christians should continue to pray for President Obama and ask God to bless the United States, but he is equally clear that neither he nor God can condone the administration's actions. Reflecting on the fact that during the inauguration ceremony, President Obama would place his left hand on the Bible and raise his right to swear an oath, Cahn asks rhetorically, "Can you invoke the name of God and ignore His word?" He argues further that at this moment in history, America has entered a period of "spiritual amnesia," coupled with warnings of coming economic and social calamity should America continue, as Israel did, down a path of rebellion against God's laws, and to harken to the voice of "political correctness." Yet, in keeping again with his narrative structure in *The Harbinger* and other writings, Cahn contends that God is not through with America and, quoting the frequently used passage from 2 Chronicles, he says, "If my people, who are called by my name, will humble themselves and pray and seek my face and turn from their wicked ways, then I will hear from heaven, and I will forgive their sin and will heal their land." God's judgment is coming because of the wickedness of America's people and their leadership, but the people of God may indeed still, and must, continue to try to correct the errors of abortion, homosexuality, and godless secularism to reestablish the nation as God's favored nation and allow it to enjoy His full blessing once more.

At another inauguration prayer breakfast, this time for President Trump in January of 2017, held at the Trump International Hotel in Washington DC, Cahn repeated much of what he said in his 2013 message.[2] He began this sermon with the same warning from his prior message that what he was going to say was not going to be "politically correct," he proceeded to repeat what he said in 2013 and wrote in *The Harbinger*. The narrative, once again, recounts Winthrop's vision, which Cahn describes as the "founding vision of America," and he claims on that basis that "in the history of this planet, only two nations have been founded solely for the Glory of God—one was Israel, and the other was America." Like Israel, Cahn argues, America was equally "consecrated to the will of God" in its founding. Yet, also like Israel, as Americans began to enjoy God's blessing, they removed Him from their political and social life and moved in "foreign idols" to replace God. America was "at war" with its founding principles and "sacrificed their children" on the altars of abortion as Israel did on the altars of Baal. Repeating all of what he previously stated in his writings and in 2013, Cahn claims that America has fallen from favor because of its collective sin and that "[s]omething happened to the city on a hill."

Cahn explains that the condition of "apostasy" in the United States cannot be attributed to the actions of one political leader, but it is "the nation that is accountable." However, he does explain that an "ungodly leader," a "Jeroboam or an Ahab," can "turn a nation from God or accelerate its departure." This is, as we know from Cahn's 2017 book *The Paradigm*, discussed in the previous chapter, for him parallels between Obama and Bill Clinton, respectively. And just as their predecessors in the paradigmatic relationship between Israel and America, they played a significant role in driving America further away from God and deeper into the judgments described in *The Harbinger*. "In the last eight years," Cahn goes on to say, "America's spiritual fall has deepened and accelerated." The Obama administration, he says, has "championed the killing of the unborn" at home and abroad, "has labored to strike down the standards of order ordained by God concerning man and woman and marriage," and brought relations between Israel and the United States to the "lowest point in the history of the two nations." In Cahn's estimation, this administration has "waged war against the Word of God" and persecuted God's people. But Cahn reminds the audience that even with the crimes the Obama administration had been guilty of in leading America further away from God and His commandments, "within an hour this administration will cease to exist."

Recalling the 2016 campaign, Cahn exclaims, "The stakes of this election could not have been higher," and goes on to argue that if Hillary Clinton had won that Obama's legacy would have been cemented, and the war on God's laws would have continued unabated. "America stood at a threshold," he claims, noting that the Supreme Court was at stake "in an election that threatened to establish for ages the wages of Godlessness." However, Cahn continues to report that amid this dire position, "and then there was Donald Trump." Despite the predictions that Clinton would win and how unorthodox Trump's campaign was, Trump won. To explain the seemingly inexplicable success of Trump's efforts to become president, Cahn quotes from Isaiah 55:9, "As the heavens are higher than the earth, so are my ways higher than your ways and my thoughts than your thoughts." God had intervened, and such a conclusion seemed evident to Cahn precisely because of the unlikelihood of the outcome. "As we can bear witness today," he states, "with God, nothing shall be impossible."

Remarking on Trump's sorted past at the 2017 Prayer Breakfast and recalling his claims from *The Paradigm* comparing Trump to Jehu, a similar move to Wallnau's comparison of Trump to Cyrus, Cahn argues that God can use those who have not known Him to further "the purposes of God." And now, he claims in the talk that Christians should pray for Donald Trump and that he should surrender his life and will to God so that he might be directed to lead the nation. More to the point of the talk's central theme, Cahn explains that as the Obama administration ends and the Trump administration begins, America and the people of God have been given a "window of mercy." In the coming years, under the leadership of President Trump, he predicts, "America will be great again" by returning it to "the One who made it great."

Cahn's message was rather more energetic and lengthy than what Trump's personal spiritual adviser and well-known prosperity gospel preacher, Paula White, prayed at the official inauguration ceremony.[3] In her short prayer, White asks God to "bind our wounds and divisions" and "to join our nation to [God's] purpose," and asks that "these United States of America be that beacon of hope to all people and nations under your dominion, a true hope for humankind." The message was shorter but no less certain that God has indeed bestowed special favor on America for His divine purpose and for the sake of His dominion over the nations.

More indicative of the salvific message of the incoming administration was Trump's own words at the inauguration, where he described an America to riddled with poverty, crime, and unsecured borders, with dangerous threats looming from abroad and distention and political corruption rampant within. However, now that he was in office, Trump was clear that a new era had begun. The tone of the speech is best summarized in his claim, "This American carnage stops right here and stops right now."[4] For Cahn, Trump's allies and supporters, and for Trump himself, the results 2016 election signaled a shift in the fortunes of forces of righteousness and marked the starting point of America's renewal. And yet, there was coinciding with this exuberance and optimism a sense of danger from within that could undo all the good that Trump was meant to accomplish.

In this chapter, I describe the ways in which the avertive apocalypticism, hopeful millennialism, and the assertive dominionism of key figures associated with the NAR molded how they understood and described Trump's presidency. Moreover, as we have seen in the previous chapter, the significant role of conspiratorial narratives about malevolent forces working to subvert Trump's efforts to save the nation also strongly shaped this discourse. NAR leaders argued that God specifically chose Trump and anointed him for the task of restoring America to Himself, which meant Trump was going to be attacked by satanic forces seeking to undermine or even destroy what he was going to do for America. Every attack was a demonstration that the enemy was indeed frightened of what God would accomplish through Trump.

Just as God's people would intercede for the president in prayer, engaging in spiritual warfare to protect him from the schemes and wiles of the Devil, so too there must be demonically inspired opposition that also would use political and spiritual means to attack him. In this vein, all opposition to Trump or his administration's agenda was seen at best as misguided attempts by politically illiterate and spiritually deluded individuals to oppose what they did not fully understand as God's plan for the nation and the world, or at worst as demonically inspired political strategies by a cabal of corrupt and perverted actors bent on destroying the United States by sabotaging what God was doing through Trump as His chosen vessel for establishing the Kingdom. And just as we saw in Chapter 2, these narratives of subversives working to undermine Trump's agenda moved in and out of various circles among Trump's base of support, his political allies in Congress and his administration, and various religious actors, though not all of them were directly associated with the NAR.

During Trump's term, we witnessed the frequent utility and popularity of conspiratorial narratives among Trump's allies and supporters that share many of the dualistic discursive structures that we find among Trump's Christian supporters. An article detailing the findings of a study by Pew Research on how America changed during the Trump years demonstrates that a measure of how polarized the country became was in part because Republicans and Democrats did not "share the same set of facts."[5] The authors of the report point to a 2019 survey, which stated that "around three-quarters of Americans (73%) said most Republican and Democratic voters disagreed not just over political plans and policies, but over 'basic facts.'" The report goes on, "Much of the disconnect between the parties involved the new[s] media, which Trump routinely disparaged as 'fake news' and the 'enemy of the people,'" and stated further that Republicans expressed distrust of the media, which they saw as the main antagonist to the president.

In a report from 2022, PRRI presented findings from a study that stated that the proportion of Republicans who believe in the QAnon conspiracies is one in four, which represented a much higher percentage than other political affiliations.[6] The report quotes Natalie Jackson, director of research at PRRI, who stated, "Our surveys show that QAnon conspiracy theories are not losing popularity over time, despite their championed leader being out of power." Further, she explains that while the percentage of Americans who believe in these "wild conspiracy theories" seems small, the total number is "around 41 million Americans."

Conspiratorial narratives permeate the discourse of NAR and other Christian Trump supporters. They employ the specific language of demonic entities and spiritual warfare in Trump's defense and to explain his opponents' objections and actions against him. We should note, too, that these narratives are set with the broader political context in which Trump's supporters and political allies in the GOP, as did Trump himself, saw Trump's opponents as operatives of the Deep State or otherwise working counter to American interests. They also agreed that in Trump's 2016 election, America was given a chance to be great again, to be fully what they regarded as the greatest force for good the world has ever known. However, they also saw in this moment of promise potential great peril because of deeply entrenched corrupt interests that had no intention of allowing Trump to succeed in his mission to save America. Trump, his political allies, and his Christian supporters might have disagreed on the reality of demonic activity, but they frequently shared the language of a cosmic battle between the forces of good and the armies of evil.

The "Deep State"

Unusual and unprecedented events typified Trump's tenure in office. He was the first president to be impeached twice.[7] He was president when the Covid-19 pandemic started. He also strained relationships with NATO and long-standing allies abroad.[8] Trump additionally oversaw changes in US policy concerning the nation of Israel, recognizing Jerusalem as the capital of the Jewish state and moving the embassy there in 2018. Christian Broadcasting News noted that Trump claimed to do so "for the evangelicals."[9] For Steve Schultz of *The Elijah List*, the recognition of Jerusalem as Israel's capital demonstrated that the "many of the prophecies" previously spoken of by Kim Clement, Johnny Enlow, and others concerning the "fortunes" of the nation of Israel as well as for America were coming true.[10] Enlow's prophecy from January 6, 2017, quoted by Schultz in the article, seemed to be more accurate given these accomplishments. It stated in part that Trump possessed a powerful discernment about the situation in Israel and that "Trump is a quick discerner of core intent and he will discover that those who represent the Palestinian people are driven by the unreasonable hatred of a demonic principality and have no real desire for peace or compromise."

President Trump embraced conspiratorial narratives in a way that was unprecedented. Infamously, he propagated the false claim that the 2020 election was stolen and continued to do so long after every court challenge to the legality of the election had been exhausted. According to the House select committee investigating the January 6 attack on the US Capitol, to quote Representative Bennie Thompson, "Donald Trump was at the center of this conspiracy, and ultimately Donald Trump, the President of the United States, spurred a mob of domestic enemies of the Constitution to march down the Capitol and subvert American democracy."[11] According to the committee, the repeated false assertion that the election in 2020 was stolen from Trump through alleged massive fraud was partly responsible for the violence that day. Even before these events, however, there was no more significant trope defining the period from 2016 through 2020 than the notion of the so-called Deep State.

To summarize, as professor of communication Robert B. Horwitz describes it, the figure of the "Deep State" was meant to convey "the accusation that the hidden elements of the federal bureaucracy, having impugned Trump's candidacy at the outset, thwarted the policy prerogatives he earned through his electoral victory"; a "polemical charge … aimed at stoking rage and promoting paranoia among [Trump's] supporters about a sinister, if largely invisible, force within the state that was capable of perverting not just the mandate they bestowed upon him but of American democracy in general."[12]

We should note that Trump was far from the first politician to incite fear among his base to mobilize them against allegedly corrupt forces subverting freedoms from within. Nor was he the first to take advantage of public mistrust of government to present himself as a reformer. However, law professor Lawrence Douglas states that Trump's style of deployment of such narratives was novel. He writes, "The political style that Hofstadter described sixty years ago as distinctly fringe now sounds disturbingly familiar," referring to when in June of 2017, "Trump became the first president to use the term 'Deep State,' retweeting a post by [Fox News host] Sean Hannity."[13] He continues, "Since then, the US president has decried the malevolent workings of the Deep State on dozens of occasions—and with potent effect." Remarking on the support Trump got from tacking this tactic, Douglas notes, "Staunch loyalists, such as the California congressman Devin Nunes and Trump's senior policy adviser Stephen Miller, have stridently attacked the investigation by Robert Mueller into Russian interference in the presidential election and the impeachment proceeding as machinations of the Deep State."

In *A Lot of People Are Saying: The New Conspiracism and the Assault on Democracy* (2019), political scientists Russell Muirhead and Nancy L. Rosenbaum speak directly about how different they find the brand of conspiracism exemplified by President Trump and his allies during his presidency compared to the kind which had long been present in American political discourse. They argue that this new conspiracism, distinct from earlier forms of these narratives, requires "no punctilious demand for proofs, no exhaustive amassing of evidence, no dots revealed to form a pattern, no examination of operators plotting in the shadows." This new form of conspiracism rests on "innuendo and verbal gesture," which they illustrate by pointing to Trump's claim that millions of illegal votes were registered for Hillary Clinton without any evidence presented to support the claim.[14] They argue that this form of conspiracism "seeks to replace evidence, argument, and shared grounds of understanding with convoluted conjurings and bare assertions" as a part of a project of "delegitimization" of existing political norms and "disorientation" of the population, which they argue strikes at the core of democracy.[15] They conclude that such claims, which function to delegitimate facts and institutions like the free press, cast experts as "the global elite" or "politically vulnerable experts" as a "cabal" with ill intentions for the nation and its people and that Trump is "only its most powerful agent."[16]

The prevalence of narratives concerning alleged "Deep State" enemies trying to destroy President Trump is easily demonstrated, even with a cursory examination of the literature expounding on this trope between 2016 and 2019. The genres where these narratives are presented include speculative fiction, politically slanted exposés, and, of course, the president's own messaging. One overtly fictional narrative that captured the general tone of the narrative is an independent author who retired from years of work as a set dresser in several

Hollywood movies named Les Pendleton wrote a political thriller titled *1600 Trump Avenue: Against All Odds* (2016). On the cover the book is described as "a political prophecy," which is reiterated on the back of the book, where it goes on to say that Trump's running for office was a response to an "angry America, electing him to office; that he vowed to unite the country and make it great again."

The novel opens with a prologue referencing President Obama, claiming that eight years prior to Trump's election, "an unvetted, socialist candidate was elected to the Presidency promising positive change." Mimicking the sentiment from Trump's own inaugural speech, the prologue continues: "The economy was in shambles for the average person," while "[political] leaders and Wall Street were going incredibly well," and "[c]rime was rampant." The government was corrupt and the average person in America suffered, while "the media appeared to be doing all it could to promote anything the average American abhorred," and even Christian churches "seemed to be caving in to political correctness," while the "great universities had become a cesspool where many liberal-minded professors that anything anti-American was correct, while not tolerating even the smallest voice to the contrary among the students entrusted to them." The prologue continues, "Middle America had endured enough," and elected Trump, who "offered them a last shot at taking their country back and reining in the radical leaders who seemed to have taken control over every institution in their country."

This prologue establishes the starting point for the narrative, which builds on the actual events of the novel, which follows a fictionalized President Trump, his family, and administration officials as they set on their course after the inauguration in 2017. Over the course of the story, a fictional general with the aid of secretive government insiders who aim to kill the president to stop his reforms initiates a bloody coup attempt. At the conclusion of the novel, the coup fails, and the general's plot is uncovered, revealing "the vast extent of the corruption that had infiltrated the ranks of virtually every agency and bureau in the government at every level."[17] Following the plot, a necessary component of the novel's dramatic action is the malevolent cabal of secretive government leaders who not only meant to subvert Trump's agenda but to kill him in a violent coup d'état.

The epilogue narrates that after the coup plot was revealed and foiled, Trump went on to serve two terms and was "considered by most Americans to be the savior of their country." In this fictional future, Trump "reinstated the rule of law, enforced the nation's borders," and "with his business savvy and influence, America re-emerged as the world's leading economy bringing stability and an improving lifestyle to all Americans, not just those favored by the ruling party." In the aftermath of the assistance that military veterans gave to the fictional Trump during the attempted coup, he would speak at their gatherings to "pay tribute to those who came to his aide and helped the country get rid of the parasites that were living in its capital while disguised as our leaders." In the scope of the narrative, Trump is destined to bring about prosperity and a renewal of a certain patriotic vision of America, while also crushing the "parasites" who have long preyed on "middle America."

It is unlikely that this novel deeply influenced anyone who did not already hold complimentary views of Trump, and reviews from readers were mixed. However, the book does represent the kind of popular narrative of what Trump's election meant to his supporters and perhaps some of their anxieties regarding the future of his administration at the beginning of his term. While one reviewer referred to it as a "delusional rant," and a "pitiful excuse of a novel" that was nothing more than a "right-wing fantasy," others saw something that resonated with their views. A reviewer named Lynn said of the book, "An absolutely amazing fictional book about our current President Donald Trump, his family and OUR [sic] America."[18] Another reviewer named Betty asks regarding the book, "A prophecy in the making? Or an entertaining spin on US politics?" She goes on to say, "This is a book of fiction, but how close to the truth is it? Who really runs the country indeed? I found this book to be entertaining, rife with possibilities, suspense and more." She concludes, "I thought it was well-produced, clean, often factual, and a great wake-up, entertaining and suspenseful."[19]

Though written as fiction, *1600 Trump Avenue* captures the general themes found in books intended as non-fiction after Trump's election. Thomas Horn, whom we mentioned in the previous chapter, produced a book titled *Saboteurs: Shadow Government in Quest of the Final World Order* (2017). He also wrote a later book titled *Shadowland* (2019), which included a foreword by Lt. Colonel Robert Maginnis and claims on the cover of the book to reveal the hidden agenda of the "occult elite" and the "deep-state actors at war with Christianity, Donald Trump, and America's Destiny."[20]

In 2018, a self-described Bible prophecy expert named Paul McGuire and investigative journalist and former executive editor of *Charisma* magazine, Troy Anderson, wrote *Trumpocalypse: The End-Times President, a Battle against the Globalist Elite, and the Countdown to Armageddon* as a follow-up to their 2015 book *The Babylon Code: Solving the Bible's Greatest End-Times Mystery*. In *Trumpocalypse*, they claim to "uncover exclusive and explosive information about the prophetic significance of Trump's presidency and what it means for America's future, the world's future, and your future," including exposés of "biblical codes" detailing Trump-related prophecies, "the revolution against the globalist elite" that "culminated with Trump's election," the "occult elite's secret plan for humanity," and a "high-level plot to assassinate the president."[21]

Referencing Lance Wallnau's language concerning Trump's candidacy, McGuire and Anderson identify Trump as the "chaos candidate," an obvious reference to Wallnau's description of Trump, and then reference Jonathan Cahn's work, concluding that the election of Donald Trump offered the nation an opportunity to return to God after the past decade, "largely during the Obama administration," during which "many Americans watched with dismay as their nation—one the Pilgrims dedicated to God in the Mayflower Compact four centuries ago—underwent a radical and malevolent transformation."[22] Now, under the leadership of Trump, the forces in the employ of the "elite globalists" face a reckoning through God's power to expose and understand the "deep corruption and spiritual darkness presently waging war against Trump, his family, and his administration."[23]

Book-length exposés about the "Deep State" and its alleged effort to impede Trump's efforts to save America were not limited to charismatic Christian authors. In 2018, Trump's one-time campaign manager for the 2016 campaign, Corey Lewandowski, and conservative activist David N. Bossie wrote *Trump's Enemies: How the Deep State Is Undermining the Presidency*, where they allege that the "Deep State" was using a "politically motivated investigation" in the Mueller report to overturn Trump's 2016 election victory, which they describe as "the greatest American political victory since the American Revolution."[24] That same year, Jerome Corsi wrote *Killing the Deep State: The Fight to Save President Trump* stating similar allegations, while former Congressman Jason

Chaffetz wrote *The Deep State: How an Army of Bureaucrats Protected Barack Obama and Is Working to Destroy the Trump Agenda*, also in 2018.[25]

In another 2018 book titled *The Plot to Destroy Trump: How the Deep State Fabricated the Russian Dossier to Subvert the President* by author and business consultant Theodore Roosevelt Malloch, Trump's longtime friend and associate Roger Stone wrote in the foreword, "Make no mistake: there was a clear attempt, call it a plot, to take down the duly elected president of the United States," setting the tone for the book's narrative.[26] Alex Jones of *InfoWars* stated on the cover, "The DEEP STATE [sic] conspired to take down TRUMP [sic]. This book fills in all the details, and names names. All Patriots [sic] need to read it." And in 2019, former campaign aid to Trump, who pleaded guilty to lying to the FBI during its investigation, wrote a book about his experiences titled *Deep State Target: How I Got Caught in the Crosshairs of the Plot to Bring Down President Trump*.[27]

One could say that among Trump's allies and supporters, the phrase "Deep State" became the term of art to frame how they perceived their political opposition and, in turn, how they saw Trump's administration and agenda set within a morally dualistic narrative. Trump's election was framed as a victory over these pernicious forces; however, now, the battle for the nation, a battle frequently compared to the American Revolution itself in these narratives, is underway, and the dark forces of the globalist cabal are still at work to destroy Trump whom these forces see as the main obstacle to their control over America and the world. This general narrative persisted among the prophets and apostles associated with the NAR but with the added elements derived from their practice of spiritual warfare. The "Deep State" cabal was indeed a central feature of their explanation of political events since the 2016 election, but behind that was a more ominous, more powerful, and more malicious supernatural force that only Spirit-filled Christians could overcome through spiritual warfare.

The POTUS Shield

President Trump's connection to Paula White, who served as his spiritual advisor throughout his administration, is well known. But she was not the only representative of charismatic Christianity in Trump's orbit during the 2016 campaign. Many such figures flocked around him after he secured the Republican nomination. One such figure was Frank Amedia, a pastor and founder of the intercessory prayer group POTUS Shield. Amedia is the senior pastor of Touch of Heaven Ministries in Canfield, Ohio, and, as he describes it, POTUS Shield came about because of the "Kingdom shift" in 2016. He explains that POTUS Shield came about as the result of a prophecy God gave him to do so. He claims that at 3:30 am on November 9, 2016, God gave him "a new assignment," in which he and the prayer warriors he would gather in this mission to protect the president would become a "spiritual strikeforce" and that they would form a "spiritual protection" for Trump as he embarked on his first term as president. Amedia further explained that God had gifted Trump with a "breaker anointing," which sounds quite close to what Wallnau said of Trump during the campaign.

Amedia, also like Wallnau, claimed to have prophesied before the election that Trump would win and that "Haman would hang on his own gallows," a reference to the story of Esther in which an enemy of God's people, Haman, was hung on the gallows he prepared for the Jewish people in an attempt to exterminate the Jewish people.[28] Amedia prophesied about the outcome of Trump's election in 2016, stating that Trump's victory would be a step in furthering God's plan to bring the United States and the world into His Kingdom. Of course, there were others more well known than Amedia in the networks of prophets who gave predictions about Trump's victory and stated something very similar about the meaning of the election's outcome; however, Amedia was closer to the 2016 campaign than most others associated so closely with the NAR.

Before Amedia received his revelation to found POTUS Shield, Trump appointed him to be his "liaison for Christian policy" within the campaign.[29] In an interview with *Religion & Ethics Newsweekly* during the campaign, Amedia explained his support for Trump. He argued, reflecting on the concern that Trump lacked Christian credentials and temperament, "when you look at the issues there's no doubt that the contrast is clear … that Trump stacks up more on the line of what are Christian fundamental doctrines and concerns than Hillary or Obama do or they have."[30] Here we can see that the issues seemed to take precedence for Amedia at least in speaking about his involvement with the campaign. However, as he has often said in his messages from POTUS Shield, there is another level to his support for Trump, one informed by a revelation regarding what God is doing that went beyond simple political issues.

Amedia continually refers to his intercessory prayer on Trump's behalf as an assignment from God. His mission in this assignment is to organize spiritual warfare to aid Trump so that he might accomplish the goals God put him in the White House to achieve. Since it began, POTUS Shield's internet broadcasts presented conspiratorial narratives about the efforts of the Deep State to subvert President Trump's agenda and destroy his presidency. Informed by millennialist expectations and avertive apocalypticism characteristic of the NAR, Amedia broadcasts alerts throughout Trump's term about the various spiritual dangers that Trump and the nation faced as connected to issues like the Supreme Court nomination process and other challenges facing the Trump administration. In this way, POTUS Shield stands as an organizational expression of the kind of networks that formed around the narratives concerning Trump in charismatic and NAR networks.

POTUS Shield is also significant because of who is associated with it. Members include Lance Wallnau and figures like former General William "Jerry" Boykin, who sits as a "council member" for the POTUS Shield.[31] Boykin also serves as Executive Vice President for the Family Research Council, a well-known Christian lobbying group that describes itself as on a "mission is to advance faith, family, and freedom in public policy and the culture from a biblical worldview."[32] In 2004, Boykin was criticized in news media for statements he made during a filmed speaking engagement at a church referring to his combat experiences in Somalia. Referring to the battle as a spiritual contest between Islam and Christianity, he said, "I knew that my God was bigger than his. I knew that my God was a real God and his was an idol."[33] Boykin is also a loyal Trump supporter who claimed on the *Jim Bakker Show* in March of 2018 that opposition to Trump was "diabolical" and described it as a "spiritual attack." Restating the claim that often came from Christian Trump supporters associated with the NAR, Boykin noted what he understood to be a prophetic element in Trump's election and reinforced the notion of a specific insight given to Christians who supported Trump, saying that Trump's critics did not understand that "God's imprint" was on this election.[34]

Another council member for POTUS Shield is a prominent figure in the NAR's prophetic networks named Lou Engle. Engle was the leader of a ministry called The Call, one of the organizations that organized Rick Perry's prayer meeting in 2011.[35] He is also known for his controversial involvement in the infamous anti-homosexuality laws in some African countries in the early 2000s.[36] Like General Boykin, Amedia, and others associated with the NAR, Engle believed that Trump needed protection from satanic enemies seeking to undermine his presidency and even destroy him personally. In an open letter in 2017 in which he called for fasting and prayer, Engle said, "Esther is a prototype of history's hinge: a courageous woman who humbly and artfully spoke truth to power." In confronting this "witchcraft," referring to the plan to destroy God's people described in the Bible, "a nation was spared annihilation."[37]

Comparing this moment in the Hebrew Bible to the opposition to Trump's election in 2016, and by so doing comparing America with Israel, Engle puts the election in terms familiar already from our discussion of Jonathan Cahn and others. Remarking on the Women's March organized to protest Trump's inauguration, he emphasizes the importance of spiritual warfare in defending Trump's presidency and the nation itself. He says, "The Women's March was the first shot across the bow, heralding a revolutionary rise against the president of the United States, 'We the people' and in reality, the foundational biblical truths upon which our nation was founded." Esther's confrontation with demonically inspired conspiracies to destroy God's people, in a similar fashion to the parallels that Cahn often evokes in his writings, is the paradigm evoked to inspire God's people to take prayerful action in opposing the "witchcraft" aimed at Trump's presidency by his political opponents. Engle is also clear in his letter that the political battle that we can all witness has a hidden dimension; it is "a spiritual battle that cannot be won on the playing field of protests and political arguments."

POTUS Shield and those associated with it consistently presented opposition to Trump and his policies as organized around a demonically inspired and irrational hatred of the president and resistance to his agenda. Political action to protect the president from such attacks was, of course, encouraged. Still, the primary tool called upon in the context of the Amedia's calls to action was spiritual warfare through intercessory prayer. Central to this narrative of demonic forces aligning against what God plans to do through Trump as his chosen leader for the United States was always laden with both an optimistic expectation that the power of God was sufficient to see Trump and the nation through any given attack. Here, the narrative meant to encourage political activism is united with the call to prayer. There is a distinction between the kinds of action, but no distinction in that they must be mutually reinforcing. Political action must be guided by prophetic insight and conducted in concert with spiritual warfare and intercessory prayer.

One can see this, for example, in the then-impending release of the Mueller report, when in January of 2018, Amedia asserted that an attempt at impeachment was inevitable but that "God is going to prevail" because of the "anointing" on Trump's life whatever "they intended for bad, God will make good."[38] This optimism continued in reference to the then longest-running government shutdown in history, about which Amedia said that this political obstacle was not, in fact, a prelude to misfortune but God's way of breaking a "spiritual stronghold." Nevertheless, in accordance with the conditional nature of avertive narratives, he exhorts his audience to pray for Trump so that God's people might yet overcome the plans of Trump's enemies and, by extension, God's political and spiritual adversaries. In many ways, POTUS Shield's calls to prayer represent the avertive and optimistic elements of NAR as well as the centrality of conspiratorial narratives in their religious and political discourse. In its very self-definition, POTUS Shield is described to have been established to specifically engage in strategic intercessory prayer for the president and act as his "spiritual shield."[39]

Two specific examples of POTUS Shield's political and intercessory activity that illustrate our point further are Amedia's calls for prayer concerning the revelations that came out from Michael Cohen, who disclosed damaging information about Trump's operations, and the confirmation process for Supreme Court Justice Brett Kavanagh. When Michael Cohen, Trump's former lawyer, spoke in a public hearing before Congress in February of 2019, Amedia had a great deal to say on the matter. Amedia knew Cohen from his time working with the Trump campaign and even claims to have offered Cohen pastoral advice, so in response to the testimony, Amedia felt that he had a measure of insight into what may have motivated what Amedia and others allied to the president described as a betrayal.[40] Cohen said in his testimony that he felt "ashamed that [he] chose to take part in concealing Mr. Trump's illicit acts rather than listening to [his] own conscience …, because [he knows] what Mr. Trump is. He is a racist, he is a con man, and he is a cheat."[41] Behind the testimony, Amedia, however, saw not a man full of regret for his past decision to work for and protect an unethical boss, as Cohen presented himself, or even a liar trying to save himself from federal prosecution, as some of Trump's defenders believed. Amedia saw a man targeted by a conspiracy that threatened him to participate in destroying Trump's administration and remove him from office.

The narrative that there was a conspiracy to unseat the president was not exclusive to Amedia. Amedia's specific description of the alleged conspiracy does reveal something about how he viewed Trump's political opposition. Though he, like Wallnau and others associated with the NAR, had stated that Trump's character and personal faith were irrelevant to the fact God chose him to be president, Amedia nevertheless offered a staunch defense of the president against Cohen's allegations. Contrary to Cohen's claims, Amedia argues that Trump was not a racist, a conman, or a cheat, and there was no evidence that Trump was guilty of the actions that Cohen alleged. Amedia, however, explains that there was a reason why Cohen would perjure himself in this way. He alleges a plan to destroy the president and the operatives of the secretive cabal, implemented by Lanny Davis, Cohen's lawyer, who also formerly served as special White House counsel for President Clinton.

Amedia describes Davis as a "Washington spin maestro" and "Clinton warrior" who was still in the employ of the interests that opposed Trump in 2016. Amedia claims that these forces saw their moment to manipulate Cohen into making defamatory claims that could damage Trump that would create the pretext for removing him from office.[42] Amedia argues that Cohen's deal that would shield him from damaging prosecution in the future was "no different than what would happen in a Deep State or CIA trying to get somebody to turn spy." As Amedia saw it, Cohen was a person being manipulated by the same cabal of political activists seeking to remove Trump from office and thereby remove a significant obstacle to carrying out their plans for the nation.

Regarding Cohen's testimony, Amedia seems more concerned with the human actors working to subvert Trump's agenda by exploiting one man's weaknesses; however, the spiritual warfare element is still central to the call to action and prayer narrative. At the conclusion of his discussion of the events surrounding Cohen's testimony, Amedia calls for prayer a beseeches God that Trump may withstand these attacks, which he regards as spiritual in nature. What some Trump supporters and political allies view as the actions of human beings involved in the Deep State plot to overthrow the president,

Amedia, through his spiritual discernment, can more accurately describe as the machinations of dark spiritual forces that seek to destroy Trump to hinder him in what God has anointed him to do.

The spiritual warfare element that is present in every POTUS Shield commentary is more clearly demonstrated in Amedia's comments about the confirmation process for Supreme Court Justice Brett Kavanagh that began in September of 2018. In an "Urgent Prayer Alert" posted on *YouTube*, Amedia called for the POTUS Shield warriors to engage in intercessory prayer for the confirmation process just after Senator Dianne Feinstein made public the letter from Christine Blasey Ford, which detailed an accusation of sexual assault allegedly committed by Kavanagh against her several years prior.[43] Amedia viewed this as an underhanded effort to discredit a qualified, pro-life justice whom the president had chosen to fulfill a promise concerning how he wanted to restructure the Supreme Court. Amedia specifically said of the letter and the announcement as "a conspiracy and plot" and a "thwart of the enemy." Appealing to the specific insight that Christians empowered by the Holy Spirit possess, Amedia stated, "We look at it spiritually ... We go into the spiritual realm that God has given us authority and dominion over." He describes what others saw as a legal and political challenge as another battle within a grander spiritual conflict over America's future.

In this call to prayer, Amedia reminded his POTUS Shield prayer warriors that what was at stake was the removal of "the curse that is upon our land"; a curse here resembling what we heard from Cahn at the prayer breakfast messages in 2013 and 2017, that resulted from legalizing abortion and removing prayer from schools. "The enemy," Amedia argued, had set up a trap for Kavanagh in the form of the "Me Too Movement," and if he were denied a place on the Court, it would endanger the interests shared by Amedia and the members of POTUS Shield for America to reverse its course on these social issues that will determine America's destiny regarding its right relationship with God. Significantly, too, such a political defeat, having Kavanagh not confirmed as a new justice on the Court, would solidify the curse that America faces and lead it into God's judgment.

Amedia exhorts the viewers of the POTUS Shield call to prayer to "bind those forces" that "come from the depths of Hell." Echoing the language common from Cohen, Strang, and others concerning the Clintons during the

2016 election, Amedia targets what he calls "the Jezebel spirit, and the Ahab spirit," that lost the election, whom he accuses of engaging "in a conspiracy to steal the results of what God has done," and asks God to "send confusion and chaos into the enemy's camp." For Amedia, the political contests and legal intrigue that characterized Trump's term in office were not only the result of Clinton's disciples, the conspiracies of the Deep State, or leftists who would keep America in its current disposition. Trump's political woes were the result of demonic spirits manipulating and empowering human agents to attack the president. To counter this activity, Amedia argues that POTUS Shield warriors must "go into the spiritual realm that God has given us authority and dominion over" to enact His divine will through prayer.

In an interview with Steven Strang for *Charisma News* in September 2018, Amedia was clear about the spiritual warfare dimensions of the fight over Kavanaugh's confirmation.[44] Strang says about Amedia that he, like Chuck Pierce and Mark Taylor, had predicted Trump's victory in 2016 and now comes with further insight into the current political moment. According to Strang, Amedia was clear that the effort to stop Kavanaugh's appointment to the court "is clearly about abortion." For Amedia, Kavanaugh's opponents are not merely motivated by political ambitions but compelled by demonic forces to stop the seating of a pro-life justice on the Supreme Court. "This is clearly about the life of the unborn child," Amedia claims. He continues, "This is clearly about the same murderous spirit that took over when Moses was being born and Pharaoh declared that all the Hebrew boys would be destroyed." To counter this, as Strang notes, "prophetic and apostolic leaders," including Cindy Jacobs and Lance Wallnau, will join Amedia to intercede in prayer to affect the outcome of the hearings, praying that the friendly senators "not to weaken" and that "Kavanaugh to stay strong."

For Amedia, this was a significant moment in the life of POTUS Shield in its assignment from God to intercede for Trump and to spiritually support the administration's political efforts. "That was the promise God gave us on Nov. 9, at 3:30 in the morning," Amedia reminds Strang in the interview, to "put up the shield." In return, Amedia says, "God will change the [Supreme] Court," establish "three new justices," and thereby "transform the laws of this nation and I will transform this court system and clean it." Strang then returns to the importance of the unlikely and even surprising use of a person like

Trump by God for this purpose. Remarking on what Trump had done with the appointments of Gorsuch and now Kavanaugh, as well as moving the embassy to Jerusalem, Strang notes:

> But although I acknowledge the good Trump has done so far, I don't ignore the hard truths. I deal honestly with his flaws, his mistakes and his checkered past. But I see a big difference in Trump; I don't think he's the same man he used to be. And if God can use an ungodly king like Cyrus from Babylon, can't He use a flawed businessman like Trump to do His will for the US?

Trump's past was no deterrent to supporting him now in what he was doing. One could see a pragmatic bent to this support as Trump was doing so much that his Christian base wanted to see from him. However, even in recalling the practical and political action Trump had undertaken, what mattered was the prophetic element and that the prophecies demonstrated that God was indeed moving in the world and prophecy voters were taking part in it.

Amedia's prayer-warrior support for Trump through POTUS Shield continued through the term through to the 2020 election. In this case, too, he saw the spiritual dimension of the forthcoming election as ultimately determinative of the outcome. In a report from October of 2020 on *Charisma News* the title of which seems to encapsulate the avertive elements of the NAR's narratives about Trump, "Frank Amedia: God Has Shown Me What Will Happen With This Election if We Do Our Part," Amedia claims to have revelation from God about the election, especially after Trump's diagnosis with the Corona Virus.[45] He claims to have received a vision from God that he would repeat before, during, and even somewhat differently after election day 2020. He says:

> The Lord had shown me earlier in the year a vision of the president stuck in the mire of quicksand, sinking and drowning in muck up to his chin. But in the vision, the thumb and finger of the Lord suddenly appeared from above and snatched him out of this death grip, hurling him high into the sky to soar.

This message takes on particular importance after the election, but at this moment, it is the capstone for how Amedia viewed Trump's tumultuous presidency. Amid the political scandals, the alleged conspiracies to personally destroy Trump, and even Trump's own failures, and now, amid the pandemic, which Amedia described as a "diabolical onslaught injected a dark fear into the world," God was doing a great work for and through President Trump. "Here is what I believe is our assignment for the president and through the election," Amedia claims. He then exhorts the audience "to push/pray that the fury of the Lord, for His own name's sake, will accomplish what He has set out to do."

Amedia contends that Trump was anointed by God himself to change America's course, particularly through the courts. In 2017, before his interview with Steven Strang, Amedia appeared on the *Jim Bakker Show* and said God told him to prophesy, "There's going to be a shift; there's going to be a change. I'm [God] going to reset the Federal Court System, and He [God] said, begin to pronounce it."[46] He goes on to advise that God further ordered that lawsuits supporting "Judeo-Christian causes" be brought before the lower courts so that the Supreme Court that Trump was going to change in favor of pro-life and other causes important to Amedia, Bakker, and their audience will win in the newly realigned Court so to "reestablish the Judeo-Christian doctrines of this country." Concluding that thought, Amedia cheerfully states, "It cannot be stopped, it cannot be stopped."

"Trump Quake!"

In a prophetic word from December 2016, Enlow exclaimed in a message titled "Trump Quake! What's Next!" that God had "intervened" in electing Trump as president and in so doing "the United States and the world itself … experienced a global-rattling earthquake, which will release tsunami waves of reformation changes for some time."[47] With this election, "He [God] placed Trump into power" and also "released unprecedented wave after wave of the hosts of Heaven" to aid Trump and empower him to bring massive changes to the United States and the world. Enlow writes:

> Trump has been anointed with an Isaiah 45, Cyrus anointing to break down the enemy's mafia-like stronghold on the mountains of government, media and economy. **As our 45th President, he will "strip kings of their armor, level the mountains, break down the double gates of resistance and cut through iron doors" (see Is. 45). He will also be given access to treasures and riches stored in secret places.**

At this moment, Enlow exclaims, God is remaking America, and beginning a particular phase in establishing His dominion. **"God is about to do a most holy thing among us as we go into the 'Promised Land' of the seven mountains, and it all starts with getting clarification on who is in charge,"** he writes.

As full of promise as this moment is for Enlow, he nevertheless warns that it is not without its dangers. He argues that however important this election was for establishing a winning front for the Kingdom of God, "The Church must continue to work at winning the battle for the hearts and minds of men and women and seeing that as a more effective long-term answer to the moral disaster of abortions." The war is not necessarily won, and the final victory is contingent on how the church behaves. "The long-term reformation of America is not just contingent on a president making political moves and creating new laws," argues Enlow, "but rather it is a vibrant, in love with God, and in love with people—Church."

In the 2016 election, Enlow explains, the demonic "principalities" that govern the areas of "government, media, and the economy" were "heavily damaged," but Trump has only just begun to battle the expanded network of corruption and demonic forces at work in the country. Enlow writes, "Three major archangels, including Gabriel, will be assigned to Trump's commission and the gates of hell will rattle, shake, and be pulverized," but that "A major black web that was over the nation has been suctioned off the land and that's just the beginning." Enlow describes Trump's election, once again, as more than a political victory that offers an avenue for revival and for God's people to move to reform the nation. Trump's victory was a triumph for God's people in the realm of spiritual warfare as the dualistic forces battled for control over the three mountains of government, media, and the economy. Trump should go on the offensive, empowered by God to "the root structures of these webs," which, Enlow believes, "will be exposed and uprooted."

Not long into the Trump presidency, the expected "tsunami" of victories seemed to ebb, and doubts emerged as the scandals that dogged him seemed to take their toll on the optimistic view of the prophecy voters. In what should be read as a response to this creeping sense that things were not going as well as expected, in May of 2017, Enlow released a prophetic word titled "God

Says, 'I Played My Trump Card, I Will Win the Hand.'"[48] Here he explains that God affirmed that what he had set out to do in making Trump the winner of the 2016 election would by no means be undone even if Trump seemed to be losing. According to Enlow, God said to him: "I played My Trump card and I will win the hand." The prophecy goes on, "This move does not require My Trump card to be perfect, as I have already taken all of that into consideration—as I always do—when I choose anyone for any assignment that I have."

This prophetic word by Enlow seems to be in reaction to the then ongoing developments around alleged Russian interference in the election and the firing of FBI director James Comey on the ninth of that month.[49] Enlow does not name any specific event that may have triggered this word, but in the text of the prophecy itself, there seems to be a doubling-down on the point that Trump was chosen for God's own purposes with the caveat that much of what is being done is not apparent at the moment. Enlow claims that God has said in this regard that He "chose Trump for purposes you must yet be patient to watch for."

No matter how the tone might have shifted from his 2016 message, Enlow is still certain at this moment that God is still supernaturally aiding Trump against the forces of darkness. Immediately following the claim that we would "have to be patiently watchful for what God is doing," the prophecy continues, "The hordes of Hell in media have rallied in mass under Leviathan but I [God] will crush them under the forces that I have released under My trusted archangel Gabriel." The prophecy goes on, "He [Gabriel] will be instrumental in devastating media outlets that do not position themselves as lovers of truth and goodness," and that for them "[t]here will be in-house fires that will not be able to be put out in some major media outlets." In a callback to the story of Esther and Haman, Enlow claims that God said, "There will be the hanging by the very noose they have created for others." "My Trump card," the prophecy continues, "is something I will continue to play, but is a card I have already played well." Referencing what he describes as the media's "backlash," assuming he is speaking to the increasingly negative news coverage around Comey's firing, Enlow claims that God says, "Much of the enemy's powerful-seeming backlash is the backlash of that which is beheaded."

This prophecy concludes with a reminder that God is beyond the "theology" and "eschatology" that people created, and the prophecy chastises anyone who would look at Trump's administration with doubt concerning God's working through it despite any misgivings that may be rising in their minds. With the promise that God is going to "overhaul" everything in the world according to his time of "accelerated change," any doubt that with God "literally ALL IS POSSIBLE [sic]" is rejected in favor of a certain faith that all ends will be accomplished according to His will. "I call on you to stop carrying anxiety, stop the finger pointing, stop the angst, stop proclaiming end of days scenarios," the prophecy continues. "Stop any and everything that takes you out of being a carrier of good news." With a final caveat concerning how the people of God must engage with this plan for it be fulfilled, the prophecy states, "Your best days are here if you are committed to faith, hope and love," and finally states, "I am using My Trump card for certain matters but you must rise up and make even the much greater Kingdom difference."

The "Cyrus Anointing"

In June of 2017, Lance Wallnau described Trump's presidency as the "era of Cyrus Trump."[50] He further defines it as an era of "a 'reset' that blocks the aspirations of world rulers who were on a fast track to build a global Babylon," where otherwise, he argues, global catastrophes "would have been accelerated by an American economic/social meltdown under the wrong leadership." In concurrence with Cohen, Amedia, Enlow, and others, Wallnau believed that the Trump Presidency averted the most dire of futures for America. It also offered the opportunity for the people of God to begin to really assert their authority over the Seven Mountains, empowered by the Holy Spirit to build the Kingdom, "IF THEY CAN SEIZE [sic] the moment." In common with other prophecy voters and with the broader base of Trump's support, Wallnau saw Trump's opponents as agents working with or for the Deep State.

In 2018, with reference again to his reading of the story of Esther, Wallnau prophesied that before "June 6, we're going to see the unraveling of the entire deep state intrigue." Echoing again one of the common references during the Trump's presidency from prophets like Frank Amedia, Wallnau claims concerning these revelations, especially in that the Mueller's investigation was a "witch-hunt," with reference to reports from *Fox News*, that Haman, whom he describes in this scenario as the intelligence community that he thinks is behind the "satanic" scandals that plague the administration will be "hung by their own tongue."[51]

In a conversation with Steve Schultz on a broadcast for *The Elijah List* posted in March of 2019, Wallnau states that God gave him authority as an "intercessor" and a "bodyguard," in a spiritual sense, for Trump.[52] He stated, "I'm convinced I got the intercessory prophetic mantle for the American government for the season we're in." Wallnau here continues to affirm that the church needs to be emboldened to "move out of the dormancy" that the "Body of Christ" has found itself in and to have "the courage and confidence to show up" in 2020 for what he calls a "collision of worldviews." Already looking at the 2020 election, Wallnau was concerned that the church remembers that her role is to support and pray for God's anointed and that the stakes for the election were very high indeed.

In a January 2, 2020 post on *YouTube*, Wallnau describes the coming election as a "spiritual battle." Referencing a then-recent editorial in *Christianity Today* arguing that President Trump should be removed from office for using his influence to coerce the President of Ukraine to find compromising material on Joe Biden's son Hunter, that this was an attack against Trump for being the "wrecking ball" that was now "hitting the religion mountain."[53] He continues, "the church itself will go through a reformation this year," and now is a particular prophetic moment for the right kind of intercessory prayer. Stating that "Christians have come out against Christians" signaled for him that "the church needed a deliverance" from a certain kind of blindness to what God was doing through Trump despite the concern for the president's actions that led to his impeachment on December 10, 2019.[54] This kind of attack signals what Wallnau describes as "Jezebel witchcraft" for which an "Elijah" is needed and that a "prophetic anointing has to come upon the church to break this halting between two opinions" concerning Trump. Referencing a previous prophetic message from Dutch Sheets, Wallnau then scolds the church for not reforming "a bloody thing" since Trump took office, remarking that Trump would have supported them to do whatever they wanted to do to that end.

Looking toward election night, Wallnau contends, "Satan wants to reset the clock and take back over this country because he plans on, well basically … fortifying a move that is going be the economic takedown of the United States," followed by the rising up of China, Iran, and the "triggering of a depression," what he calls, referencing Cahn's book, "a harbinger scenario."[55] In what he describes as a "collision of voices" between the "prophets of Baal," among whom he counts the Christian critics of President Trump, and the "spirit of Elijah," or God's prophets speaking against the "antichrist," the 2020 election is for him a "governmental battle for the future of the United States." Referencing Exodus 23, wherein God promises Moses that he will send an angel before him to the land promised to Israel, Wallnau states that any opposition to what God is doing through Trump will be met by the judgment of God and that God will "wipe them all out." Despite these assurances, Wallnau quickly points out that God's people ought not to become "lethargic" and that the effort at reelecting Trump would require them to "acquire one million new voters" to not lose. Despite God's supernatural power, the election's outcome is in part determined by the actions of God's people. Wallnau states, "if they [Christians]" have their "ear tuned to what the angel of the Lord is saying" and act accordingly, then victory will be achieved.

While Wallnau emphasizes the contingencies regarding the 2020 election in his January 2020 message posted on *YouTube*, he speaks with equal confidence of God's "doctrine" overcoming the "witchcraft" in Washington. This avertive narrative permeates the rhetoric of the prophets during the 2020 campaign. If the church was complacent, and the malevolent forces of the Deep State left unchallenged, Trump could lose. However, the prophets were convinced that Trump would miraculously win the election by supernatural means. Frank Amedia, Johnny Enlow, and another prophet, Jerimiah Johnson, all declared that they received a vision in which God told him that Trump was indeed going to win. Johnson claimed that God told him, "The enemy has intended to strike out Donald Trump at a very critical hour in history. But behold, supernatural help is on the way, for I will slow down the advancement of the enemy and allow him to knock this out of the park. For it is simply a matter of time before the victory."[56]

Nevertheless, as confident as these prophets were, regardless of how fervently the prayer warriors interceded, Trump lost. What remained was for the prophecy voters to account for how and why that might have happened. More importantly, they had to determine what the election loss and their failed predictions meant for their ministries going forward.

.

5

The 2020 Election—Spiritual Warfare by Other Means

Trump's campaign for reelection officially started in June of 2019 with a rally in Florida, where he announced his candidacy. During that speech, he demonstrated that he was perfectly willing to use again the apocalyptic language of his 2016 campaign. He warned his audience, "Our radical Democrat opponents are driven by hatred, prejudice, and rage," and that they "want to destroy you and they want to destroy our country as we know it," but exclaimed, "Not acceptable. It's not going to happen."[1] He went on to list several grievances, including the "hoax" of the Mueller investigation and falsely claiming that there were attempts to steal the 2016 election in favor of Hillary Clinton. He also asserted that if he lost in 2020, things would get much worse for America, claiming, "A vote for any Democrat in 2020 is a vote for the rise of radical socialism and the destruction of the American dream."[2] In 2016, Trump ran on a promise to "Make America Great Again," and in 2020, he was running on the promise to "Keep America Great." But his ambitions for national greatness and prosperity were not guaranteed. If Trump's supporters did not mobilize, if the secretive and malicious cabal of Trump's opponents were successful in their efforts to impede his reelection, disaster would overwhelm the nation, and they would reverse any gains Trump achieved in the previous four years.

The conspiratorial narratives that shaped the discourse among the prophecy voters during the 2016 election and Trump's presidency persisted throughout the 2020 campaign and beyond. However, these narratives, as we can see from Trump's own rhetoric, were not localized to those associated with the NAR. Notwithstanding the growing popularity of QAnon during the latter part of Trump's presidency, some of the most prominent leaders among the base of Trump's Christian support frequently expounded on descriptions of alleged subversive plots to destroy the president and all the good he intended for America. For example, in May 2019, Franklin Graham called for what he described as a "Special Day of Prayer," scheduled for June 2 of that year.[3] In what he termed "a special day of prayer for the President, Donald J. Trump," he argues, "President Trump's enemies continue to try everything to destroy him, his family, and the presidency." Graham claimed, similarly to what President Trump had often claimed of himself, that "no president has been attacked as he has." He concluded his appeal for prayer on Trump's behalf with the same passage from Ephesians so frequently quoted in the context of spiritual warfare: "For we do not wrestle against flesh and blood, but against principalities, against powers, against the rulers of the darkness of this age, against spiritual hosts of wickedness in the heavenly places."

Graham's call to prayer was no minor event, attracting the support of the most prominent figures in the American Christian right. Among the more than 300 Christian leaders who signed Graham's statement associated with the call to prayer were former congressional representative Michelle Bachmann, one-time presidential aspirant and conservative activist Gary Bauer, Jerry Falwell, Jr., and Dr. James Dobson of Focus on the Family. Signatories also included Mike Bickle and POTUS Shield council members Bishop Harry Jackson, Lance Wallnau, and Alveda King, the niece of Dr. Martin Luther King, who is also the director of the anti-abortion activist organization, Civil Rights for the Unborn.

Calls to spiritual warfare on Trump's behalf were frequent and common among various persuasions of conservative American Christianity in the months leading to the 2020 election. At the same time Graham issued his call to prayer, Lance Wallnau was selling the "13 Cyrus Trump Bundle," which included a book, a video, and a coin that featured the images of King Cyrus and President Trump. This collection was meant to give those who donated sufficient funds the spiritual power and discernment that the items can impart so that they might more effectively engage in intercessory prayer for Trump's, and by extension, America's benefit. The ad on the *Jim Bakker Show* website claimed, "*The hour is urgent—but the Saints are not. Christian civilization is at a historic crossroad. Unprecedented REVIVAL and the upheaval of REFORMATION are converging as spiritual powers collide over the destiny of nations.*[4] Trump's spiritual advisor Paula White engaged in this discourse with intensity and frequency. During a reelection rally in Orlando, Florida, on June 10, 2019, she prayed:

> Right now, let every demonic network who has aligned itself against the purpose, against the calling of President Trump, let it be broken, let it be torn down in the name of Jesus … I declare that President Trump will overcome every strategy from hell and every strategy from the enemy—every strategy—and he will fulfill his calling and his destiny.[5]

The prophetic narrative groundwork established in the 2016 election was in some ways repeated during the 2020 election, certainly in part because of the conviction of the prophets that Trump was still God's anointed leader. Many Christian leaders had become apologists for the President and his record, though as the election neared, Trump's handling of the pandemic and other issues received a great deal of criticism. His NAR supporters, however, did not waver. Ché Ahn, for example, streamed a Sunday service on September 13, 2020, titled "Promises Made, Promises Kept," clearly echoing one of the Trump 2020 campaign slogans.[6] Noting the importance of life to God, referencing abortion, he encourages the congregation to "vote biblically." In the context of describing enriching judgment and the coming of the Lord, pointing to the wildfires and riots in California at the time noted Trump's appointees to key judgeships that he expects to protect "religious freedom" in the future and the appointment of "Evangelicals to key positions" in the government, including Mike Pompeo and Vice President Pence, whom he describes as "Spirit-filled," and Betsy Devos, whom he describes as charismatic Christian.

Ahn goes on to tout Trump's "deregulation" of the market that he claims led to great economic benefit for all, which he describes as God's blessing. He goes on to praise the president for achieving "historic unemployment," especially for "ethnic minorities," "standing with Israel," the executive order to disempower the Johnson Amendment, confronting NATO, establishing the Space Force, The United States' withdrawal from the Iran Deal, and a "wise Covid 19 response" including economic stimulus money and "Operation Warp Speed" promising a vaccine before the end of 2020. All these accomplishments signaled to Ahn that under Trump, God has blessed America. Adding to his assurance of the positive progress on dealing with Covid, Ahn further explains that he had issued an "apostolic decree" after receiving a word from the Lord a few weeks before the lockdown began. He claims that this prophetic word stated, "Covid will come to an end either supernaturally or a vaccination would be supernaturally given to some company some individual," and that Trump was crucial in laying the "infrastructure" for recovery after the pandemic ends.

In closing the sermon, after directing the audience once again to vote "biblically," Ahn exclaims, rephrasing Joshua 24:15, "As for me and my house, we are voting for Trump." In his closing prayer after the sermon, Ahn reminds the audience, too, that the context for the "taking the land" of Canaan was that "all the saints did their part to transform Canaan, to transform the land," and asks God to empower them to do the same for America through voting, which he counts as a gift from God to further carry out the "Great Commission," but not just to save souls but to transform the nation and the world.

NAR affiliates, like Ahn, often spoke specifically about what Trump accomplished for them and what this meant to further God's Kingdom. Paramount among these critical issues for them was abortion. Ahn posted on Facebook the video of Trump's appearance in January of 2020 at the "March for Life," an annual gathering of pro-life advocates, where he described his attendance as a "profound honor." Trump, the first president to attend the event, is recorded in the video stating to the delight of the marchers, "unborn children have never had a stronger defender in the White House."[7] However, apart from what he accomplished, what mattered for the prophets associated with the movement was, as Trump himself claimed before the press on August 21, 2019, that he was "the chosen one."[8]

As the Covid crisis deepened and Trump's path to reelection seemed more uncertain, prophets began to weave concern for the increasingly negative prospects for Trump's reelection with certainty as to the need for and confidence in supernatural intervention to ensure Trump would be victorious in 2020. As we know, Trump did not win, despite fervent claims by Trump, his allies, and his supporters, including those associated with the NAR, that the election was stolen. Trump's clear loss was followed by several failed legal attempts to overturn the election results. Nevertheless, many NAR-affiliated

Trump supporters were adamant that Trump had actually won, in part because of how confident they were in the prophecies given concerning the election. Even after the violence following the "Stop the Steal" rally on January 6, 2020, many of Trump's NAR supporters continued to deny the reality of the election's outcome and even wove the violence of that day into their conspiratorial narratives about what took place during the election and what may come because of the truth being revealed.

As some prophecy voters continued to insist that the election was stolen and that further actions by God or the courts might help to expose and correct what they regard as a perversion of the election system, prominent prophets took another look at their prophecies and concluded something different. Some insisted that the prophecies were always conditional. Others stated that they read the vision incorrectly. Yet at least one other dissolved his ministry and apologized. Others were still concerned that with so many apparently false prophecies, there was a broader crisis of confidence in prophetic ministries. What resulted was a debate about what it could mean that the prophets who were so certain of Trump's victory in 2020 were wrong, something that challenged their understanding of prophecies as a fundamental component of the dominionist ambitions at the core of the NAR.

In this chapter, we will look closely at the narratives presented by prophets associated with the NAR before, during, and after the election to see how, in some ways, these narratives were a continuation of the claims in 2016 and throughout Trump's presidency. We will also see that in many ways, these prophecies were different in that they continually adapted to the tumult of the months leading up to the election and after, one might say, to adjust their prophetic outlook to challenging and ever-shifting circumstances during the 2020 election. Moreover, in the case that the election's outcome was not favorable, consumers or producers of the prophecies that foretold a miraculous victory for Trump as God's chosen leader, what would they then have to do to adjust to that outcome? The election was expected to confirm the ambitions of those who saw Trump as God's anointed leader for this moment in American history—a new King Cyrus or a Jehu-like reformer—became a moment to question their own prophetic vision and, in some cases, the future of prophetic ministries.

Trump Prophecies—"2019 & Beyond"

Though Trump officially launched his reelection campaign in 2019, his introduction and remarks at the "Evangelicals for Trump" rally held on January 3, 2020, at El Rey Church in Miami, Florida established his friendship with and reliance upon prophecy voters. To open the rally, Paula White welcomed the attendees and the president, describing her relationship with Trump these past years as witnessing a "course of destiny" that began with their friendship in 2011 to see him become the 45th President of the United States.[9] In describing Trump, White states that he is "a great father … fearless leader" and "a man of courage." She goes on to explain that while he is "competitive" as well as a "very giving person," whom she describes as "compassionate unless you start the fight with him and he will finish it." She further describes President Trump as "a man that loves God, family, faith, people, and. Most of all, he stands strong for America," calling him "a champion for faith."

After these introductory remarks, White calls the president to the stage and asks that all in attendance pray for him to Lee Greenwood's classic "God Bless the U.S.A." playing over the speakers. First among those who prayed over Trump with the laying on of hands was Jentezen Franklin, senior pastor of Free Chapel, a Holiness affiliated church in Gainesville, Georgia, and an evangelical adviser to President Trump. His prayer began with thanks to God for "this nation that was born in 1776," and that "in 2020 that it would be born again." Moving from thanksgiving to repentance, he stated that "we repent for personal sin, national sin, and we humbly ask that [God] bless our nation and our president."

Pastor Franklin goes on to thank God that "America did not need a preacher in the oval office," nor did it need "a professional politician"—explicit references to both Trump's lack of Christian bearings and political experience. Instead, he qualifies Trump as a "fighter" who "does not claim to be perfect" but someone who was a passionate "champion for freedom," for whom Franklin thanks God, and who was "passionate to stop the merciless killing of the unborn." He goes on to describe Trump as having "raised people from poverty" and "passionate to see our Supreme Court filled with men and women who will stand for justice for all." In concluding his prayer, pastor Franklin asks for supernatural power be given to the president and that God would thereby demonstrate His power, even to the point of amazing the "pundits on TV" demonstrating that "God is great in America again."

Apostle Maldonado, the leader of El Rey, prayed next for the president. After reciting the Lord's Prayer, stating that God's kingdom would come, he issued several proclamations that God would strengthen the president and that He would give Trump "boldness" and the power to "defy and challenge giants in the world and to defy and challenge enemies in this nation." After declaring solidarity with the president, Maldonado referenced the now-familiar comparison between Trump and Cyrus from Isaiah 45. He prayed, "Father, we give you the praise and the honor and we ask you, Father, that [Trump] can be the Cyrus to bring reformation change to this nation and all the Earth will say, 'America is the greatest nation of the Earth.'" Paula White continued the intercessory prayer immediately after Maldonado, stating, "we secure your purpose, your calling," here referring to God's chosen purpose and calling on the president in confirmation of the prophetic anointing that Trump as said to enjoy. "Victory after victory, victory after victory, victory after victory," she prayed, and continued, "We declare no weapon against him will prosper and every demonic altar erected against him will be torn down."

Though those gathered at the Evangelicals for Trump rally were, as Paula White noted, from diverse denominational backgrounds, the rhetoric and practices most familiar to Third and Fourth Wave charismatic Christians dominated the stage at the event. That said, we should also recognize that theological divisions concerning gifts of the Spirit never seemed to be terribly important for Trump's Christian supporters. For example, Paula White's prominence in the prosperity gospel movement did not inhibit her allegiance with Sothern Baptist Robert Jeffress or Franklin Graham to support Trump's reelection, each of whom was equally committed to political support and prayer on Trump's behalf. That said, those associated with the network of prophets of the NAR stood out with their prophetic claims as to what would happen in the 2020 election.

One of the figures to gain attention for prophesying Trump's victory in 2020 was prophet Jerimiah Johnson. Like many other prophets associated with the NAR, Johnson claims to have had a word from the Lord regarding Trump during the 2016 campaign, which he discussed in an interview with Michael L. Brown on his show *Ask Dr. Brown* on November 15, 2016.[10] Brown acknowledged in the program that he had reservations about Trump but then asked Johnson to explain the word he received from "the Spirit of God." Johnson then stated that God spoke to him, explaining that Donald Trump was going to be a "trumpet to the American people," in some ways echoing the alleged word of prophecy by Kim Clement discussed in Chapter 3. Johnson explains he received this word on the morning of July 15, 2015, while in "a time of prayer." He states that he received a vision that made clear to him that Trump was, in fact, chosen to become president because of the qualities that Trump possessed that were "hard to find even in God's people." Key among these, again similar to what other Christian Trump supporters noted, was that Trump was a fighter.

Johnson explains that God told him that "Trump does not fear man and then he wouldn't allow deception and lies to go unnoticed; he was going to expose the darkness in America, but that he would be like a bull in a china closet." Like those prophecies given to Lance Wallnau and others, Johnson's vision was of Trump as a wily and disruptive force, but one that God would ultimately use for His purposes. Johnson explains that in the vision, God told him that "many will want to throw [Trump] away because he will disturb their sense of peace and tranquility," but that we must "listen through the bantering to discover the truth" that God is going "to speak to him." And, again, like others, Johnson explains that God spoke to him about Cyrus, that "as the Lord raised up Cyrus to fulfill His purposes, that He would raise up Trump to fulfill His purposes prior to the 2016 election."

Johnson goes on in the concluding moments of the interview to explain that he had another dream on November 5 in which he saw "a baby with the face of Donald Trump was handed to a mother in a church nursery." In the dream, Johnson explains, the mother began rocking the baby and weeping, and she said to the child with Trump's face four times, "You have a crooked way in you but through the intercession of the Church God will change you." Johnson states that he woke up with a "sense that God was going to give Donald Trump as gift to the church" and that Trump's 2016 victory was "primarily a gift from God to the church and God was entrusting Donald Trump to the church that we must be faithful in prayer and intercession" on his behalf. Johnson ends with the warning that the church cannot "sleep" because Trump "does have a crooked way in him," but that "at best [Trump] is baby Christian," but in any case, he "needs our prayers." In a sense, the very qualities that made Trump God's chosen candidate in one vision, in the later vision were things to be mitigated through intercessory prayer.

One way to understand the message across the two visions is precisely what Brown himself noted in the program, that Trump's candidacy presented concerns related to his character that could not be easily satisfied for all Christian observers even if they were inclined to support him. Another way to understand it is to look to the avertive apocalyptic narratives inherent in the eschatology of the NAR being scripted into the very prophecies concerning Trump's possible election in 2016. For NAR prophets, God's promises concerning Trump, there was always a sense of danger that Trump could fail precisely because of his temperament, and this sense of a caveat, at least for a time, pervaded prophecies concerning 2020 as well.

Johnson published two books discussing his prophetic dreams concerning Trump before the 2020 election. The first was *Trump, 2019, & Beyond* in 2019, and its sequel, *Trump and the Future of America* published in 2020. In *Trump, 2019, & Beyond*, Johnson begins much like Mark Taylor does regarding his Trump prophecy, that in November of 2012, Johnson claims to have had a "very powerful and detailed prophetic dream" in which he saw the United States and kept hearing the sounds of a woman in labor and a voice declaring "Braxton Hicks" four times, and then that the 2012 election was "false labor."[11] He claims further that God spoke to him and explained that the next four years would be "years of complication" and that what was going to be released after four years giving the American church that time to "change its position on five strategic areas that are upon [God's] heart."[12] Those areas are abortion, "sexual immorality," and particularly homosexuality, "tolerance and rebellion," "Hillary Clinton," and Israel, meaning America's need to defend it against its enemies.[13]

Johnson goes on to describe again the trumpet prophesy from 2015 and then to describe the prophetic significance of the 2016 election. He states that according to the dream in which a baby with Trump's face was given to a woman, "Donald Trump has clearly been given by God as a gift to the Church and she must engage in intercession in order to drive out the rooked way that is inside him."[14] The meaning of this is consistent with what Johnson explained in his 2016 interview with Michael Brown, that the church has a responsibility to pray for Trump precisely because of the qualities that seemed to make him fit to lead America at this moment.

Johnson goes into detail about a dream from 2018 that he calls "The Nebuchadnezzar Warning."[15] In this dream, Johnson claims that God warns he has "raised Trump up for four years as a battering ram and trumpet in this nation, but without a serious sanctification and softening of his heart and words, there will be great trouble and danger that will mark his run for a second term."[16] To mitigate this danger, Johnson says, God has raised up what he calls "The Daniel Company," people who "carry" a specific "anointing" to guide, advise, and pray for Trump.[17] Johnson states, "God has revealed to me that **Sarah Huckabee**, **Nikki Haley**, and Mike Pence [emphasis in the original]" to fulfill this task of guiding Trump away from danger as the 2020 election approaches.[18] Johnson is clear, as are the other prophets who describe Trump as having a special calling from God to be president, that "Donald Trump is not the savior of America," but he is equally clear, as are the others, that Trump "has been raised up by God for divine purposes and the enemy will attempt to thwart his destiny without the prayers and prophetic intelligence of the saints."[19]

Once again, all the themes from the NAR that typified their discourse concerning the 2016 election and Trump's presidency persist—a prophetic word of victory that must be acted upon with intercession and other action to be fully realized, along with the conspiratorial element inherent in the dualism of spiritual warfare regarding what God's plans are for Trump, whom He has "raised up" in this hour for a divine purpose. However, there are some elements worth considering in this book addressed in the sequel. Johnson warns that if any in the "Daniel Company" were to "resign, are fired, or if there is tension or disagreement" between them and Trump that "it could be an indicator that trouble is ahead" for the reelection.[20] In closing, Johnson also sternly warns the church to be more prayerful and look for "a cleansing and purification of the Church" ahead.[21]

The main message of *Trump, 2019, & Beyond*, apart from recounting the previous prophecies that he regards as having been fulfilled, was to offer a warning to those advising Trump and for those praying for him that there were signs of trouble for the president. The sequel carries on from this more general point to offer specific details about the 2020 election. Where the warning remains, Johnson provides direction regarding strategy for Trump and for the church. In *Trump and the Future of America*, Johnson begins with references to *Trump, 2019, & Beyond*, particularly the Nebuchadnezzar dream.[22] Worrying still about Trump's "pride and arrogance," Johnson states that "intercessors and watchmen" should make this the focus of their prayers.[23] Noting that both Nikki Haley and Sarah Huckabee had resigned by the time he published this book, he warned, "We must pray for an increase in the strategic placement of godly men and women around Donald Trump who will faithfully deliver the word of the Lord to him as he seeks to guide our nation in the days ahead."[24]

In the subsequent chapters, Johnson describes other prophetic dreams regarding the president and the upcoming election. In one, he describes a dream in which he is advising Trump about the "principalities," or demonic spirits, that he must confront: "racism," "radical feminism," and "Molech," which we know is the common reference to abortion, which, as Cohen described it, is thought to be ritualistically offering children to the demonic spirit that bears that name.[25] Johnson then goes on to be more specific regarding what these principalities mean in the context of the advice he has regarding the meaning of the dream. He explains that he indeed does believe, as he stated before, that Trump was "strategically and divinely placed" in leadership at this "time of crisis" for the United States and compares him to Abraham Lincoln in importance to the future of the nation.[26] Indeed, he rebuffs many claims that the Founding Fathers and Lincoln were themselves men of faith but were "shallow" in their faith.[27]

The point for Johnson is that while President Trump is not known for his Christian bearing, just as was the case for some of the founding fathers and President Lincoln, they were, like Trump, used by God to accomplish His purpose. Johnson states that while questioning God about what he discovered in his historical research, he wondered what it could mean that contrary to the claims among conservative American Christians, America was not a Christian nation and that important American leaders were not Christians. He claims that God replied, "He raised up Abraham Lincoln, an imperfect man of religious faith during the Civil War to issue the Emancipation Proclamation in an attempt to free the slaves and call for a National Day of Prayer, Humiliation, and Fasting," that so too "He has raised up Donald Trump." This time, however, God's chosen leader of the nation would use this "man of imperfect faith, during the greatest holocaust the world has ever witnessed the shedding of over sixty million babies' blood," to end abortion. He goes on to say that at this moment Christians should "be fervently praying, fasting, and crying out for the ending of *Roe v. Wade*" rather than worrying that Trump's depth or sincerity of faith.[28]

Johnson spends the next several pages addressing abortion, which he connects to another prophetic dream titled "The Antichrist Spirit," before moving on to "radical feminism."[29] With reference to a book written by Michael Brown titled *Jezebel's War with America* (2019), Johnson asks whether this "aggressive" spirit is manifested through Alexandria Ocasio-Cortez and Nany Pelosi.[30] Referencing Brown's book, the conversation turns from feminism to abortion. In the book's very brief discussions of racism and feminism, the focus returns time and again to abortion, the importance of supporting Trump in 2020 to ensure that abortion is abolished, and Roe v. Wade overturned. Abortion is clearly the most important issue for Johnson as he recounts his prophetic dreams and their interpretation.

Johnson then turns again to express trepidation regarding Trump's efforts at reelection and offers advice again about how Christians should intercede on Trump's behalf. With a specific reference to the "Entertainment Mountain," Johnson states that he had a prophetic dream in 2019 in which he, Trump, Kanye West, and Justin Bieber appeared on stage before a crowd that "manifested demons" and began to demand that West and Trump "demonstrate greater spirituality," before Bieber appeared and "threw the crowd into utter chaos" before the event was ended.[31] In the dream, he says to West, "just as the Lord raised up Donald Trump to be a wrecking ball to this nation, so God has raised you up as another wrecking ball for such a time as this"; that "Trump has wrecked the political landscape in America, but you shall wreck the religious one."[32]

Johnson then turns to Bieber and asks him, "the spirit of Elijah is resting upon you, to turn the hearts of the fathers back to the sons and the hearts of the sons back to the fathers."[33] Johnson then explains that in the dream, he prophesied to Trump, "Donald, says the Lord, I have given you Kanye and Justin as gifts to help bring a greater influence that you will need heading into the 2020 elections." In this prophesy delivered to Trump within the dream, God promises that he is "moving in the media and the Church" to supply him with the needed to conduct a successful reelection campaign.[34] Johnson takes this vision into his discussion of the 2020 election nearer the end of the book to remind the reader that while Trump may be an "immature Christian," he is "pro-life," and that, like Abraham Lincoln, Trump is God's chosen leader at this moment and that as Trump was a political "wrecking ball," so too Kanye West will also play that role and "help bring a mighty harvest of souls to this nation."[35]

In the book's final pages, Johnson returns to abortion as a central issue. He urges intercessory prayer on Trump's behalf and for Kanye West but also notes that "Baby Boomers" will play a decisive role precisely because of their historical position as having been young at the time Roe v. Wade was decided.[36] At this moment, if they act to support Trump, Johnson claims, they could reverse the course of the nation by reelecting Trump. However, he warns, "Should Baby Boomers fail to respond to this call, the cost exacted from them will be the lives of their children and grandchildren," and that "It would be a terrible price to pay."[37]

The prophecies concerning Kanye West and Justin Bieber may seem odd, but we should look past what may strike us as ridiculous to note the way in which Johnson interweaves the various Mountains of NAR dominionism into the prophecy. Specifically, he positions Trump's place in the Government Mountain as supported by the Media and Entertainment Mountains, specifically related how Kanye is someone who will trouble the Religion Mountain. We should also see how the later point about the boomers aligns with the book's continued focus on overturning Roe v. Wade. Even when discussing the other two "principalities" of radical feminism and racism, Johnson immediately focuses on "Molech," or the demon to which abortionists offer children. For Johnson, racism and feminism are inextricable in their complicity in abortion under the guidance of demonic spirits that control these vices. The 2020 election is no less a front for an ongoing spiritual war than was 2016.

In the context of the pandemic, Johnson had more to say about Trump's reelection. In March of 2020, *Charisma News* shared a story in which Johnson described a dream he had regarding Trump's reelection.[38] In the report, he says:

> I knew in the dream that the demon-possessed pitcher intended to throw a fastball right past Donald for a strikeout … As I held my breath and watched the pitch come out, I was suddenly stunned to watch the ball be slowed down

by a supernatural force in the air. And by the time the ball got to Trump, it was going very slowly, and he hit the ball out of the park for a big home run ... In the dream, I heard the voice of God say, "The enemy has intended to strike out Donald Trump at a very critical hour in history. But behold, supernatural help is on the way, for I will slow down the advancement of the enemy and allow him to knock this out of the park. For it is simply a matter of time before the victory."

Prior to this, Johnson had offered more of a caveat for Trump's prospects. In *Trump, 2019, & Beyond*, "Do not be deceived by the wealth and change that Donald Trump has and will bring to America," he claims the Lord told him, "for I am after far more than the gifts I have irrevocably given him, I must have his heart so that I can order his steps."[39] However, in light of this dream, Johnson expresses no doubt that Trump will be supernaturally assisted in achieving victory in the election.

Frank Amedia was also confident of victory going into the 2020 election, prophesying that Trump would indeed win. In a report from *Charisma News* on August 11, 2020, taken from an interview conducted earlier by Stephen Strang, Amedia shares his vision of what God is doing regarding the election and the surety he had that God was moving to reelect Donald Trump. In describing his vision, he says, "I saw, and what I'm sharing is that I saw Donald Trump and all of our hopes sinking into the quicksand."[40] With the chaos of the previous year, particularly the recent riots and the then ongoing pandemic, it seemed that Trump's chances at reelection were looking bleak. However, Amedia goes on: "I saw [Trump] up to his chin ... And then I saw the thumb and forefinger of the hand of the Lord come and pluck him by his head, right by the very thing that identifies him ... and flick him into the air, [to] pull him out of that." This vision assured Amedia that God was going to supernaturally intervene to ensure Trump's reelection. In the interview, Amedia offers other reasons for his confidence. "God has heard the prayers of many years," and references especially those associated with POTUS Shield, like Avelda King, "who have been on the forefront of the cry for life against abortion for years." Amedia exclaims that God is "going to answer those prayers."

Amedia also ties his certainty of Trump's reelection to support for Israel. "Part of what's going to fuel Trump back to this victory is because God's

Word is true from Genesis 12 on those who bless [Israel] shall be blessed." Contrasting the Obama administration with Trump's, Amedia states that while in the previous administration "there was no love for Israel, and especially the Prime Minister, Benjamin Netanyahu," Trump's support of Israel and relationship with Netanyahu "brought this country that blessing" that comes from a close allyship and support for Israel. This is also why Biden could not win the election, in Amedia's view, because he was part of the former administration that opposed Israel and maintained a poor relationship with its prime minister. Amedia closes this claim that Trump "is not finished" with his work on behalf of the nation of Israel and that "We," Christian supporters of Trump, "have open assignments."

Amedia ends his message with prayer for Trump, beseeching God that he would receive divine assistance in winning reelection. Amedia concludes, referring to his fellow Christians engaged in warfare on Trump's behalf, "We're the birthers; we're the ones who are the midwives of this move of God, that's going to happen" in the coming months. Alas, that help was not given and Trump lost. What followed was denial, panic, and, finally, for some, a reevaluation of prophecy.

"I Hear the Sound of Victory"

On election night, when it seemed that Trump was losing, Paula White openly engaged in spiritual warfare to attempt to turn the tide in Trump's favor. During a prayer service streamed on Facebook on November 4, 2020, White prayed fervently, "I hear the sound of victory," and repeatedly said as if to invoke a win, "For I hear victory, victory, victory, victory, victory in the corridors of heaven, in the corridors of heaven—victory, victory, victory, victory, victory, victory, victory." During this prayer, she claims to have a special revelation that "demonic confederacies" were at work "attempting to steal the election." Still, nevertheless, God was sending angels to aid in the supernatural battle raging over the election, breaking into tongues or glossolalia, praying more fervently for divine intervention. Despite zealous prayer, and though she claimed that "the Lord says it is done," Biden defeated Trump to become President of the United States.[41]

There was, indeed, a great deal riding on this election for many Christians. Stephen Strang, echoing much of what Ché Ahn said about the importance of praying for and voting for Trump in 2020, wrote two books on the topic: *God, Trump, and the 2020 Election: Why He Must Win and What's at Stake for Christians If He Loses* and a slim edition to follow titled *God, Trump, and Covid-19: How the Pandemic Is Affecting Christians, The World, and America's 2020 Election*, both published in 2020 before the election.[42] Several influential Christian leaders wrote approvingly of the first book, including Paula White, who said she was "grateful for voices in the media like Stephen Strang who understand the very real spiritual battle behind the 2020 race for the White House" and that the book sheds light "on what's really at stake for our country in the next election."[43] In the foreword to the book, Eric Metaxas, a controversial figure in his own right, references the Cyrus discourse around Trump, especially in his defense of "religious liberty" and "the unborn," and says that Strang "challenges us to look beyond the polarizing news stories to see Donald Trump through a spiritual lens."[44]

Like Paula White, Metaxas presents a dichotomy in the election, stating the stakes as between "two futures" and that "Donald Trump is the best hope of keeping America from sliding into oblivion."[45] In the book itself, Strang describes Trump's opposition in familiar terms, as the "extreme" Left becoming more extreme and makes early references to George Soros, who have "become emboldened and more radical, espousing an agenda from a conservative Christian perspective is downright evil."[46] Adding to this dualistic and conspiratorial tone, he references David Horowitz's 2018 book *Dark Agenda: The War to Destroy Christian America*, calling it "required reading for anyone wanting to understand objectively what is going on in our mixed-up culture."[47] He then notes key issues that he thinks are of concern to motivate the "Right," first among them is abortion. He argues that Trump's inclination to nominate pro-life Supreme Court Justices, and particularly the importance of this as of 2019 when "bills that can ban abortion once a fetal heartbeat is detected … were passed partly to bring the issue before the Supreme Court."[48] Other issues include Israel and Middle East Policy, religious freedom, immigration, justice issues like prison reform, and, he notes again, the Supreme Court. Regarding the Supreme Court, Strang notes the importance of judges who will have what he considers a proper perspective on abortion and gay marriage.[49]

The same issues that motivated Christian support for Trump more broadly were also important to Strang. However, as Paula White noted in her comments about the book, Strang never abandons the spiritual warfare element of the election in drawing attention to political issues. He argues, for example, "The Democrats will unite and throw everything they have at the next election, and if Christians decide not to rally together and vote according to biblical values, we could see our spiritual enemy win some major battles—in our policies, our leadership, and our rights."[50] Strang concludes the book with a "Call to prayer and action."[51] Tying spiritual warfare and voting closely together in the 2020 election, he argues, "The Bible says, 'Faith without works is dead,'" and continues, "So we can pray, but we must work, and we must vote."[52] He goes on to encourage the reader to register to vote and to get involved with community organizing, stating in avertive terms, "Donald Trump cannot win without [their] help," and that each must "do [their] part" and that "God demands no less."[53]

In the much shorter follow-up to *God, Trump, and the 2020 Election*, Strang reiterates the key points that he believes would motivate conservative voters and argues that while in the 2016 election that opposition to Hillary Clinton was so strong that "the American people took a chance on a political outsider." This time, however, he argues that Trump is the experienced and "dynamic leader" who can "help our country get back to normal" after the pandemic subsides.[54] As the title of the book suggests, there is a great deal about the pandemic and the challenges it may present for the 2020 election. Moreover, there is a rather lengthy discussion of the pandemic affirming popular conspiracy theories about its origins and how it may be used by the "Deep State" to subvert Trump's efforts at reelection. In the concluding paragraphs of the book, Strang argues, "Now the Deep State, Chinese Communists, Hollywood, and the entire one-party establishment," referring to Democrats and moderate Republicans, "are still colluding to take Trump down," and argues that they are doing so because Trump is "the first president since Kennedy who is trying to dismantle their control." Should Trump lose this election, he argues, these anti-Trump forces will take control and "Christians will be target number one!"[55]

For many of Trump's Christian supporters, the 2020 election was filled with peril as much as it was with promise, even if they had prophetic words that were meant to motivate them and reassure them that Trump was going to win reelection. Lance Wallnau, for example, spoke of a word of prophecy in February of 2019 while in conversation with Andrew Wommack on a video interview for the Truth & Liberty Coalition, for which Wallnau serves as a board member.[56] In the interview, Wallnau shares that he was talking with someone he calls "a White House communications" whom he calls a "dear friend," who shared a dream that she had before working at the White House. He explains, "she had a dream that there were going to be years of plenty before there was going to be years of challenge and that she came into Trump's administration with the belief that we're going to have two terms for this president because the Lord showed it to her."

Just as Mark Taylor had prophesied, she claims that Trump was going to have two terms. Wallnau uses the occasion of this prophetic dream to explain that he, too, believed that God was working to allow "the enemy to produce a manifestation … a crisis of decision so that we can choose life and not death." He exclaims how radical the opposition has become, "And in the boundaries of God's time for America, I believe Donald Trump will be put back in office because the left, like the devil, is overextending its hand." However optimistic he is, Wallnau still warns in the talk about the "hate from the Left" because of the "threat" that Trump poses to "the global order" to such a degree that "high-level conspiratorial elements" determined to remove Trump from power.

Wallnau later published a book in 2020 on the forthcoming election titled *God's Chaos Code: The Shocking Blueprint That Reveals 5 Keys to the Destiny of Nations*, a title that is clearly playing on his previous book, *God's Chaos Candidate* (2016). In it, he discusses the popularity of his claim that Trump was like a new King Cyrus and expanded on that claim to argue for a wave of leaders that also will act as Cyrus figures, including far-right leaders such as Hungarian Prime Minister Viktor Orbán and President of Brazil Jair Bolsonaro.[57] More broadly, Wallnau claims in the book that there are patterns in scripture, similar to what Jonathan Cahn claimed in his work, that is being repeated in 2020, and in this context reiterates the importance of the Seven Mountains and the importance of activism and spiritual warfare to that mandate.[58] Looking toward the 2020 election, Wallnau writes, "The battle over America is not just about America; it is about the destiny of nations in an era of increasing global governance," and claims further that the "United States under Donald Trump is a restraining force."[59] Continuing in this claim about the importance of nationalism to God's plan, Wallnau argues that what is at stake in the 2020 election is the "endgame" for "the destiny of nations."[60] The election is nothing short of a key battle in a long war against a global government to maintain the independence of what he calls "sheep nations" who are struggling to maintain their autonomy from the "empire ambitions of a one-world government."[61]

Later in the book, Wallnau claims, "Tuesday, November 3, 2020, will be the most consequential day of your lifetime" and that "November 4 will be more dramatic yet." He goes on to warn that if "the race is tied or if Donald Trump should win, the left will demonstrate its characteristic grace and composure by tearing the nation apart in rage until they have harvested enough votes to keep the revolution going." He presents an even darker, far more frightening vision of the future should Trump lose. Referring to the secularists as "fundamentalists," he argues that they will leverage control over the powers of the government to enact "varying levels of persecution" of Christians.[62] Referencing another book by David Horowitz, Wallnau, like Strang, presents their political opposition in the most vile terms.[63] In comparing the events of 9/11 to the 2020 election, Wallnau states, "Now we face new religion," by which he means secularism, "that has captured the minds of radicals who have stormed the 'cockpit,' and once again, we risk losing the White House." Continuing this theme, he closes the chapter by echoing a common theme of both the 2016 election and the later fight to overturn the election results in 2020 among Trump supporters by saying, "It's time to take America back."[64]

For Wallnau, like Strang, the election's outcome in 2020 will determine not just the nation's political future, but its destiny regarding God's plan for the nations, and, importantly for them, the future of Christianity in America. For both Wallnau and Strang, a Biden victory would not simply mean that the dominionist ambitions of the NAR would be forestalled but that actual persecution of Christians would ensue. And for both men to avoid this future is for Trump's Christian supporters to vote. Wallnau repeats very closely what Strang says in his book by quoting the Second Epistle of James, "faith without works is dead," and argues, "If we are going to fight for the destiny of America, we are going to have to take some sort of spiritual action, and that action is manifest when we vote for candidates that honor the policies that honor God."[65]

Wallnau emphasizes for the reader the importance of action in the close of this section of the book. He states, "your vote is a spiritual veto or authorization," and further, that a vote is "a tangible declaration that says 'Regardless of the outcome, I am planting a seed for God's will to be done in America!'"[66] For Wallnau, as it is for others associated with the NAR, voting in the 2020 election, and indeed in any election and on any issue, is not merely a political act. It is a prophetically informed act of spiritual warfare.

Anger, Accountability, and Apologies

For many charismatic Christians, especially those associated with the NAR, the stakes were as high as they possibly could be in 2020. Wallnau wrote in *God's Chaos Code*, "An entire world order is wanting to shift, and America, if given more time, can restrain a measure of this chaos and allow the Church in emerging sheep nations to learn from the errors of the Church in America and stand with the Cyrus rulers God gives them."[67] The dominion mandate was at stake in the 2020 election for prophecy voters. However, responses to the 2020 election results were not uniform.

Ché Ahn released a message on YouTube on February 12, 2021, titled "Prophetic Update on California and the State of the Church."[68] In this talk, Ahn describes the struggles of the pandemic and the subsequent economic downturn in the United States, particularly its effects in his home state of California. He also notes the disappointment of the election loss, which he describes as "discouraging and depressing" and representative of the "deep darkness" that the church is meant to overcome through the power of the Holy Spirit. However, he goes on to explain that "in spite of the disappointments from the Covid 19, or economic shakedown, or even the riots over George Floyd's death, I want to encourage you that His light is shining, and the Bible promises that all nations will come to his light and the kings to the brightness of His dawning."

Although clearly not pleased with the election's outcome, Ahn accepted it. Others, however, were not so easily persuaded to accept the results. Lance Wallnau in *God's Chaos Code* and Stephen Strang in *God, Trump, and the 2020 Election* warned that Democrats would attempt to steal the election if Biden lost. After the election's results were reported, Wallnau, as did many of Trump's base, refused to believe that the election was, in fact, lost. However, apart from the many proclamations that the evidence of the election being stolen would emerge and that Trump would be reinstalled as president, Wallnau also had moments in which he became more reflexive about the meaning of Trump's defeat.

On January 20, 2021, in a Facebook live video, referencing a message from Rick Joyner, Wallnau addressed the meaning of the 2020 election result for the church.[69] Though as late as April of 2022, Wallnau was podcasting about how the election was stolen from Trump, in his Facebook live video he had another message.[70] He said concerning responses to the lost election, "The Lord said, 'There is a lot of prayer, but few are humbling themselves,' and even less were turning from their wicked ways. … We don't even know what is grieving His Spirit. Many people sought for an outcome, but they were not seeking His face." He goes on to say that "God is not done yet," and that he believes "that what we are experiencing is a discipline. Judgment begins in the house of God. Maybe we are experiencing a little adjustment now." This is a moment, after the election, he argues, for Christians to reassess their placement of trust in political figures and their attitude toward Trump in light of God's withholding of a favorable outcome. But far from giving up on prophetic guidance as an avenue for seeking proper action in the future, he argues that this "circumstance" will be an "occasion for deliverance."

For some of the prophets that stated that had heard a word from the Lord that Trump was going to win through supernatural intervention, there was more concern regarding the meaning and consequences of why they were so wrong. Frank Amedia did, for a time, join the chorus of Trump's supporters and allies to claim that the election had been stolen; however, he did not focus all of his remarks on that issue alone. After a relatively long hiatus from his show, Amedia returned to broadcasting on February 22, 2021, in an episode titled "For Sake of His Word and His Glory."[71] In this episode, Amedia explains that Trump lost the election, despite the expectations and prophetic statements that he would win, because of his own pride. He states that President Trump had done many important things that were good for the Kingdom of God, but that Trump had increasingly accepted the praise heaped upon him rather than giving glory to God.

Amedia, therefore, does not see his prophecy that Trump would be delivered from his enemies as a failed one but as an example of God changing

His mind. "I missed God, but I didn't miss God. God spoke, and God changed, and God is allowed to change," Amedia explains. He then recalls the prophecy he gave then-candidate Trump and Corey Lewandowski, Trump's campaign manager, in 2015, that if Trump "would humble [himself] before God," Trump would then "be the next President." He goes on to explain that Trump did indeed come to repentance at that time, and God made a way for him to be the President. Reflecting on this "condition of humility" before God, Amedia explains that Trump lost his way, noting in the debates and in the rallies leading up to the 2020 election that he called attention to himself rather than to God and did not give glory to God, but increasingly spoke of himself pridefully. Amedia does not mention Jerimiah Johnson's prophecies in his two books, but his explanation for the election loss signaled that Trump had fallen prey to his own arrogance and, as a result, lost God's favor.

Amedia also has some harsh words for the church in this message, whom he faults for becoming a mere "political asset." Moreover, he criticizes many of Trump's advisors, some of whom he says are in the "faith community," who allowed access to the president those who were feeding his arrogance and leading him astray, disallowing "prophetic voices" that may have warned the president from his erring ways. Amedia states that God indeed wanted a second term for Trump so that what was underway in the first term could continue, but God cannot "bless pride and haughtiness." Concerning Trump's Christian supporters, Amedia states, "We allowed a man to be lifted up higher than God." From Amedia's perspective, this loss is a vindication of God's righteousness and a lesson for the church about their support for a political candidate. As Rick Joyner and Lance Wallnau described it, the defeat in 2020 was a moment of discipline for God's people. "It is time," Amedia states in his broadcast, "for us to be the people of God who seek the Kingdom of God." Patriotism, he argues, is a virtue but not one that should overshadow God's glory. He reasserts that his political views have not changed; he is still committed to "defending the unborn" and other issues that have long motivated Christian conservatives. However, he states, "We are not a political asset ... We are God's people, God's children."

For Jerimiah Johnson, there seemed no justification for his false prophecy that Trump would win in 2020. As with the other cases, Johnson initially responded to the election loss with denial. On November 4, 2020, Johnson sent out a message that Trump had actually won the election. In a statement that would be echoed in numerous stories about the failed Trump prophecies, Johnson argued rhetorically, "Either a lying spirit has filled the mouths of numerous trusted prophetic voices in America or Donald J. Trump really has won the Presidency and we are witnessing a diabolical and evil plan unfold to steal the Election," and affirmed, "I believe with all my heart that the latter is true."[72] This denial, however, did not hold. On January 7, 2021, the day after the shocking display of violence in the US Capitol, he released a letter titled "My Public Apology and Process."[73]

In this letter, Johnson directly states that he repents for falsely prophesying that Trump would win the election. He goes on to explain that he was not going to blame Trump's loss on the lack of prayer. Nor was he going to claim any longer "that Trump actually won" and that his prophecy was still correct because the election "was stolen." This, of course, was his November fourth explanation. In the remainder of the document, he recounts the various prophesies he received about Trump from 2015 up to the election of 2020, most of which seem to, in his view, that he was hearing God's voice for the most part. Among them are references at length from *Trump, 2019, & Beyond* and *Trump and the Future of America*. He quotes from the latter in his statement that God said to him, "I warn you Jerimiah, that as Trump tries to drain the swamp. The Swamp is draining him." He thereby claims that God warned him that Trump was under significant demonic attack and that his heart was in danger of being "hardened."

This statement is similar, again, to what we saw from Amedia—that Trump became boastful about his accomplishments and thus lost favor with God. In this case, however, Johnson overrode those caveats with later claims in that chapter of his book in which, like the baseball dream from 2020, there was going to be supernatural intervention to rescue the president and assure him the election. To explain Trump's defeat, Johnson again returns to this point. He argues, "God Himself anointed Donald Trump in 2016 and then removed him from office in 2020 because of his own pride and arrogance." Far from disconfirming Johnson's faith in God, the failed prophecy reestablished for him God's sovereignty over all, even over the President of the United States.

Like what we heard in Amedia, Joyner, and Wallnau, Johnson also affirms in his statement that this great disappointment is a means by which God will discipline his people. He states, "Joe Biden's becoming the 46th President of the United States is meant to humble not only Donald Trump but all those who worshipped him more than they kept their focus on Jesus Christ." Johnson argues that God wants Christians who supported Trump to refocus on the Gospel of Jesus Christ and that he, Johnson, intends to dedicate himself to this mission. His commitment to certain political issues had not waned, nor has his certitude that prophecy is a gift of the Holy Spirit for the good of the church. On the contrary, this was a moment to refocus prophetic ministries while continuing to engage in social transformation with their conservative political convictions intact.

Conclusion: Reframing Visions

In their classic study published in 1956 titled *When Prophecy Fails*, social psychologists Leon Festinger and Stanley Schachter and psychologist Henry W. Riecken state, "A man with a conviction is a hard man to change." They go on to posit that even when confronted by evidence or even "facts or figures," the person so convinced by their beliefs "fails to see your point." They argue that such defensiveness goes beyond "simply protecting a belief" and that often this belief is accompanied by "irrevocable actions" driven by this belief so that when confronted with its falsity, this person will "frequently emerge, not only unshaken but even more convinced of the truth of [their] beliefs than ever before."[74] There is no small measure of affinity between this claim and Michael Barkun's description of "stigmatized knowledge" discussed in Chapter 2. The seeming refutation of obviously unsupportable claims does not necessarily convince the believer that their convictions were misplaced.

In her 2005 study *When Prophecy Never Fails*, owing no small debt to Festinger, Schachter, and Riecken's work, social psychologist Diana G. Tumminia argues, "Some people might think that certain beliefs are so fragile that they will break in the face of contradictory information about their validity."[75] She goes on to argue that "belief in the spiritual power behind disconfirmed events hinges upon the maintenance of solid social support," and that "[b]elief systems stay alive in social settings that generate cohesion and provide emotional succor."[76] Others see unreasonable beliefs embedded in larger social frameworks that support continued engagement with the community of people with shared perceptions of the world. In short, a social element is at play in the seemingly discredited beliefs. This speaks to what psychologist Daniel Bar-Tal describes "societal beliefs," which "represent the social reality" of the members and act as "lenses through with [they] look at their own society," and "make an important contribution to [their] social identity."[77] Such commitments, we should note, are not easily abandoned.

Though Tumminia focuses her remarks on the Unarians, her conclusion about the movement's failed prophecies also offers some helpful insight for the Trump prophecies in 2020. She argues that prophecy among the Unarians works with other kinds of "taken-for-granted specialized understandings" that help the members to establish their "lifeworld," or their "embodied social world."[78] Accordingly, "A lifeworld frames a consistent world of imperative validation," with references to "their mythology to make sense out of random occurrences in the world."[79] Though the Unarians' mythology is very different from those associated with the NAR, there is a commonality here highlighted by the use of prophecy in concert with other narrative techniques that in both circumstances frame the world for the respective movements. Further, in both cases, the broader mythology is used to explain why prophecies have not come true as expected. Prophecy does not exist in a vacuum bereft of social dimensions. It is set within a larger narrative frame that incorporates other commitments that can be deployed to explain why a specific prophecy did not come to pass in the way it was expected.

However, this process of explaining failed prophecies does not alleviate all contests or controversy. There was significant backlash against Johnson for his apology and statement. *Charisma News* announced in a story lifted from *Christianity Today* that on March 8, 2021, Johnson posted on his Facebook account, which has since been deleted, that he was dissolving Jerimiah Johnson Ministries.[80] He argued that his apology was not enough to rectify his false prophecy. More to the point about what may come after the failed prophecies predicting Trump would win reelection, he stated:

> We need to recognize that God is up to something far greater in the prophetic, charismatic movement that I believe is beyond what many even recognize. We need to stop, we need to take a breather and we need to come back to a place where we can begin to dialogue about these issues rather than be so triggered.

He went on to say that "I believe that it is a tremendous mistake to take the next four years to argue and debate and cause division and grow more prideful talking about how we think the election was taken from Donald Trump." He went on to say that Christians "need to take the next four years and humble ourselves."

The meaning of Trump's defeat and the number of failed prophecies that promised victory were a source of debate in the broader charismatic community. A document dated April 29, 2021, titled the "Prophetic Standards Statement," whose signatories included many prominent charismatic movement leaders, including Steven Strang, and was authored by Michael Brown and Bishop Dr. Joseph Mattera, was issued to, in part, respond to the discussions regarding these failed prophecies. In an article from *Charisma News*, Mattera says that part of dealing with this fallout was to offer some greater structure and accountability concerning prophecy in the future. "The gift of prophecy is given to the whole church," he argues, "and so it behooves apostles, pastors, and teachers especially to understand this and sign off on protocols."[81]

The statement itself makes several points, affirming prophecy as a valid gift of the Holy Spirit, and that it is important to the church's future. It also affirms that prophetic language can be "symbolic" and "mysterious" and should therefore be carefully evaluated over time but not rejected unless the utterances contradict the Bible.[82] However, the statement argues that if prophecies contain specific information and dates that do not come to pass, the prophet should take "full responsibility" and apologize to the community to whom the false word was given.

This standard seems shy of Deuteronomy 18:20, which says, "But the prophet who speaks a word presumptuously in My name which I have not commanded him to speak, or which he speaks in the name of other gods, that prophet shall die."[83] However, the authors state they recognize

> distinctions between a believer who gives an inaccurate prophecy (in which case they should acknowledge their error), a believer who consistently prophesies inaccurately (in which case we recognize that this person is not a prophet and we urge them to stop prophesying), and a false prophet (whom we recognize as a false believer, a lost soul, calling them to repent and be saved)

As with Wallnau, Amedia, and Johnson, the authors' political stances have not changed because of the 2020 election, but in its aftermath, they seek to reassure their followers that "[p]rophetic ministry is of great importance to the Church and must be encouraged, welcomed, and nurtured."

The apparent disappointment of the Trump prophets in 2020 was a moment of reconfiguration and reframing of prophecy more generally. It was also a moment when those previously dedicated to prophetic ministry reaffirmed their commitments. God still speaks to His people, and the gift of prophecy is still at work. God has not abandoned His people but is chastising them, affirming that they are still His children, as Amedia, Johnson, Wallnau, and Joyner affirmed. Furthermore, the prophecy voters did not retreat a single inch from affirming the dominionist mandate or their commitment to social change. Far from refuting the beliefs of the prophecy voters, the failed prophecies provided an opportunity to reaffirm their theological views and their political commitments. Trump may not be in office, but God is still on His throne.

Conclusion: Prophetic Politics after Trump

As of the writing of this book, Trump's intentions regarding running for President again in 2024 remain unclear. We can be certain, however, that if he decides to run, he will heavily court those Christians who supported him throughout his presidency. Signaling this reliance on conservative Christians for any possible political future, Trump proudly boasted of an initiative announced on September 2, 2021, the establishment of a "National Faith Advisory Board."[1] Its website states, "The National Faith Advisory Board will proudly continue the work we began at The White House, through partnering and bringing together a diverse coalition of faith leaders to amplify their voices to impact our nation."[2] It lists Paula White as the president and founder of the organization and says concerning the other members leading it, "The same trusted team that served in the halls of the White House for 4 years will continue to advocate for the issues you hold dear."[3] Trump said of the board, "One of my greatest honors was fighting for religious liberty and for defending the Judeo-Christian values and principles of our nation's founding," and listed accomplishments that should excite conservative Christians about this new organization: his Supreme Court appointments, moving the embassy to Jerusalem, and "totally obliterating" the Johnson Amendment.[4]

The last point, of course, is not true, but that hardly matters. Trump's argument is that he has been a reliable friend to conservative Christians and the staunchest ally the Religious Right could hope for; a point that was affirmed in late June of 2022 when the Supreme Court overturned Roe v. Wade with the necessary aid of the new justices Trump appointed. After the ruling, Trump said of his role in the outcome, "I delivered everything as promised, including nominating and getting three highly respected and strong Constitutionalists confirmed to the United States Supreme Court."[5] When the Fox News reporter asked him to explain his contribution to the decision more clearly, Trump simply replied, "God made the decision."[6] For those who supported Trump from among the broad spectrum of traditions and persuasions of American Christianity, no matter how bitter his defeat or controversial his actions or legacy, he was a gift from God. The Supreme Court's ruling revoking Roe solidified for the prophecy voters that despite his flaws, despite his loss in 2020, Trump was indeed their Cyrus.

Mere hours after the Supreme Court released its ruling overturning Roe v. Wade on June 24, 2022, Jerimiah Johnson issued an email through his new ministry containing what he wrote in a brief article posted on its website.[7] In the announcement, Johnson reminds the reader of his prophecy concerning Trump's reelection. He claims that he was given a three-part prophetic dream in which after Amy Coney Barrett was confirmed as a Supreme Court Justice. One aspect of the dream concerned Trump's reelection; another was that "revival" would "hit California," and finally that he "would see Roe v. Wade overturned in [his] lifetime." Indeed, he took Coney Barrett's confirmation to court as "the sign that God would overturn Roe v Wade in America." As far as getting the election prediction wrong, he says, "It was about humbling myself, dying to my public reputation, and a massive shift and purification that was coming to the prophetic movement." However, on the news of Roe v. Wade, he writes:

> As Roe v Wade has been overturned today, hundreds and hundreds of messages, texts, and phone calls are pouring in already. 😄 "See Jeremiah! You were right! The 2020 election was stolen and you should have never apologized. You are a true prophet and all 3 events you saw and predicted came to pass" they say.

He offers a modest response to such messages, stating, "I simply obeyed God the best I knew how. We see in part and know in part." But what remains clear here from his short response to the news, Johnson is certain in his commitment to prophetic ministry as is his audience. Echoing the apocalyptic language common to many Christian traditions, he ends his letter by stating, "A Bride is being prepared in the earth for the Second Coming of Jesus Christ and I'm all in."

A chorus of familiar voices joined Johnson's celebration. The website for Steven Strang's Charisma House noted that Jonathan Cahn received the news from the Supreme Court with joy.[8] He said:

> Now that the Supreme Court followed through and overturned Roe v. Wade, it is the first but major step in turning back that which history will judge as a great evil. In the Bible, the fiftieth year is the Jubilee—the year of restitution, when that which taken is restored, and that which was done is reversed. The fiftieth Jubilean Year of Roe v. Wade in America is this year! It comes to an end January 22, 2023. We pray that it be a true year of Jubilee, of the saving of lives, and of restoration.

This notice served as a message of hope amid their fight to abolish abortion in the United States and to promote Cahn's books, especially *The Harbinger* and its 2020 sequel, *Harbinger II*.

Advertising aside, Cahn expressed the commonly held sense that the fight against abortion has yielded a victory but an incomplete one, a sentiment echoed throughout conservative Christians' responses to the Supreme Court's decision. As Franklin Graham said of the leaked draft of the decision a month prior to the actual decision, "If *Roe v. Wade* is overturned, abortion will become a state issue—and unborn lives will still be in danger. We must continue to cry out on their behalf. … The battle is not over!"[9] He maintained a sense of cautious celebration after the decision, expressing concern over the court leaving the decision to outlaw abortion to the individual states.[10]

Michael Brown seems to agree that the Supreme Court decision is a victory but one that is partial. Just hours after the ruling, like Johnson, Brown issued a message celebrating the Supreme Court's decision. He admits the limited effect of the ruling and goes on to say that this was "just the beginning of a new battle to be fought for the unborn, state by state." And he is unambiguous in his attribution of this victory to Trump. "It was only because President Trump (himself an unlikely hero in this story) was able to appoint 3 justices to the Court, all of who voted the right way."[11] This new Cyrus, though flawed, delivered on one of his most important promises by appointing justices in the Supreme Court that seemed to be following through in spectacular fashion on what Trump's Christian supporters wanted to see, and some of whom prophesied may happen.

For Lance Wallnau, speaking on a Facebook video posted that afternoon, the court's decision was a stunning reversal of fortunes for the forces of good owing to Trump's appointees on the court. He argues in the first place that the decision rightly places the determination of access to abortion to the states, which will be the best protected there after this recent election because of ID laws and other measures put in place since then. Secondly, he argues that what will happen as a result is what he calls the separation of the various states into "sheep and goat states," indicating, as he explains it, a period of decision and judgment to follow. The sheep states will, he explains, protect religious freedom, the First and Second Amendment rights, and, of course, outlaw abortion. The goat states will, in his narrative, be their antithesis in all respects, "clamping down" on freedoms at the behest of "elites." Moreover, he encourages his audience to see the reaction of those upset by the ruling as evidence that the "principality" has fallen. "The Devil is manifesting," he exclaims. Comparing this reaction to an exorcism, he explains that when one sees "the demon manifesting it's probably coming out." He goes on to explain that "the screeching, the screaming, the anger" is the expression of defeated demonic spirits. Consequently, for him, the "pushback" and "pontificating" by those who oppose the decision should not "obscure the fact that it's all a manifestation of spiritual warfare in the face of a great victory."

This praise should not obfuscate the mixed feelings that some Christians have expressed about Trump, even those like Michael Brown, who credited Trump for making the Supreme Court's reversal of Roe v. Wade possible. In his 2020 book, published just before the election, *Evangelicals at the Crossroads: Will We Pass the Trump Test?*, Brown writes, "There can be little doubt that Donald Trump has been a wrecking ball, especially when it comes to political correctness"; however, he continues, "the problem with a wrecking ball is that it swings forward and backward, knocking down everything in its path."[12] Brown goes on to explain that while Trump's recklessness indeed helped to expose corruption and the "existence of the Deep State," "liberal bias" in the media, and the "radical nature of the Democratic Party," Trump's presidency also exposed "some real hypocrisy and shallowness in parts of the Church."[13]

A significant part of this concern about hypocrisy was that Christians had previously rejected Bill Clinton because of his immorality and low character but excused Trump for similar shortcomings. Further, almost like what Frank

Amedia had said after the election, Brown argues that having excused Trump's behavior to have "a seat at the table of political influence," Christians becoming divided "over a man rather than uniting around Jesus," their "equating patriotism with the kingdom of God," and "putting our hope in a human being to the point of giving him almost cult-like veneration" and even "emulating the behavior and speech of the president," all contribute to the conclusion that some evangelical Christians "have failed the Trump test."[14] He continues to advise that Christians can still vote for Trump in 2020 but that they should realign their priorities, maintaining their commitment to ensuring that people come to know Jesus.

These critiques seem even more significant given that Brown was one of the authors of the Prophetic Standards Statement and that much of what he said before the election is said later by those who continued to worry about Trump's hold on the conservative Christian imagination and the effect this has on churches. These fears reflected concerns he wrote about in his 2018 book *Donald Trump Is Not My Savior: An Evangelical Leader Speaks His Mind about the Man He Supports as President*. In that book, Brown describes the relationship between evangelicals and this "least 'Christian' candidate" to have gained their support as potentially costly for their witness to the broader society.[15] However, despite the dangers associated with supporting Trump, he remarks here that he has been positive for their interests in that, among other things, he "appears to be taking many steps in the right direction, at least in terms of pro-Christian policies, for the good of the nation."[16] Though Brown firmly rejected his association with NAR, which he regarded as nothing more than a fictitious and slanderous category, he held many of the same views as those associated with the movement and those involved in the Trump Prophecies phenomenon in 2016 and 2020. Nevertheless, he was concerned at the cost of a certain kind of support for a political figure like Trump as much as he was concerned later about the excesses of the prophetic movement that spoke wrongly about Trump's reelection.

While Brown felt the Trump prophecies for 2020 reflected something deeply problematic in prophetic ministries, Johnny Enlow's reaction to the failed prophecies was quite different. Enlow related prophetic visions as late as August of 2021 that he then described as foretelling a "reset," a "new world coming," in which he saw a "confident looking" President Trump sitting next to a "huge" stack of "trump cards."[17] He explains that the vision told him that Trump had not used any of his cards, insinuating that there were further moves to reseat Trump as president. Additionally, in an open letter dated February 11, 2021, which he posted on his website Restore 7 titled "An Apostolic Rebuke and Entreaty for Those Blaming the Prophets," Enlow has very strong words for those whom he thought had defamed the prophets and rejected the word given to them by God.[18] Stating that though he has been called a prophet that his "primary gift is apostolic," and in that capacity, he argues:

> If you can't believe with the FAITHful that God still has a Cyrus that is not yet finished—and behind the scenes being positioned for the next part of his assignment—then at minimum turn your fury away from the FAITHful and target Satan and his evil destructive agenda for USA and the nations. STOP CONGRATULATING JB!!! Rescind any congratulations you have previously given! It is personally way more serious TO YOU than you know. You cannot congratulate blatant evil! Wake up!!

He goes on to address those who, like the signatories of the "Prophetic Standards Statement," argued for more accountability for prophets. "The LEAST [sic] important matter presently on the planet is 'prophetic accountability' and you are allowing yourself to be [a] tool of the enemy if you don't see it," he argues.

For Enlow, the more important matter is that Christians stop "bashing the prophets still contending for your nation," which he claims at this moment is endangered by satanic forces and Joe Biden. For him, the real issue is not that the prophets were wrong, but certainly, not that changes should be made within prophetic ministries for greater accountability. What is important is that the fight over the 2020 election and the fate of the nation is still ongoing and that prophets and apostles like himself are still leading the fight.

However confident Enlow was in the moment he chastised those criticizing the prophets, some, like Brown, continued to be concerned about the state of prophetic ministries. In a book released in 2022 and very much in response to the controversy of the failed 2020 Trump prophecies, a respected Christian writer and former pastor of Westminster Chapel, R.T. Kendall, argued that prophetic Christian ministries did now face significant challenges. In *Prophetic Integrity: Aligning Our Words with God's Word*, he argues, "We face a severe crisis … We have a crisis of leadership within the charismatic movement that predicts one thing while another thing happens." He adds, "How long will we let this continue?"[19] He adds that the issue is perhaps larger than that specific question, stating, "the greater crisis is theological because God cannot be all-knowing and mistaken about who will be president."[20] In the foreword to the book, Michael Brown supports Kendall's argument and especially agrees that the charismatic movement is now in a state of duress. In a blurb included in the first pages of the book, John E. Thomas, the founder of a prophetic ministry Stream Ministries, states clearly, "I have cried over the state of the prophetic movement—we are supposed to represent God, but we have proven to represent party lines and opinions; we are supposed to be the ones who stand before God, but we have sold ourselves to stand in front of men."

These messages of lamentation are coupled with a hope that the ministries so damaged by the Trump prophecies as well as the deeply polarizing politicization of the Trump years will yet yield to the power of God's mercy. Both Michael Brown and John E. Thomas affirm that this is their wish as well as their expectations in their short commentaries on Kendall's book. Kendall himself concludes the book with a note of optimism. Despite the state of affairs with prophetic ministries and the condition of the country in general he argues, "I am convinced that a major awakening is coming."[21] "The simultaneous combination of the Word and Spirit will cause spontaneous combustion," he claims, and that Muslims will "come to Christ" and the "blindness on many Jews will be lifted."[22] And while he expresses sympathy for "prophets who got it wrong about Donald Trump being reelected on November 3, 2020," he claims, similarly to others, that this is now a moment for Christians to "humble ourselves" or "God will humble us."[23] In the final chapter before the conclusion, Kendall calls for repentance and a reaffirmation of humility in prophetic ministry. He warns that without this humility and repentance, "revival will be postponed or we may be prevented from seeing the next spiritual awakening."[24]

This is a far cry from Johnny Enlow's proclamation and admonition of those critical of the prophets, and yet it echoes what others have said concerning the failed prophecies. And still, despite his criticism, there is no sense that Kendall's affirmation of the value and validity of the gift of prophecy has receded or become obsolete. Trump's failed attempt at reelection did not signal the end of a great move of God any more than did the fact that the prophets failed to see his loss. God is still at work, a great revival is still on the way, and the prophets still can guide God's people into proper action.

Pentecostal theologian Amos Yong writes in a 2014 essay concerning "prophetic politics" that "prophecy can involve either the fore-telling of a future otherwise unknown to human beings or the forth-telling of a divine message for a specific place, time, and situation," but also in the sense that the prophets "warned kings and governments, questioned existing sociopolitical developments, and advocated for the poor, women, and other oppressed groups, often challenging the status quo."[25] This sense of prophetic politics may indeed continue to be a part of how NAR-affiliated Christians think and act politically, especially as they see themselves as the embattled remnant of God's people in a corrupt nation. However, the stigmatized knowledge central to the way prophecy voters see their world, especially in how they value spiritual insight and discernment, blended with a discourse that casts current events as opportunities to engage in spiritual warfare, signals that there is yet another way in which the prophetic can inflect politics. In the context of their dominionist perspective, prophecy sacralizes political action and renders the effort to achieve political victories through voting and activism as a natural extension of spiritual warfare practices.

We could see the struggles of Wallnau, Amedia, Johnson, and others to account for the Trump years and the failed prophecies associated with the end of Trump's presidency as a means of making new sense of their worldview in the face of challenges to their faith. We could also see religious these and other entrepreneurs' explanations as a cynical ploy to secure their brand. After all, Jerimiah Johnson shuttered Jerimiah Johnson Ministries only to launch a new ministry called The Altar after moving to Charlotte, North Carolina, in 2020. Perhaps it is an admixture of both motives to varying degrees. However, what is clear to me as I think about the prophecy voters is that their narratives were about reframing the prophetic roadmap for American political life and a developing strategy for affecting it according to how they understand God would want them to. The legacy of the Trump years for the prophecy voters is they have a clear sense that such change is possible. His will could still be done on Earth as it is Heaven if, among other things, they vote correctly.

There is yet another legacy of the Trump years for American Christians beyond the boundaries of those associated with the New Apostolic Reformation.

Conclusion: Prophetic Politics after Trump

Christianity Today featured a story on November 1, 2021, that argued that Trump's political career has profoundly affected evangelicals. In it, Alabama pastor and freelance journalist David Roach argues that while "[p]olitical polarization has subsided in most American churches a year after the 2020 presidential elections, but goes on to state that "there are notable exceptions to that trajectory, and new research has found lingering effects of evangelical support for former president Donald Trump."²⁶ The article references a report from Pew Research from September of 2021 that found, "Among White respondents (including both voters and nonvoters) who did not identify as evangelicals in 2016 and who expressed a warm view of Trump at some point during the timespan of this study, 16% began describing themselves as born-again or evangelical Protestants by 2020."²⁷

In many ways, these developments are not surprising. What it means to be a Christian was always flexible in the American context. The word "Evangelical" is similarly complex, with multiple communities claiming the title for varying traditions. As we noted in the introduction, Kristin Kobes Du Mez argued, "In the past some issues that divided evangelicals, such as speaking in tongues, End Times theology, Calvinism—all of those things have receded, and it's now these social and political issues that define allegiances."²⁸ Reflecting again on what Anthea Butler wrote about the "full-fledged marriage" between the Republican Party and the Religious Right after evangelicals who "overlooked" Romney's Mormon faith and supported him in 2012, it would seem that the evangelical tent has come to include even the unchurched during Trump's term in office.²⁹

In October 2022, one of Trump's staunchest critics from within the Southern Baptist Convention, Russell Moore, spoke in an interview with Chuck Todd on NBC's *Meet the Press Reports* and said, "The use of religion as a means to an end ... for an end of politics, for various sorts of ends that really can transform and change the nature of Christianity itself."³⁰ Moore continued, "So if you look at, for instance, some of the tactics often used by people who are claiming to be evangelical Christians, they're often quite short of the Sermon on the Mount." He noted, too, "I'm talking every day to churchgoing evangelical Christians who don't want to use the word 'evangelical' because it's become merely a political word. And then those who don't go to church but who are using 'evangelical' in a political sense as a way to 'own the libs'—that's not ... a good development in my view." Referring to the data reported by Pew 2021, he calls this phenomenon "the secularization of evangelicalism."

Moore argues that this surrender of principles for political expediency sacrifices moral development and harms the church's witness for the Gospel. "Once evangelical Christianity is defined not by the Gospel but by some sort of cultural or political movement, we're in a really dangerous place," He explains. "Evangelical Christianity is meant to be the good news of Jesus Christ, and handing that over to a political agenda, no matter what the political agenda, is a bad idea." I think what Moore perhaps misses concerning the dominionist claim is that for those who adhere to this ideology, as Wagner proclaimed, the "political agenda" of the prophecy voters is the fullest expression of the Gospel. They are not simply meant to save souls but to change society via social and political power and influence.

The apparent political schism among evangelical churches has not gone unnoticed by other observers. In June of 2022, during the congressional hearings on the January 6 insurrection were being conducted, Illinois Republican Representative Adam Kinzinger, who had previously remarked about divisions over Trump in his own family, noted, "There are a number of churches that have basically become, you know, from a house of worship of Christ and of God to a house of worship of Donald Trump."[31] He went on to say, "I think the church played a huge role in how we got to where we are," and that ultimately, "the church generically, and I think the church will have to play a huge leadership role in getting us out of this moment." Journalist Tim Alberta, writing a month earlier in *The Atlantic*, states, "Having grown up just down the road, the son of the senior pastor at another church in town, I've spent my life watching evangelicalism morph from a spiritual disposition into a political identity."[32] In the article, with interviews of pastors of differing dispositions, Alberta notes that the effect of this on the church itself is profound.

Splits over Trump, the outcome of the 2020 election, the January 6 riots, and Covid have taken their toll as well. Alberta recalls that one pastor told him that some churches have grown due to congregants feeling "betrayed by their pastors" on political and social issues. "That trend looks to be holding steady," he argues. Alberta continues:

> More people will leave churches that refuse to identify with a tribe and will find pastors who confirm their own partisan views. The erosion of confidence in the institution of American Christianity will accelerate. The caricature of evangelicals will get uglier. And the actual work of evangelizing will get much, much harder.

Not everyone agrees with Alberta's claim that this phenomenon is entirely novel.

Referencing Alberta's article report, historian of religion Mark Silk argues that the religious right "has never limited itself to religious issues." Whether opposing abortion, homosexuality, feminism, or pornography, he notes, "The trick has always been to turn secular issues into religious ones, to sacralize them in a way that ensures that partisan politics is understood as holy war."[33] In a sense, as Silk notes, the politicization of evangelicalism is nothing new. I argue, though heuristically useful at times, that separating religion from politics when discussing the Religious Right obscures an important point. For those associated with the NAR, the mandate to establish cultural and political dominion for the purposes of social transformation negates the idea that religion and politics are separate in their thought. The broader spectrum of the Religious Right seems to substantiate this point in their frequent attacks on "secularism," making clear that they do not want the kind of separation Jefferson described in his letter to the Baptists of Danbury, Connecticut and that many Americans might take for granted. Calls from current Republican congressional representatives to abandon "this separation of church and state junk" or who proclaim themselves to be unapologetic Christian nationalists, though their theological bone fides seem as questionable as Trump's.[34]

We should conclude that the glue of the modern Religious Right is not theology but a political vision that shares a dominionist perspective, and the NAR contributes to the formation of that perspective. Even within the sphere of charismatic Christianity, as these Christians continue to debate the controversies surrounding the prophets predicting a Trump victory in 2020, Frank Amedia, Lance Wallnau, Jerimiah Johnson, and Johnny Enlow continue to agree on the basic premise of gaining control over the major institutions of American society to transform it through social and political power. We should remember, particularly for the prophecy voters, that this dominionism is an extension of what they understand to be Jesus's command in the Great Commission. They are not simply fulfilling their duties as citizens when they vote for a candidate or promote legislation but realizing the fullness of their convictions as followers of Jesus. In this sense, the sacred is the profane insofar as they can capture the realms of everyday social and political life to bring them under the lordship of Jesus Christ. It is clear that they seek to transform America in a way that reflects their commitment to politics that promotes what they regard as biblical values; specifically, opposition to abortion, opposition to gay marriage and trans rights, support for Israel, and, of course, supporting candidates that share their views. Moreover, none of these positions are alienating to other conservative Christians, even those who are critical of charismatic movements and of the NAR.

In this context, Christians with little theological affinity with one another continued mutual support for Trump throughout the 2016 campaign, his presidency, and through the 2020 election. The differences in positions concerning eschatology and the cessation of the office of apostle or spiritual gifts seemed not to matter when it came to their mutual agreement on the immediate need to support for Trump. Sociologist D. Michael Lindsay wrote in *Faith in The Halls of Power: How Evangelicals Joined the American Elite* (2007), "American evangelicalism has the ability to maintain a core set of convictions without being so rigid that it cannot cooperate with others who do not share them."[35] He calls this "elastic orthodoxy" and describes it not as "a softening of conviction or a blurring of the lines of the lines that make Christianity distinct."[36] Referencing interviews conducted for the book, Lindsay argues that "the strength of evangelicals' religious convictions … has compelled them to work with others."[37] In concluding his thoughts on this elasticity, Lindsay writes, "instead of emphasizing doctrinal differences, modern evangelicals have looked for points of agreement with those who might be brought under the evangelical tent," and further that such ecumenism has "been the movement's strength."[38]

Lindsay's comments in his book come before some critical moments that I argue shed a different light on the elasticity he notes. One of those moments is the 2012 election in which Christian conservatives were given a choice to vote for Mitt Romney, a Mormon, or Barak Obama, a professed Protestant. Pastor Robert Jeffress, while backing Rick Perry in the primaries, famously called Mormonism a "cult."³⁹ Remarking further on these comments, Jeffress pointed out that most evangelicals would agree that Mormonism is not Christianity. "This idea that Mormonism is a theological cult is not news either," he said, and continued, "That has been the historical position of Christianity for a long time."⁴⁰ However, when commenting on the possibility of voting for Romney or Obama, Jeffress stated, "I'm going to instruct, I'm going to advise people that it is much better to vote for a non-Christian who embraces biblical values than to vote for a professing Christian like Barack Obama who embraces un-biblical values."

If we attend to this recent history, the cooperation between Jeffress and other Southern Baptists, Paula White, and those more closely associated with the NAR to support someone like Trump should not seem perplexing. As Butler noted in her 2012 article mentioned in our introduction, such connections across these theological and denominational lines are not unprecedented in the Republican Party. I argue that her point remains particularly prescient now, and I would add that it is certainly no longer something we should consider anomalous.

I agree with Butler's point about the NAR that I referenced in the first chapter, where she noted that the NAR does not exist in a vacuum.⁴¹ The NAR in many ways anticipated and embodied the changes in ecclesiastical organization referenced in Christerson and Flory's work on the topic of network Christianity. Moreover, those associated with the movement represent the increasingly popular style of charismatic Christian worship found in adjacent Christian movements like the Vineyard movement the prosperity gospel. In this sense, the NAR represents an intersection of perhaps differing yet corresponding networks related to charismatic Christian beliefs and practices. As the sociologist Michael Wilkinson noted, while NAR figures may differ from others with whom they might appear in joint events, "the relational component highlights points of overlap theologically, missionally, and relationally."⁴² For Wilkinson, this "overlap" relates specifically to how these diverse charismatic movements may find commonality in the context of worship and fellowship. For our consideration, however, we find overlap, too, in the political objectives regarding support for Trump that extends beyond even that into an alliance with non-Charismatics and even those for whom the term "evangelical" designates political affiliation and not a specific and personal relationship with Jesus Christ.

Part of the connection between those associated with the NAR and other Christians who supported Trump I would argue lies in the more fundamental popularity of the narrative elements deployed by NAR-affiliated Trump supporters. The figures discussed in this book modify and deploy older tropes of subversion and the promised cataclysm of the nation turning its back on God so often deployed, as we have seen, by Billy Graham in the context of the Cold War, and Pat Robertson and Jerry Falwell after 9/11. The jeremiads concerning the fate of an apostate America likened to Israel and threatened with the same judgments are not innovations of Lance Wallnau's or Jonathan Cahn's imaginations. The conspiratorial tropes of a secret cabal working to undermine the nation from within are also much older than the NAR and are as much the fodder of political discourse as they are readily used as plot devices in popular fiction. In brief, the import of the narratives coming from the NAR is that they both reflect and adapt existing narratives that have been potent in Americans' imaginations and are steadily deployed in American political discourse.

In the context of the Trump years till now, we must also consider the ease with which news media can fuel apocalyptic speculation to the degree that reporting, political messaging, and works of fiction are hardly distinguishable. As journalist Chris Stirewalt notes in his 2022 book *Broken News*, "What we think of as 'bad news' can score like gangbusters if it is scary and anger-inducing."[43] One does not need to purchase a DVD from Lance Wallnau, go to a Seven Mountains seminar, or read Jonathan Cahn's latest novel to receive the message that America is under assault by the "Deep State." The broader deployment of apocalyptic language with references to conspiratorial and malevolent forces at work to destroy America fits as easily within the NAR's political discourse as it does among the broader spectrum of Trump's supporters. This discursive overlap shows that even if Christians do not openly embrace the NAR, or, in Brown's case, they deny its existence, the key constituent elements of dominionism, apocalypticism, and conspiracism are particularly relevant to America's political future.

With the 2022 midterm elections nearing their conclusion, the viability of Trump-supporting candidates in general elections is uncertain. In key primaries, so-called "MAGA Republicans" won their races, and, of course, Liz Cheney, who was one of the leading voices in the January 6 hearing seeking to hold Trump accountable for his role in the violence, lost her seat to a Trump-backed challenger.[44] However, it seems the coalition of Christians, including key figures associated with NAR, is standing ready to support them. In the context of the governor's race in Pennsylvania, for example, Republican Doug Masistrano, who has also questioned the validity of the separation of church and state, has not only demonstrated his appeal to "MAGA" voters but has gotten the attention of figures associated with the NAR. Most significantly, perhaps, Lance Wallnau has appeared at rallies supporting Mastriano. At one rally, Wallnau spoke to the crowd and stated that he believed that "Col. Mastriano is anointed to lead an as-one movement," and that "The whole country will be affected by what happens in Pennsylvania."[45] These claims are not too far indeed from what he claimed of Trump in 2016 and 2020.

Five days after this story describing his support for Mastriano appeared in the *Pittsburgh Post-Gazette*, Wallnau sent a general email to his subscribers describing the expectations for the coming November elections. "We should expect to gain ground in November," he remarks, "BUT the U.S. economy is tanking, violent crime is surging, America's borders are overrun, and children in kindergarten on up are being forced to deal with pornography and questioning their gender."[46] He follows with a rhetorical question, "How could the land of the Statue of Liberty and the Liberty Bell be taken over by the demonic principalities of bondage and servitude?"

In what follows in Wallnau's email, we see a similar reminder of the judgment that would come should God's people fail to act, accompanied by repeated references to the historical pattern of the judgments against Israel for committing similar apostasies and abominations. Near the end of this message of prophetic warning is a call to spiritual warfare and a confident exclamation that "God is delivering an Elijah blow to the power of witchcraft that is operating like a veil over the mind of America," and that he, Wallanua, has not "had a word like this since [he] prophesied Trump in 2016." He continues, "We are about to see the power of God in a new way!" The rest of Wallnau's email titled "Is America Under Judgement?" advertises an event featuring Wallnau and Mario Murillo, whom he describes as teaming up with him to "push back against the Jezebel Spirit of darkness covering our land," at the Hertz Arena in Estero, Florida on October 24 and 25, 2022.[47]

There is certainly more to be said about the NAR and its varying relationships to other Christian organizations and its place in even broader networks of Christian nationalist activism. We can also be certain that the NAR will be affected by demographic changes in the United States, in particular, dwindling numbers of Americans identifying as Christians.[48] What we can say now is that Christians, broadly speaking, supported Trump for a number of reasons. I have argued, therefore, Christian support for Trump is a complex issue that should be considered in multiple ways, including by focusing on less recognizable movements whose adherents aligned themselves with Trump's agenda despite their uneasy relationship with other Christians who likewise supported him. For the prophecy voters, supporting Trump was a means to further engage in spiritual warfare against demonic forces and save America by establishing dominion over specific institutions, particularly the presidency. Support for Trump was for these Christians part of a broader strategy of gaining institutional power with promises of averting catastrophic judgments of God on the country and ushering in the fullest realization of the Kingdom of God in fulfillment of the Great Commission.

There is no sign that such ambitions by advocates of the Seven Mountains Mandate have abated. There is also no indication that diverse coalitions of self-described Christians, some of whom are perhaps using the term "Evangelical" as a sign of political alignment rather than affiliation with a tradition, will allow theological disagreements or even accusations of heresy by their fellow conservatives to dissolve political alliances in an effort to advance their vision of establishing America as a Christian nation governed by "biblical" principles. As a historian of religions, I try to abstain from prophesying too confidently about what the future brings. However, I think that we can conclude that just as Butler argued that we "will need to pay attention to the theological, religious, and ethnic diversity among evangelicals, Pentecostals, and non-denominational churches" to "understand the last 10 years of the religious right movement," we should continue to think about this complexity, including the role of the prophecy voters, to understand the next ten to twenty years as well.

Notes

Introduction

1. C. Peter Wagner, *Churchquake! How the New Apostolic Reformation Is Shaking up the Church as We Know It* (Ventura, CA: Regal Books, 1999), 31.
2. C. Peter Wagner, "Year in Review: The New Apostolic Reformation Is Not a Cult," *Charisma News*, August 24, 2011, accessed June 12, 2021, https://www.charismanews.com/opinion/31851-the-new-apostolic-reformation-is-not-a-cult.
3. C. Peter Wagner, *Dominion! How Kingdom Action Can Change the World* (Grand Rapids, MI: Chosen Books, 2008), 12.
4. Damon Berry, "Voting in the Kingdom: Prophecy Voter, the New Apostolic Reformation, and Christian Support for Trump," *Nova Religio: The Journal of Alternative and Emergent Religions*, Vol. 23, No. 4, 69–93.
5. Lance Wallnau, "Trump Is a Modern Cyrus," video, Lance Wallnau, December 21, 2017, accessed May 12, 2021, https://lancewallnau.com/trump-is-a-modern-cyrus/.
6. Berry, "Voting in the Kingdom," 74.
7. "Reagan Ending Make America Great Again," video, C-SPAN, May 24, 2022, accessed June 12, 2022, https://www.c-span.org/video/?c5016373/reagan-ending-make-america-great.
8. Chris Cillizza, "Donald Trump Leads in the Polls, but Ted Cruz Looks More Like the Favorite," *The Washington Post*, December 9, 2015, accessed March 10, 2020, https://www.washingtonpost.com/news/the-fix/wp/2015/12/09/fact-ted-cruz-is-in-the-catbirds-seat-to-win-the-republican-nomination/.
9. Gregory A. Smith, "Churchgoing Republicans, Once Skeptical of Trump, Now Support Him," Pew Research Center, July 21, 2016, accessed March 10, 2021, https://www.pewresearch.org/fact-tank/2016/07/21/churchgoing-republicans-once-skeptical-of-trump-now-support-him/.
10. "Trump in 1999: 'I Am Very Pro-Choice,'" Meet The Press, July 8, 2015, accessed March 10, 2020, https://www.nbcnews.com/meet-the-press/video/trump-in-1999-i-am-very-pro-choice–480297539914.

11 Meghan Keneally, "Donald Trump's Evolving Stance on Abortion," *ABC News*, March 31, 2016, accessed March 10, 2020, https://abcnews.go.com/Politics/donald-trumps-evolving-stance-abortion/story?id=38057176.

12 Brian Naylor, "Trump Backtracks on Comments about Abortion and 'Punishment' for Women," NCPR, March 30, 2016, accessed March 10, 2020, https://www.npr.org/2016/03/30/472444293/trump-calls-for-punishing-women-who-have-abortions-then-backtracks.

13 Dan Mangan, "Trump: I'll Appoint Supreme Court Justices to Overturn Roe v. Wade Abortion Case," October 19, 2016, accessed March 10, 2020, https://www.cnbc.com/2016/10/19/trump-ill-appoint-supreme-court-justices-to-overturn-roe-v-wade-abortion-case.html.

14 Maureen Mackey, "Roe v. Wade Overturned: Rev. Franklin Graham, Other Faith Leaders React to 'Significant' Abortion Ruling," *Fox News*, June 24, 2022, accessed June 24, 2022, https://www.foxnews.com/lifestyle/franklin-graham-faith-scotus-abortion-ruling.

15 Daniel Silliman, "Goodbye Roe v. Wade: Pro-Life Evangelicals Celebrate the Ruling They've Waited For," *Christianity Today*, June 24, 2022, accessed June 25, 2022, https://www.christianitytoday.com/news/2022/june/roe-v-wade-overturn-abortion-supreme-court-ruling-pro-life.html.

16 Daniel Cox and Robert P. Jones, "The 2016 Religion Vote," PRRI, October 27, 2018, https://www.prri.org/spotlight/religion-vote-2016/; Robert P. Jones, "Donald Trump and the Transformation of White Evangelicals," November 19, 2016, accessed May 11, 2020, http://time.com/4577752/donald-trump-transformationwhite-evangelicals/.

17 Robert P. Jones, "How 'Values Voters' Became 'Nostalgia Voters,'" *The Atlantic*, February 23, 2016, https://www.theatlantic.com/politics/archive/2016/02/thetrump-revelation/470559/.; Robert P. Jones, *The End of White Christian America* (New York: Simon & Schuster, 2016).

18 Jones, *White Christian America*, 230–1.

19 Stephen Mansfield, *Choosing Donald Trump: God, Anger, Hope, and Why Christian Conservatives Supported Him* (Grand Rapids, MI: Baker Books, 2017), 15.

20 Lance Wallnau, "Episode #603: Is Roe about to Be Overturned?!," audio, Lance Wallnau, May 4, 2022, accessed June 24, 2022, https://www.christianitytoday.com/news/2022/june/roe-v-wade-overturn-abortion-supreme-court-ruling-pro-life.html.

21   Ed Stetzer and Andrew MacDonald, "Why Evangelicals Voted Trump: Debunking the 81%," *Christianity Today*, October 18, 2018, https://www.christianitytoday.com/ct/2018/october/why-evangelicals-trump-vote-81-percent-2016-election.html.

22   Philip Schwadel and Gregory A. Smith, "Evangelical Approval of Trump Remains High, but Other Religious Groups Are Less Supportive," Pew Research Center, March 18, 2019, accessed May 11, 2020, https://www.pewresearch.org/fact-tank/2019/03/18/evangelical-approval-of-trump-remains-high-but-other-religiousgroups-are-less-supportive/.

23   Michelle Boorstien, "For Some Christians, the Capitol Riot Doesn't Change the Prophecy: Trump Will Be President," *The Washington Post*, January 14, 2021, accessed July 12, 2021, https://www.washingtonpost.com/religion/2021/01/14/prophets-apostles-christian-prophesy-trump-won-biden-capitol/.

24   Danielle Kurtzleben, "How Is The GOP Adjusting to a Less Religious America?," NCPR, June 4, 2021, accessed June 10, 2022, https://www.npr.org/2021/06/04/1002841048/how-is-the-gop-adjusting-to-a-less-religious-america?utm_term=nprnews&utm_source=facebook.com&utm_medium=social&utm_campaign=politics&fbclid=IwAR3DsbLAzerDJjaetaEDnoO03blCJ2FtydIV0d7leMeo_0-RGv18d0Mp4Gg.

25   Kristin Du Mez, *Jesus and John Wayne: How White Evangelicals Corrupted a Faith and Fractured a Nation* (New York: Liveright Publishing, 2020) kindle page 3 o4 iv location 293.

26   Chris Cillizza, "The Secret of Why Evangelicals Love Herschel Walker (and Donald Trump)," CNN Politics, June 22, 2022, accessed June 23, 2022, https://www.cnn.com/2022/06/22/politics/herschel-walker-donald-trump-evangelicals-republicans/index.html?fbclid=IwAR1Uf6rIM65XM4b5KP6zN-2Faqg4aSiso8jNkKQy1laCVbHsDq7FoQtMPdc.

27   Andrew L. Whitehead and Samuel L. Perry, *Taking Back America for God: Christian Nationalism in the United States* (New York: Oxford University Press, 2020), 10.

28   Ibid., 16.

29   Ibid., 151.

30   Amos Yong, *In the Days of Caesar: Pentecostalism and Political Theology* (Grand Rapids, MI: William B. Eerdmans Publishing Company, 2010), 130.

31   Ibid., 131.

32 Michelle Boorstein, "As Southern Baptists Gather, Right-Wing Faction Sounds Alarms," *The Washington Post*, June 13, 2022, accessed June 20, 2022, https://www.washingtonpost.com/religion/2022/06/13/southern-baptists-john-macarthur/?fbclid=IwAR1R6stKXHJBxXbV0veNPJlhyh19iUP37oMNTsT6oyNEQKkziVUYHTrR3f4.

33 Bruce Lincoln, "Theses on Method," *Method & Theory in the Study of Religion*, Vol. 17, No. 1 (2005): 8–10. Accessed June 10, 2021. http://www.jstor.org/stable/23551717.

34 Hugh B. Urban, *Zorba the Buddha: Sex, Spirituality, and Capitalism in the Global Osho Movement* (Berkley, CA: University of California Press, 2016), 4.

35 Anthea Butler, "From Republican Party to Republican Religion: The New Political Evangelists of the Right," *Political Theology*, Vol. 13, No. 5 (2012): 635–51, 650. https://doi.org/10.1558/poth.v13i5.634.

Chapter 1

1 John Weaver, *The New Apostolic Reformation: History of a Modern Charismatic Movement* (Jefferson, NC: McFarland & Company, 2016); André Gagné, *Ces évangéliques derrière Trump: Hégémonie, démonologie et fin du monde* (Genève: Labor et fides, 2020).

2 Damon Berry, "Prophecy Voters, the New Apostolic Reformation, and Christian Support for Trump," *Nova Religio*, Vol. 23, No. 4 (2020): 69–93. https://doi.org/10.1525/nr.2020.23.4.69; Arne Helge Teigen, "Profetiene om Donald Trump, USA og NAR-bevegelsen En kritisk undersøkelse av profetier om Donald Trump, USA og Guds rike innen New Apostolic Reformation-bevegelsen," *Theofilos*, Vol. 12, No. 2–3 (2020): 291–309. DOI: https://doi.org/10.48032/theo/12/2/8.

3 James Davidson Hunter, *To Change the World: The Irony, Tragedy, and Possibility of Christianity in the Late Modern World* (New York: Oxford University Press, 2010), 129.

4 Quoted in Hunter, *To Change the World*, 130.

5 "A Leading Figure in the New Apostolic Reformation," *NPR*, October 3, 2011, Accessed July 31, 2020, https://www.npr.org/2011/10/03/140946482/apostolic-leader-weighs-religions-role-in-politics.

6 Sarah Posner, "Rick Perry and the New Apostolic Reformation," *Religion Dispatches*, July 19, 2011, accessed July 1, 2020, https://religiondispatches.org/rick-perry-and-the-new-apostolic-reformation/.

7   Forrest Wilder, "Rick Perry's Army of God," *Texas Observer*, August 3, 2011, accessed July 1, 2020, https://www.texasobserver.org/rick-perrys-army-of-god/.
8   Chris Mahoney, "Rachel Tabachnick—Exposing Dominionism," *Point of Inquiry*, September 12, 2011, accessed July 2, 2020, https://pointofinquiry.org/2011/09/rachel_tabachnick_exposing_dominionism/.
9   Rachel Tabachnick, "Spiritual Warriors with an Antigay Mission: The New Apostolic Reformation," *Public Eye*, March 22, 2013, accessed July 2, 2020, https://politicalresearch.org/2013/03/22/spiritual-warriors-with-an-antigay-mission.
10 Quoted in Tabachnick, "Spiritual Warriors."
11 Ken Silva, "Influences: Rick Warren and C. Peter Wagner of New Apostolic Reformation," Apprising Ministries, May 23, 2010, accessed July 2, 2020, https://www.apprising.org/2010/05/23/influences-rick-warren-and-c-peter-wagner-of-new-apostolic-reformation/.
12 R. Douglass Geivett and Holy Pivec, *A New Apostolic Reformation? A Biblical Response to a Worldwide Movement* (Wooster, OH: Weaver Book Company, 2014); Gievette and Pivec, *God's Super Apostles: Encountering the Worldwide Prophets and Apostles Movement* (Wooster, OH: Weaver Book Company, 2014).
13 Gievette and Pivec, *God's Super Apostles*, 126–7.
14 John F. Macarthur, Jr., *Charismatic Chaos* (Grand Rapids, MI: Zondervan, 1992), 11.
15 Ibid., 164.
16 John MacArthur, *Strange Fire: The Danger of Offending the Holy Spirit with Counterfiet Worship* (Nashville, TN: Nelson Books, 2013), 88–9.
17 "Strange Fire," *Grace To You*, accessed June 8, 2020, https://www.gty.org/library/strangefire.
18 Costi Hinn and Anthony G. Wood, *Defining Deception* (El Cajon, CA: Southern California Seminary Press, 2018), 55.
19 Ibid.
20 Anthea Butler, "Heresy, Bad Taste, or Capitalist Adventure: Is It Still Pentecostalism?," *Religion Dispatches*, September 14, 2009, accessed July 12, 2020, https://religiondispatches.org/heresy-bad-taste-or-capitalist-adventure-is-it-still-pentecostalism/.
21 Anthea Butler, "Beyond Alarmism and Denial in the Dominionism Debate," *Religion Dispatches*, April 17, 2012, accessed July 12, 2020. https://religiondispatches.org/beyond-alarmism-and-denial-in-the-dominionism-debate/.

22. See also, Anthea Butler, "From Republican Party to Republican Religion: The New Political Evangelists of the Right," *Political Theology*, Vol. 13, No. 5 (2012): 634–51. doi.org/10.1558/poth.v13i5.634.
23. C. Peter Wagner, *Churchquake! How the New Apostolic Reformation Is Shaking up the Church as We Know It* (Ventura, CA: Regal Books, 1999), 31.
24. C. Peter Wagner, "YEAR IN REVIEW: The New Apostolic Reformation Is Not a Cult," *Charisma News*, August 24, 2011, accessed July 7, 2020, https://www.charismanews.com/opinion/31851-the-new-apostolic-reformation-is-not-a-cult.
25. Michael Brown, "Dispelling the Myths about NAR (the New Apostolic Reformation)," *Christian Post: Voices*, May 3, 2018, accessed July 7, 2020, https://www.christianpost.com/voice/dispelling-myths-new-apostolic-reformation-michael-brown.html.
26. "What Is IHOPKC's Stance on the New Apostolic Reformation?" International House of Prayer, accessed July 7, 2020, https://www.ihopkc.org/press-center/faq/ihopkc-part-new-apostolic-reformation/.
27. Brad Christerson and Richard Flory, *The Rise of Network Christianity: How Independent Leaders Are Changing the Religious Landscape* (New York: Oxford University Press, 2017), 10–11. See also my discussion of this in "Voting in the Kingdom," 73–4.
28. Christersen and Flory, *The Rise of Network Christianity*, 10.
29. Ché Ahn, *Modern-Day Apostles: Operating in Your Apostolic Office and Anointing* (Shippensburg, PA: Destiny Image Publishers, Inc.), 15.
30. Weaver, *New Apostolic Reformation*, 40.
31. Wagner, *The Third Wave of the Holy Spirit: Encountering the Power of Signs and Wonders* (Ann Arbor, MI: Servant Books, 1988), 15 and 18.
32. Weaver, *New Apostolic Reformation*, 61–9.
33. Jon Bialecki, *A Diagram for Fire: Miracle and Variations in an American Charismatic Movement* (Oakland, CA: University of California Press), 175.
34. Wagner, *The Third Wave*, 27.
35. Wagner, "The New Apostolic Reformation," in *The New Apostolic Churches: Rediscovering the New Testament Model of Leadership and Why It Is God's Desire for the Church Today*, edited by C. Peter Wagner (Ventura, CA: Regal Books), 15.
36. Ibid., 16.
37. Ibid., 17.
38. Ibid., 18.
39. Ibid.

40   C. Peter Wagner, *Wrestling with Alligators, Prophets and Theologians: Lessons from a Lifetime in the Church—A Memoir* (Grand Rapids, MI: Chosen Books, 2010), 213.
41   Ibid.
42   Ibid., 218.
43   Ibid., 218–19.
44   Wagner, "The New Apostolic Reformation," 18.
45   Wagner, *Churchquake*, 31.
46   Ibid., 8–9.
47   Ibid., 107, 109–10, 118, and 120.
48   Ibid., 35, 45, 64–5, and 70.
49   Ibid., 70.
50   Ibid.
51   C. Peter Wagner, *Apostles Today: Biblical Government for Biblical Power* (Bloomington, MN: Chosen Books, 2006), 27.
52   Ibid.
53   Ibid., 28–9.
54   Ibid., 33–4.
55   Ibid., 77.
56   Ibid.
57   Ibid., 77–8.
58   Ibid., 78.
59   Ibid., 79.
60   Ibid.
61   Ibid., 80.
62   Ibid., 108.
63   Ibid.
64   Ibid., 109.
65   Ibid., 113–14.
66   Ibid., 115.
67   Quoted in Wagner, *Apostles Today*, 115.
68   Wagner, *Apostles Today*, 116–17.
69   Ibid., 117.
70   Wagner, *Wrestling*, 261–2.
71   Ibid., 262–3.
72   Quoted in Wagner, *Wrestling*, 263.
73   Wagner, *Wrestling*, 263.

74 Lance Wallnau, "The Seven Mountain Mandate," in *The Reformer'sPledge*, compiled by Ché Ahn (Shippensburg, PA: Destiny Image Publishers, Inc., 2010), 187.
75 Wallnau, "Seven Mountain Mandate," 188, 189, and 190–1.
76 "Introduction," in *Invading Babylon: The Seven Mountain Mandate*, edited by Lance Wallnau and Bill Johnson (Shippensburg, PA: Destiny Image Publishing), 14.
77 Ibid., 13.
78 Ibid., 17.
79 Michael J. McVicar, *Christian Reconstruction: R.J. Rushdoony and American Religious Conservatism* (Chapel Hill, NC: University of North Carolina Press, 2015), 5.
80 McVicar, *Christian Reconstruction*, 200. See note 13 in Dylan Pahman, "Toward a Kuyperian Ethic of Public Life: On the Spheres of Ethics and the State," *Journal of Reformed Theology*, Vol. 12 (2018): 413–31, for a discussion of the ambiguity of this term, ("sphere sovereignty," or souvereiniteit in eigen kring) for Kuyper. On p. 138 of *Contours of the Kuyperian Tradition: A Systematic Introduction* (2017), Craig G. Batholomew notes that for Kuyper "[h]uman life is an infinitely complex organism made of many spheres," which include morality, family, social life, and so further each sharing in a separate domain, but interlocking with one another in the proper functioning of a society. See also Gangé, *Ces évangéliques derrière Trump*, 48–9.
81 Wagner, *Dominion! How Kingdom Action Can Change the World* (Grand Rapids, MI: Chosen Books, 2008), 12 and 147.
82 Ibid., 59–60.
83 Ibid., 72–3.
84 Ibid., 102, 72–3, and 37.
85 Ibid., 55.
86 Quoted in Wagner, *Dominion!*, 56.
87 Wagner, *Dominion!*, 56–7.
88 Ibid., 181.
89 Weaver, *New Apostolic Reformation*, 149–50.
90 Quoted in Wagner, *Dominion!*, 182.
91 Wagner, *Dominion!*, 183. Wagner also wrote a book on this topic titled *The Great Transfer of Wealth: Financial Release for Advancing God's Kingdom* (New Kensington, PA: Whitaker Hourse, 2015), wherein he elaborates on this point.
92 Jonny Enlow, *The Seven Mountain Prophecy: Unveiling the Coming Elijah Revolution* (Lake Mary, FL: Creation House, 2008), 104–5.
93 Ibid., 110.

94 Ibid.
95 Ibid., 118.
96 C. Peter Wagner, "Forward," in *Possessing The Gates of The Enemy: A Training Manual for Militant Intercession*, Cindy Jacobs 4th edition (Bloomington, MN: Chosen Books, 2018), 9; "Word of The Lord for 2022," Generals International, accessed January 16, 2022, https://www.generals.org/blog/word-of-the-lord-for-2022.
97 Weaver, *New Apostolic Reformation*, 146–7.
98 Wagner, *Dominion!*, 13 and 15.
99 Ibid., 15.
100 Daniel Gabriel, "'Our Dominion Mandate' | C Peter Wagner | 2010," YouTube Video, August 16, 2019, accessed May 12, 2020, https://www.youtube.com/watch?v=Xz-T2U31FZ4&t=701s.
101 Ibid.
102 Wagner, *Dominion!*, 12 and 18.
103 Ibid., 14.
104 Lou Engle, "Forward," in *Possessing the Gates of the Enemy: A Training Manual for Militant Intercession*, Cindy Jacobs, 4th edition (Bloomington, MN: Chosen Books, 2018), 16.
105 C. Peter Wagner, "Preface," in *Breaking Spiritual Strongholds in Your City*, edited by C. Peter Wagner (Shippensburg, PA: Destiny Image Publishers, Inc.), 12–13.
106 Ibid., 13–14.
107 George Otis Jr., "Chapter One: An Overview of Spiritual Mapping," in *Breaking Spiritual Strongholds in Your City*, edited by C. Peter Wagner (Shippensburg, PA: Destiny Image Publishers, Inc.), 35.
108 Ibid., 37.
109 Ibid., 45.
110 C. Peter Wagner, "The Visible and the Invisible," in *Breaking Spiritual Strongholds in Your City*, edited by C. Peter Wagner (Shippensburg, PA: Destiny Image Publishers, Inc.), 51.
111 Ibid., 59–60.
112 Ibid., 60.
113 Ibid., 70.
114 Ibid.
115 C. Peter Wagner, *Warfare Prayer: What the Bible Says about Spiritual Warfare* (Shippensburg, PA: Destiny Image Publishers, Inc., 2009), 17–18.
116 Enlow, *The Seven Mountain Prophecy*, 43.

Chapter 2

1. Catch the Fire Toronto, "Session B (Pastors & Leaders 2010) C. Peter Wagner," YouTube Video, September 14, 2012, accessed May 12, 2020, https://www.youtube.com/watch?v=2Dd0G5BV-Q4&t=5184s.
2. Damon Berry, "Voting in the Kingdom: Prophecy Voters, the New Apostolic Reformation, and Christian Support for Trump," *Nova Religio*, Vol. 23, No. 4 (2020): 76. https://doi.org/10.1525/nr.2020.23.4.69.
3. Damon Berry, "A Storm Is Coming: Horror and Hope in QAnon Apocalypticism," *Public Eye*, June 17, 2021, accessed July 17, 2021, https://politicalresearch.org/2021/06/17/storm-coming.
4. Alison McQueen, "The Apocalypse in U.S. Political Thought," *Foreign Affairs*, July 28, 2016, accessed June 6, 2020, https://www.foreignaffairs.com/articles/united-states/2016-07-18/apocalypse-us-political-thought see also Berry, "A Storm Is Coming."
5. Alison McQueen, *Political Realism in Apocalyptic Times* (New York: Cambridge University Press, 2018), 22.
6. This summary is my own, however for a more thorough treatment, see Amy Johnson Frykholm, *Rapture Culture: Left behind in Evangelical America* (Oxford, UK: Oxford University Press, 2004).
7. Frykholm, *Rapture Culture*, 15–18.
8. Tristan Sturm and Jason Dittmer, "Introduction," in *Mapping the End Times: American Evangelical Geopolitics and Apocalyptic Visions*, edited by Jason Dittmer and Tristen Sturm (Burlington, VT: Ashgate, 2010), 14.
9. Stephen Hunt, "The Rise, Fall and Return of Post-Millenarianism," in *Christian Millenarianism: From the Early Church to Waco*, edited by Stephen Hunt (Bloomington, IN: Indiana University Press, 2001), 55.
10. Johnny Enlow, *The Seven Mountain Mantle: Receiving the Joseph Anointing to Reform Nations* (Lake Mary Florida: Creation House, 2009), 134.
11. "A Leading Figure in the New Apostolic Reformation," *NPR*, October 3, 2011, accessed July 31, 2020, https://www.npr.org/2011/10/03/140946482/apostolic-leader-weighs-religions-role-in-politics.
12. Lance Wallnau, "Forget 'Rapture' as an Escape," Facebook, October 2, 2019, accessed June 12, 2020, https://www.facebook.com/LanceWallnau/posts/10157681918864936:0.
13. Lance Wallnau, "Enoch and Noah: Two Stages of Overcomer's!" Lance Wallnau, accessed June 12, 2020, https://lancewallnau.com/enoch-and-noah-two-stages-of-overcomers/.

14　C. Peter Wagner, *Dominion! How Kingdom Action Can Change the World* (Grand Rapids, MI: Chosen Books, 2008), 206.
15　André Gagné, *Ces évangéliques derrière Trump: Hégémonie, démonologie et fin du monde* (Genève: Labor et fides, 2020), 141. Translation is my own.
16　C. Peter Wagner, *Churchquake! How the New Apostolic Reformation Is Shaking up the Church as We Know It* (Ventura, CA: Regal Books, 1999), 70.
17　Catherine Wessinger, "Millennialism in Cross-Cultural Perspective," in *The Oxford Handbook of Millennialism*, ed. Catherine Wessinger (New York: Oxford University Press, 2011), 5.
18　Catherine Wessinger, "Millennialism with and without the Mayhem," in *Millennium, Messiahs, and Mayhem: Contemporary Apocalyptic Movements*, edited by Thomas Robbins and Susan J. Palmer (New York: Routledge, 1997), 50.
19　W. Michael Ashcraft, "Progressive Millennialism," in *The Oxford Handbook of Millennialism*, edited by Catherine Wessinger (New York: Oxford University Press, 2011), 44.
20　Daniel Wojcik. "Avertive Apocalypticism," in *The Oxford Handbook of Millennialism*, edited by Catherine Wessinger (New York: Oxford University Press, 2011), 66.
21　Wojcik, "Avertive Apocalypticism," 69.
22　Ibid., 84.
23　Berry, "Voting in the Kingdom."
24　Hunt, "Rise, Fall, and Return," 55.
25　Lance Wallnau, *God's Chaos Candidate: Donald J. Trump and the American Unravelling* (Keller, TX: Killer Sheep Media Group, 2016), 18.
26　N.T. Wright, "Revelation and Christian Hope: Political Revelations of St. John," in *Revelation and the Politics of Apocalyptic Interpretation,* edited by Richard B. Hayes and Stefan Alkier (Waco, TX: Baylor University Press, 2012), 107.
27　Colin McAllister, "Introduction," in *The Cambridge Companion to Apocalyptic Literature*, edited by Colin McAllister (New York: Cambridge University Press, 2020), 8.
28　"Millenialism and Violence?," The Religious Studies Project, podcast transcript, May 18, 2017, accessed April 12, 2021, https://www.religiousstudiesproject.com/wp-content/uploads/2017/05/CenSAMM-conference-Millennialism-and-Violence-1.1.pdf.
29　Bernard McGinn, *Visions of the End: Apocalyptic Traditions in the Middle Ages* (New York: Columbia University Press, 1998), 31.

30 Enlow, *The Seven Mountains Mantle* (Lake Mary, FL: Creation House, 2009), 123.
31 Cindy Jacobs, "Dealing with Strongholds," in *Breaking Spiritual Strongholds in Your City*, edited by C. Peter Wagner (Turnbridge Wells, UK: Monarch, 2015), 80–1.
32 Ibid., 83–4.
33 Ibid., 84.
34 Ibid.
35 Ibid.
36 Ibid., 86.
37 Ibid., 87.
38 Ibid.
39 Quoted in Jacobs, "Dealing with Strongholds," 91.
40 David Robertson, Egil Asprem and Asbjørn Dyrendal, "Introducing the Field: Conspiracy Theory in, about, as Religion," in *Handbook of Conspiracy Theory and Contemporary Religion*, edited by David Robertson, Egil Asprem, and Asbjørn Dyrendal (Boston, MA: Brill, 2018), 1.
41 Katheryn S. Olmsted, "Conspiracy Theories in U.S. History," in *Conspiracies and the People Who Believe Them*, edited by Joseph E. Uscinski (New York: Oxford University Press, 2019), 295–6.
42 Jovan Byford, *Conspiracy Theories: A Critical Introduction* (Basingstoke, UK: Palgrave Macmillan, 2015), 23.
43 Ibid., 151.
44 Cass R. Sunstein, *Conspiracy Theories and Other Dangerous Ideas* (New York: Simon & Schuster, 2016), 7.
45 Byford, *Conspiracy Theories,* 93.
46 Ibid.
47 Ibid.
48 Michael Barkun, *A Culture of Conspiracy: Apocalyptic Visions in Contemporary America* (Berkley, CA: University of California Press), 3 and 178.
49 Ibid., 3–4.
50 Ibid., 4.
51 Lance Wallnau, "5 Steps to Powerful Kingdom Activism," Lance Wallnau, accessed July 6, 2022, https://lancewallnau.com/5-steps-to-powerful-kingdom-activism/.
52 Matthew Avery Sutton, *American Apocalypse: A History of Modern Evangelicalism* (Cambridge, MA: Harvard University Press, 2017).

53 Richard V. Pierard, "Billy Graham and the U.S. Presidency," *Journal of Church and State*, Winter 1980, Vol. 22, No. 1 (Winter 1980): 107–27. 109.
54 Grant Wacker, *America's Pastor: Billy Graham and the Shaping of a Nation* (Cambridge, MA: The Belknap of Harvard University Press, 2014), 16.
55 Ibid.
56 Ibid., 231.
57 "Why Communism Is Gaining," Billy Graham Evangelistic Association, audio recording, accessed August 9, 2021, https://billygraham.org/audio/why-communism-is-gaining/.
58 "Franklin Graham: American Freedom Is Being 'Defeated from Within,'" Billy Graham Evangelistic Association, audio recording, accessed August 9, 2021, https://billygraham.org/story/franklin-graham-american-freedom-is-being-defeated-from-within/.
59 Lance Wallnau, "The Crimes of Our Educators: Brainwashing America's Kids into Communists | Lance Wallnau," YouTube Video, July 9, 2020, accessed August 10, 2021, https://www.youtube.com/watch?v=gpn0imAbNwA.
60 "The Crimes of Our Educators: Brainwashing America's Kids into Communists," Lance Wallnau, accessed August 10, 2021, https://lancewallnau.com/the-crimes-of-our-educators-brainwashing-americas-kids-into-communists/.
61 Daniel Wojcik, *The End of the World as We Know It: Faith, Fatalism, and Apocalypse in America* (New York: New York University Press, 1999), 21.
62 Daniel T. Rodgers, Appendix, "John Winthrop, 'A Model of Christian Charity': A Modern Transcription," in *As a City on a Hill: The Story of America's Most Famous Lay Sermon* (Princeton, NJ: Princeton University Press, 2018), 289–308.
63 Quoted in Marc Ambinder, "Fallwell Suggests Gays to Blame for Attacks," *ABC News*, September 14, 2001, accessed August 13, 2021, https://abcnews.go.com/Politics/story?id=121322&page=1.
64 Peter Carlson, "Falwell's Folly," *The Chicago Tribune*, November 26, 2001, accessed August 13, 2021, https://www.chicagotribune.com/news/ct-xpm-2001-11-26-0111260117-story.html.
65 Lou Engle, "Creating a Culture of Life," in *The Reformer's Pledge*, edited by Ché Ahn (Shippensburg, PA: Destiny Image Publishers, Inc., 2010), 113.
66 Psalm 94, NASB.
67 Lance Wallnau, "The Problem, Then and Now," Lance Wallnau, accessed August 3, 2021, https://lancewallnau.com/11806-2/.

68. Lance Wallnau, "A People Who Could Govern Themselves," Lance Wallnau, accessed August 3, 2021, https://lancewallnau.com/a-people-who-could-govern-themselves/.
69. Dutch Sheets, "Dutch Sheets: An Important Message from Dutch Sheets," *Elijah List*, March 17, 2010, accessed August 4, 2021, https://elijahlist.com/words/display_word/8589.
70. Jonathan Cahn, *The Harbinger* (Lake Mary, FL: FrontLine, 2011), 1 and 4.
71. Ibid., 17.
72. Ibid., 21.
73. Ibid., 25.
74. Ibid., 29–30.
75. Ibid., 49.
76. Ibid., 128.
77. Ibid., 161.
78. Ibid., 189.
79. Ibid., 215.
80. Lance Wallnau, "Meeting Donald Trump an Insiders Report," Lance Wallnau, accessed August 2, 2021, https://lancewallnau.com/meeting-donald-trump-an-insiders-report/.
81. Jonathan Cahn, "'The Smiles of Heaven' Speech on Capitol Hill," YouTube Video, May 8, 2014, accessed August 3, 2021, https://www.youtube.com/watch?v=6up4fVPaqQs.
82. Matthias Riedl and David Marno, "Introduction," in *The Apocalyptic Complex: Perspectives, Histories, Persistence*, edited by Nadia Al- Bagdadi, Matthias Riedl, and David Marno (Budapest, HU: Central European University Press, 2018), x. http://www.jstor.org/stable/10.7829/j.ctvbd8k9h.3.
83. Jerome Corsi, *Obamanation: Leftist Politics and the Cult of Personality* (New York: Poketstar Books, 2008).
84. Jerome Corsi, *Where's the Birth Certificate? The Case Barak Obama Is Not Eligible to Be President* (Washington, DC: WND Books, 2011).
85. Janell Ross, "Donald Trump's History of Birtherism, Selective Résumé Checks and the Thread That Connects It All," *The Washington Post*, September 16, 2016, accessed August 12, 2021, https://www.washingtonpost.com/news/the-fix/wp/2016/09/16/donald-trumps-history-of-birtherism-selective-resume-checks-and-the-thread-that-connects-it-all/.
86. Wallnau, *God's Chaos Candidate*, 29.
87. Ibid., 144.

Chapter 3

1. Sean McCloud, *American Possessions: Fighting Demons in the Contemporary United States* (New York: Oxford University Press, 2015), 115.
2. Quoted in McCloud, *American Possessions*, 115.
3. Daniel Silliman, *Reading Evangelicals: How Christian Fiction Shaped a Culture and a Faith* (Grand Rapids, MI: William B. Eerdmans Publishing Company), 211.
4. Ibid., 215.
5. André Gagné, *Ces évangéliques derrière Trump: Hégémonie, démonologie et fin du monde* (Genève: Labor et fides, 2020), 100.
6. Ibid., 101.
7. Mark Godin, "Make-Belief Translation: Fictive Truths and World-Building from *The Lord of the Rings* to Theological Institutions," *Literature and Theology*, Vol. 35, No. 1 (March 2021): 56. https://doi.org/10.1093/litthe/fraa037.
8. Kat Kerr, "Watch and Pray! Prophetic Word about Donald Trump and the Elections—From Kat Kerr!" *Elijah List*, October 26, 2016, accessed May 20, 2021, https://www.elijahlist.com/words/display_word.html?ID=16855.
9. Rob Poindexter, "Kim Clement Prophesying about Donald Trump 2007," YouTube Video, November 24, 2016, accessed April 12, 2021, https://www.youtube.com/watch?v=eFfFtq1fljY&t=5s.
10. Sarah Mae Saliong, "Kim Clement Prophecy in 2007: President Trump Will Be Baptized in the Spirit, Build the Wall, and Be Re-Elected," *Christianity Daily*, November 20, 2021, accessed February 10, 2022, https://www.christianitydaily.com/articles/13999/20211120/kim-clement-prophecy-in-2007-president-trump-will-be-baptized-in-the-spirit-build-the-wall-and-be-re-elected.htm.
11. James A. Beverly, "Trump and Prophecy," *Faith Today*, January 25, 2017, accessed May 20, 2021, https://www.faithtoday.ca/Magazines/2017-Jan-Feb/Trump-and-Prophecy.
12. "Strang Report: Kim Clement Prophesied Trump's Presidency Years before His Election," Strang Report, audio recording, June 11, 2019, accessed May 20, 2021, https://strangreport.libsyn.com/kim-clement-prophesied-trumps-presidency-years-before-his-election.
13. Sarah Mae Saliong, "Christian Businessman Shares How the Movement to ReAwaken America Back to God Came to Be," *Christianity Daily*, December 7, 2021, accessed February 10, 2022, https://www.christianitydaily.com/articles/14188/20211207/christian-businessman-shares-how-the-movement-to-reawaken-america-back-to-god-came-to-be.htm.

14. Stephen Strang, *God and Donald Trump* (Lake Mary, FL: FrontLine, 2017), 69.
15. Quoted in Strang, *God and Donald Trump* (2017), 70.
16. Ibid.
17. "Chuck Pierce: Playing the Trump Card," Strang Report, audio recording, accessed May 17, 2022, http://www.charismapodcastnetwork.com/show/strangreport/e545de53c481719e6c755200e7ec102f/Chuck-Pierce%3A-Playing-the-Trump-Card.
18. Strang, *God and Donald Trump*, 178.
19. Mark Taylor, *The Trump Prophesies: The Astonishing True Story of the Man Who Saw Tomorrow … and What He Says Is Coming Next* (Crane, MO: Defender, 2019) revised and updated edition, 3.
20. Sid Roth's program It's Supernatural!, "Mark Taylor & Mary Colbert Part 1 | Something More," YouTube video, November 3, 2017, accessed May 20, 2021, https://www.youtube.com/watch?v=WqNAbKCg4Rw&t=811s.
21. Taylor, *The Trump Prophesies*, 4.
22. Ibid., 5. Emphasis in the original.
23. CBN News, "He Predicted Trump Would Be President 6 Years Ago; Now Says Trump Is in for Two Terms," YouTube Video, December 12, 2017, accessed May 20, 2021.
24. Sid Roth's It's Supernatural!, "Mark Taylor & Mary Colbert Part 1."
25. Taylor, *The Trump Prophesies*, 44.
26. Jeremy Peter and Rachel Shorey, "Trump Spent Far Less Than Clinton, but Paid His Companies Well," *New York Times,* December 9, 2016, accessed May 21, 2021, https://www.nytimes.com/2016/12/09/us/politics/campaign-spending-donald-trump-hillary-clinton.html.
27. Taylor, *The Trump Prophesies*, 49.
28. Ibid., 91.
29. Ibid., 92.
30. Ibid., 104.
31. Ibid., 94–5.
32. Ibid., 95.
33. Ibid., 189.
34. Ibid.
35. Ibid., 190 and 192.
36. "Who We Are," SkyWatchTV, accessed May 21, 2021, https://www.skywatchtv.com/about/.

37. Thomas Horn, *Saboteurs: How Secret, Deep State Occultists Are Manipulating Society through a Washington-Based Shadow Government in Quest of the Final World Order!* (Crane, MO: Defender Publishing, 2017), cover.
38. Donna Howell, introduction to *The Trump Prophesies*, xi.
39. Taylor, *The Trump Prophesies*, 51–2.
40. Matthew7–24MonteCarlo24–7, "12/9/16 The Prophet Mark Taylor On The Donald Trump Prophecy: The Full 3 Days = Jim Bakker Show," YouTube Video, December 9, 2016, accessed May 2, 2021, https://www.youtube.com/watch?v=bVzJX3vUD4M&t=1348s.
41. Lance Wallnau, "Is Donald Trump America's Cyrus? with Lance Wallnau," interview by Stephen Strang, Strang Report, audio, May 10, 2016, accessed May 12, 2021, https://radiopublic.com/strang-report-WkwVMW/ep/s1!173f4."
42. Lance Wallnau, *God's Chaos Candidate: Donald Trump and The American Unravelling* (Keller, TX: Killer Sheep Media Group, 2016), 21.
43. Lance Wallnau, "Chaos Candidate: Is Trump a Modern-Day King Cyrus?," *CBN*, November 4, 2016, accessed May 20, 2019, https://www1.cbn.com/content/chaos-candidate-trump-modern-day-king-cyrus.
44. Wallnau, *God's Chaos Candidate*, 137.
45. Ibid., 144.
46. Ibid., 13.
47. Ibid., 18.
48. Ibid., 133.
49. Ibid., 18.
50. Ibid., 144.
51. Ibid.
52. Ibid., 155.
53. Ibid., 150 and 29.
54. Ibid., 29.
55. "The Harbinger Book & The Harbinger DVD Special Offer," Jonathan Cahn, accessed March 12, 2022, https://www.theharbinger-jonathancahn.com/Book/.
56. "Jonathan Cahn Reveals in 'The Paradigm' the Ancient Reason Trump Won," Charisma House, March 18, 2020, accessed May 12, 2021, https://charismahouse.com/jonathan-cahn-reveals-in-the-paradigm-the-ancient-reason-trump-won/.
57. Jonathan Cahn, preface to *The Paradigm: The Ancient Blueprint That Holds the Mystery of Our Times* (Lake Mary, FL: FrontLine, 2017), vii.

58 James Patrick Holding, "An Unpersuasive Paradigm," Christian Research Institute, November 13, 2017, accessed May 12, 2021, https://www.equip.org/article/an-unpersuasive-paradigm/.
59 Cahn, preface to *The Paradigm*, vii.
60 Cahn, *The Paradigm*, 1.
61 Ibid., 2.
62 Marilyn Hickey Ministries, "The Paradigm with Jonathan Cahn—Part 1," YouTube Video, January 29, 2018, accessed May 22, 2021, https://www.youtube.com/watch?v=Y0gf_b5RXLw.
63 Cahn, *The Paradigm*, 2–3.
64 Ibid., 6.
65 Ibid., 6–7.
66 Ibid., 7.
67 Ibid., 8–9.
68 Ibid., 9.
69 Ibid., 9.
70 Ibid., 10–11.
71 Ibid., 12–13.
72 Ibid., 13.
73 Ibid., 14–17.
74 Ibid., 23.
75 Ibid., 24 and 26.
76 Ibid., 26–7.
77 Ibid., 29.
78 Ibid., 30.
79 Ibid., 41.
80 Ibid., 35.
81 Ibid.
82 Ibid., 37.
83 Ibid., 42.
84 Ibid., 42–5.
85 Ibid., 61.
86 Ibid., 63.
87 Ibid., 104 and 107.
88 Ibid., 110.
89 Ibid., 114.
90 Ibid., 115.

91 Ibid., 116.
92 Ibid., 146.
93 Ibid., 148.
94 Ibid., 149.
95 Ibid., 151–2.
96 Ibid., 153.
97 Ibid., 154.
98 Ibid., 155.
99 Ibid., 181.
100 Ibid., 211.
101 Ibid., 224.
102 Ibid., 225.
103 Rebecca Barrett-Fox, "A King Cyrus President: How Donald Trump's Presidency Reasserts Conservative Christians' Right to Hegemony," *Humanity & Society*, Vol. 42, No. 4 (November 2018): 502–22, 505. https://doi.org/10.1177/0160597618802644.
104 Ibid., 243.
105 "We Are in the Spiritual Fight of Our Lifetime!," Lance Wallnau, accessed June 12, 2022, https://lancewallnau.com/we-are-in-the-spiritual-fight-of-our-lifetime/.

Chapter 4

1 Learning2vocalize, "The Presidential Inaugural Prayer Breakfast Guest Speaker Rabbi Jonathan Cahn … Jan 21, 2013," YouTube Video, January 25, 2013, accessed May 9, 2022, https://www.youtube.com/watch?v=voDD85JcR6I.
2 Aileen Delgado, "Rabbi Jonathan Cahn Speaks at the Trump Presidential Inaugural Prayer Breakfast," YouTube Video, January 21, 2021, accessed May 9, 2022, https://www.youtube.com/watch?v=URxfXcZxTYI; "Inaugural Prayer Breakfast," Presidential Inauguration, accessed May 9, 2022, http://www.presidential-inauguration.com/inaugural-prayer-breakfast/.
3 PBS NewsHour, "Pastor Paula White-Cain Delivers Invocation at Inauguration Day 2017," YouTube Video, January 20, 2017, accessed May 10, 2022, https://www.youtube.com/watch?v=YBzHgy3y2Kw.
4 "Full Text of President Donald Trump's Inauguration Speech," *Fox News*, January 20, 2017, accessed May 9, 2022, https://www.foxnews.com/politics/full-text-of-president-donald-trumps-inauguration-speech.

5   Michael Dimock and John Gramlich, "How America Changed during Trump's Presidency," Pew Research Center, January 29, 2021, accessed May 9, 2022, https://www.pewresearch.org/2021/01/29/how-america-changed-during-donald-trumps-presidency/.

6   "New PRRI Report Reveals Nearly One in Five Americans and One in Four Republicans Still Believe in QAnon Conspiracy Theories," PRRI, February 24, 2022, accessed May 10, 2022, https://www.prri.org/press-release/new-prri-report-reveals-nearly-one-in-five-americans-and-one-in-four-republicans-still-believe-in-qanon-conspiracy-theories/.

7   Jacob Pramuk, "Donald Trump Becomes First President to Be Impeached Twice," *CNBC*, January 14, 2021, accessed May 8, 2022, https://www.cnbc.com/2021/01/13/house-to-impeach-trump-for-inciting-capitol-riot.html.

8   See Jefferey A. Engel, "No More Mulligans: Donald Trump and International Alliances," *The Presidency of Donald J. Trump: A First Historical Assessment*, edited by Julian E. Zelizer (Princeton, NJ: Princeton University Press, 2022), 238–58.

9   Elily Jones, "Trump Says He Moved US Embassy to Jerusalem 'For the Evangelicals,'" *CBN News*, August 18, 2020, accessed May 8, 2022, https://www1.cbn.com/cbnnews/israel/2020/august/trump-says-he-moved-nbsp-us-embassy-to-jerusalem-lsquo-for-the-evangelicals-rsquo?msclkid=c30dfe51c41111ec96aa7151f58be6ef.

10 "3 Prophets Who Prophesied about Jerusalem, Israel and the USA!," *Elijah List*, December 8, 2017, accessed August 7, 2021, https://www.elijahlist.com/words/display_word.html?ID=19309&msclkid=c30e6b70c41111ecad3ff01c4e3c9bc7.

11 "Transcript: The First Jan. 6 Committee Hearing on Its Investigation," *NPR*, June 10, 2022, accessed June 20, 2022, https://www.npr.org/2022/06/10/1104156949/jan-6-committee-hearing-transcript.

12 Robert B. Horwitz, "Trump and the 'deep state,'" *Policy Studies*, Vol. 42, Nos. 5–6 (2021): 473–90, 474, DOI: 10.1080/01442872.2021.1953460.

13 Lawrence Douglas, "Paranoid Politics: The Malign Myth of the American 'Deep State,'" *TLS. Times Literary Supplement*, Vol. 21, No. 6132 (2020): 21. Gale Literature Resource Center, accessed April 16, 2022. https://link.gale.com/apps/doc/A639265762/LitRC?u=cant66762&sid=ebsco&xid=d8012f6b.

14 Russell Muirhead and Nancy L. Rosenblum, *A Lot of People Are Saying: The New Conspiracism and the Assault on Democracy* (Princeton, NY: Princeton University Press, 2019), 3.

15 Ibid., 9.

16 Ibid., 171.
17 Les Pendleton, *1600 Trump Avenue: Against All Odds—A Political Prophecy* (New Bern, NC: Essie Press, 2016), 263.
18 Bill Tillman, "Bill Tillman's review of *1600 Trump Avenue: Against All Odds—A Political Prophecy*," Goodreads, November 7, 2016, accessed May 11, 2022, https://www.goodreads.com/review/show/1806120733; Lynn, "Lynn's review of *1600 Trump Avenue: Against All Odds—A Political Prophecy*," Goodreads, April 14, 2019, accessed May 11, 2022, https://www.goodreads.com/review/show/2786033720.
19 Betty Smithers, "Betty's Review of *1600 Trump Avenue: Against All Odds—A Political Prophecy*," Goodreads, November 12, 2016, accessed May 11, 2022, https://www.goodreads.com/review/show/1815695835.
20 Thomas Horn, *Shadowland* (Crane, MO: Defender Publishing, 2019).
21 Paul McGuire and Troy Anderson, *Trumpocalypse: The End Times, a Battle against the Globalist Elite, and the Countdown to Armageddon* (New York: FaithWords, 2018).
22 Ibid., 1 and 7.
23 Ibid., 296–7.
24 Corey R. Lewandowski and David Bossie, *Trump's Enemies: How the Deep State Is Undermining the Presidency* (New York: Center Street, 2019), 260 and 105.
25 Jerome Corsi, *Killing the Deep State: The Fight to Save President Trump* (West Palm Beach, FL: Humanix Books, 2018); Jason Chaffetz, *The Deep State: How an Army of Bureaucrats Protected Barack Obama and Is Working to Destroy the Trump Agenda* (New York: HarperCollins, 2018).
26 Roger Stone, "Foreword," in *The Plot to Destroy Trump: How the Deep State Fabricated the Russian Dossier to Subvert the President*, edited by Theodore Roosevelt Malloch (New York: Skyhorse Publishing, 2018), xxii.
27 George Papadopoulos, *Deep State Target: How I Got Caught in the Crosshairs of the Plot to Bring Down President Trump* (New York: Diversion Books, 2019).
28 Frank Amedia, "POTUS Shield—Frank Amedia—The Birth of POTUS Shield," YouTube Video, February 14, 2017, accessed May 11, 2022, https://www.youtube.com/watch?v=ZuWDqsF7VGQ.
29 "Candidates Reach out to Evangelicals," *Religion & Ethics Weekly*, May 26, 2016, accessed May 11, 2022, https://www.tpt.org/religion-ethics-newsweekly/video/religion-and-ethics-newsweekly-candidates-reach-out-evangelicals/.
30 "Evangelicals and Donald Trump," *Religion & Ethics News Weekly*, June 17, 2016, accessed April 24, 2022, https://www.pbs.org/wnet/

religionandethics/2016/06/17/evangelicals-donald-trump/30959/?msclkid=bc69 40b3c3fd11eca98a36fcd529b206.

31 "Council," POTUS Shield, accessed May 9, 2021, https://www.potusshield.com/council.

32 "Vision & Mission Statement," Family Research Council, accessed May 9, 2021, https://www.frc.org/mission-statement.

33 Rebecca Leung, "The Holy Warrior General Called a Religious Fanatic Finally Speaks Out," *60 Minutes*, September 15, 2004, accessed May 9, 2021, https://www.cbsnews.com/news/the-holy-warrior/.

34 Michael W. Chapman, "Lt. Gen. Boykin: 'God's Imprint Was On' Trump's Election Win," *CSNnews.com*, March 28, 2018, May 9, 2021, https://www.cnsnews.com/blog/michael-w-chapman/lt-gen-boykin-gods-imprint-was-trumps-election-win see also Voting in the Kingdom.

35 "The Evangelicals Engaged in Spiritual Warfare," *NPR*, audio, 39:11, August 19, 2011, https://www.npr.org/2011/08/24/139781021/the-evangelicals-engaged-in-spiritual-warfare.

36 See Adrian Jjuuko and Monica Tabengwa, "Expanded Criminalization of Consensual Same-Sex Relations in Africa: Contextualizing Recent Developments," in *Envisioning Global LGBT Human Rights: (Neo)colonialism, Neoliberalism, Resistance and Hope*, edited by Nancy Nicol, Adrian Jjuuko, Richard Lusimbo, et al. (London, UK: Human Rights Consortium School of Advanced Study, University of London, 2018), 63–97.

37 Lou Engle, "Lou Engle Sounds Urgent Call for 3-Day Esther Fast over America," *Charisma*, accessed May 17, 2019, https://www.charismamag.com/blogs/prophetic-insight/32093-lou-engle-sounds-urgent-call-for-3-day-esther-fast-over-america.

38 Stephen Strang, "Frank Amedia Prophesies [sic]: February, March Will Be Months of Chaos For Trump," *Charisma*, accessed May 17, 2019, https://www.charismamag.com/blogs/the-strang-report/40163-frank-amedia-prophesies-february-march-will-be-months-of-chaos-for-trump.

39 "What Is POTUS Shield?," *POTUS Shield*, accessed May 30, 2019, https://www.potusshield.com/.

40 "Exclusive Report: In Depth with Frank Amedia on the Michael Cohen Hearing," Strang Report audio recording, March 1, 2019, accessed May 11, 2021, https://strangreport.libsyn.com/exclusive-report-in-depth-with-frank-amedia-on-the-michael-cohen-hearing.

41 "Michael Cohen Testifies against Trump in Public Hearing," *NPR*, audio, 21:53, February 27, 2019, https://www.npr.org/templates/transcript/transcript.php?storyId=698803678.
42 "Exclusive Report: In Depth with Frank America on the Michael Cohen Hearing."
43 Touch of Heaven Ministries, "POTUS Shield Alert 092018," YouTube video, September 20, 2018, accessed May 11, 2021, https://www.youtube.com/watch?v=za3W04YOJlE&feature=youtu.be.
44 Frank Amedia: Murderous Spirit that Came Against Moses, Jesus Now Attacking Kavanaugh—*Charisma News*.
45 Steve Strang, "Frank Amedia: God Has Shown Me What Will Happen with This Election if We Do Our Part," *Charisma News*, September 25, 2018, accessed May 11, 2021, https://www.charismanews.com/politics/73326-frank-amedia-murderous-spirit-that-came-against-moses-jesus-now-attacking-kavanaugh.
46 The Jim Bakker Show, "Sweeping the Courts—Pastor Frank Amedia on the Jim Bakker Show," YouTube Video, July 4, 2017, accessed September 20, 2021, https://www.youtube.com/watch?v=b3a3vuuQusg.
47 Johnny Enlow, "Johnny Enlow: 'Trump Quake! What's Next?,'" *Elijah List*, December 6, 2016, accessed September 20, 2021, https://www.elijahlist.com/words/display_word.html?ID=17084.
48 Johnny Enlow, "Johnny Enlow: God Says, 'I Played My Trump Card, I Will Win the Hand,'" *Elijah List*, May 20, 2017, accessed September 20, 2021, https://www.elijahlist.com/words/display_word.html?ID=18025.
49 David A. Graham, "The Many Scandals of Donald Trump," *The Atlantic*, May 15, 2017, accessed June 20, 2021, https://www.theatlantic.com/politics/archive/2017/05/donald-trump-presidential-scandals/522468/?msclkid=f3faa8e3c42911eca3ca700073e5cbed.
50 "Era of Cyrus Trump," Lance Wallnau, accessed June 15, 2021, https://lancewallnau.com/era-of-cyrus-trump/; Lance Wallnau, "Era of Cyrus Trump," YouTube Video, June 12, 2017, accessed June 15, 2021 https://www.youtube.com/watch?v=Wb3NK3GJhLU&t=1s.
51 Lance Wallnau, "STRANGE COINCIDENCE—OR PROPHETIC TIMING? —Dr. Lance Wallnau | May 23, 2018," YouTube Video, May 24, 2018, accessed June 12, 2021, https://www.youtube.com/watch?v=ZG8DxqUs2YA&t=124s.
52 Lance Wallnau, "The Cyrus Anointing, President Trump and America," Elijah Streams, March 26, 2019, accessed June 12, 2021, https://elijahstreams.com/watch/watch.php?ID=798.

53 Lance Wallnau, "Lance Wallnau's 2020 Prophecy—Relating to Kim Clement and Chuck Pierce," YouTube Video, January 2, 2020, accessed May 3, 2022, https://www.youtube.com/watch?v=X5uS_rLLjYM&t=7s. See also, Mark Galli, "Trump Should Be Removed from Office," *Christianity Today*, December 19, 2019, accessed May 3, 2022, https://www.christianitytoday.com/ct/2019/december-web-only/trump-should-be-removed-from-office.html.

54 Nicholas Fandos and Michael D. Shear, "Trump Impeached for Abuse of Power and Obstruction of Congress," *New York Times*, December 18, 2019, updated February 10, 2021, accessed February 11, 2021, https://www.nytimes.com/2019/12/18/us/politics/trump-impeached.html.

55 Wallnau, "Lance Wallnau's 2020 Prophecy—Relating to Kim Clement and Chuck Pierce."

56 Stephen Strang, "Prophetic Dream Reveals What God Is Saying about Trump and the Corona Virus," *Charisma News*, April 25, 2020, accessed May 12, 2021, https://www.charismanews.com/opinion/80473-prophetic-dream-reveals-what-god-is-saying-about-trump-and-the-coronavirus.

Chapter 5

1 Jeremy Diamond, "Trump Launches 2020 Bid with Familiar Refrains on Immigration and Trade," CNN Politics, June 18, 2019, accessed March 14, 2020, https://www.npr.org/2019/06/19/733904818/trump-launches-reelection-bid-with-promises-of-greatness-and-familiar-grievanceshttps://www.cnn.com/2019/06/18/politics/trump-orlando-rally-reelection/index.html.

2 Jessica Taylor and Tamara Heith, "Trump Launches Reelection Bid with Promises of Greatness and Familiar Grievances," *NPR*, June 19, 2019, accessed March 14, 2020, https://www.npr.org/2019/06/19/733904818/trump-launches-reelection-bid-with-promises-of-greatness-and-familiar-grievances.

3 Franklin Graham, "Along with 250+ Christian leaders, I am asking followers of Christ across our nation to set aside next Sunday," Facebook, May 26, 2019, accessed May 15, 2020, https://www.facebook.com/FranklinGraham/posts/2497135067009326?__tn__=-R. See also the announcement on the website for the Billy Graham Evangelistic Society at https://billygraham.org/story/special-day-of-prayer/?fbclid=IwAR1w4zs2TOCI2q6ccL6__Oi_bWiZOLTUaloWGe2m1KfIXw-zSeUX7JAtUuE.

4   "13 Cyrus Bundle," *The Jim Bakker Show*, accessed August 20, 2019, emphasis in the original https://store.jimbakkershow.com/product/13-cyrus-trump-bundle/.
5   Megan Flynn, "Trump's Spiritual Advisor Seeks His Protection from 'Demonic Networks' at Reelection Rally," *The Washington Post*, June 19, 2019, accessed August 20, 2019, https://www.washingtonpost.com/nation/2019/06/19/paula-white-donald-trump-orlando-rally-demonic-networks/?arc404=true.
6   Ché Ahn, "Promises Made, Promises Kept | Che Ahn | Sunday Service," YouTube Video, September 13, 2020, accessed June 20, 2022, https://www.youtube.com/watch?v=TsAxFidkz34.
7   Ché Ahn, "President Trump Called It His 'Profound Honor' on Friday, January 24, 2020, to Be the First President to Attend the Annual Pro-Life Gathering," Facebook Video, September 14, 2020, accessed June 20, 2022, https://www.facebook.com/watch/?v=1481895732007968.
8   Donald Trump, "President Trump: I Am the Chosen One," *CNN*, video, 1:47, accessed August 22, 2019, https://www.cnn.com/videos/politics/2019/08/21/president-trump-us-china-trade-war-chosen-one-sot-ip-vpx.cnn.
9   "President Trump Remarks at Evangelical Rally," *CSPAN*, video, January 3, 2020, accessed May 12, 2022, https://www.c-span.org/video/?476813-1/president-trump-speaks-evangelical-rally-miami.
10 "Jeremiah Johnson's Prophetic Word about Donald Trump," Ask Dr. Brown Video, November 15, 2016, accessed May 12, 2020, https://askdrbrown.org/library/jeremiah-johnsons-prophetic-word-about-donald-trump.
11 Jerimiah Johnson, *Trump, 2019, & Beyond* (Lakeland, FL: Jerimiah Johnson Ministries, 2019), 15.
12 Ibid., 16.
13 Ibid., 25–6.
14 Ibid., 41.
15 Ibid., 43.
16 Ibid.
17 Ibid., 47.
18 Ibid.
19 Ibid., 49.
20 Ibid., 51.
21 Ibid., 67.
22 Jerimiah Johnson, *Trump and the Future of America* (Lakeland, FL: Jerimiah Johnson Ministries, 2020), 3.
23 Ibid., 4.

24 Ibid.
25 Ibid., 8.
26 Ibid., 10.
27 Ibid., 11.
28 Ibid., 16.
29 Ibid., 24.
30 Ibid., 33.
31 Ibid., 36–7.
32 Ibid., 37.
33 Ibid., 37–8.
34 Ibid., 38.
35 Ibid., 51.
36 Ibid., 54.
37 Ibid., 55.
38 Stephen Strang, "Prophetic Dream Reveals What God Is Saying about Trump and the Corona Virus," *Charisma News*, March 25, 2020, accessed June 12, 2021, https://www.charismanews.com/opinion/80473-prophetic-dream-reveals-what-god-is-saying-about-trump-and-the-coronavirus.
39 Johnson, *Trump, 2019, & Beyond*, 43–4.
40 Stephen Strang, "Prophet, Pastor Frank Amedia: President Will 'Trump This Election' Too," *Charisma News*, August 11, 2020, accessed June 12, 2021.
41 Paula White-Cain, "Paul White Prayer Service from City of Destiny," Facebook Video, November 4, 2020, accessed June 20, 2021, https://www.facebook.com/realpaulawhite/videos/1280577475630326.
42 Stephen Strang, *God, Trump, and the 2020 Election: Why He must Win and What's at Stake for Christians if He Loses* (Lake Mary, FL: FrontLine, 2020); Stephen Strang, *God, Trump, and COVID-19: How the Pandemic Is Affecting Christians, the World, and America's 2020 Election* (Lake Mary, FL: FrontLine, 2020).
43 Paula White, front matter blurb, *God, Trump, and the 2020 Election: Why He Must Win and What's at Stake for Christians if He Loses* by Stephen Strang (Lake Mary, FL: FrontLine, 2020).
44 Eric Mataxas, Forward, *God, Trump, and the 2020 Election: Why He Must Win and What's at Stake for Christians if He Loses* by Stephen Strang (Lake Mary, FL: FrontLine, 2020), xi–xii.
45 Strang, *God, Trump, and the 2020 Election*, xii–xiii.

46 Ibid., 2–3.
47 Ibid., 9.
48 Ibid., 7.
49 Ibid., 7–8.
50 Ibid., 12.
51 Ibid., 196.
52 Ibid., 198.
53 Ibid., 199.
54 Strang, *God, Trump, and COVID-19*, xvii.
55 Ibid., 96.
56 Truth & Liberty Coalition, "Lance Wallnau on the State of Our Union and More!," YouTube Video, February 11, 2019, accessed June 20, 2021, https://www.youtube.com/watch?v=WE0uLn1fwsA; "Our Leadership—Board of Directors," Truth and Liberty Coalition, accessed June 20, 2021, https://truthandliberty.net/about/our-leadership/.
57 Lance Wallnau, *God's Chaos Code: The Shocking Blueprint That Reveals 5 Keys to the Destiny of Nations* (Keller, TX: Killer Sheep Media, Inc., 2020), 15–16.
58 Ibid., 35 and 44.
59 Ibid., 69.
60 Ibid., 72.
61 Ibid.
62 Ibid., 126.
63 Ibid., 127.
64 Ibid., 132.
65 Ibid., 162.
66 Ibid., 164.
67 Ibid., 188.
68 Ché Ahn, "A Prophetic Update on California and the State of the Church | Che' Ahn" – YouTube Video, February 12, 2021, accessed June 2, 2022, https://www.youtube.com/watch?v=l7Ep0u9hvS8.
69 Lance Wallnau, "What Now?" Facebook Video, January 12, 2021, accessed June 2, 2022, https://www.facebook.com/LanceWallnau/videos/994199231108186. See also, Shawn Akers, "Lance Wallnau Says This Is Where Believers Went Wrong in Praying for the Election," *Charisma Magazine*, January 31, 2021, accessed June 2, 2021, https://www.charismamag.com/life/politics/47927-lance-wallnau-says-this-is-where-believers-went-wrong-in-praying-for-the-election.

70 Lance Wallnau, "Bombshell Election Fraud Update," The Lance Wallnau Show, audio, April 21, 2022, accessed July 19, 2022, https://lancewallnaushow.libsyn.com/bombshell-election-fraud-update.

71 Touch of Heaven Ministries, "For the Sake of His Glory," YouTube Video, February 22, 2021, accessed June 2, 2021, https://www.youtube.com/watch?v=K6CMDTUT-oI.

72 Quoted in Stefani McDade, "How Could All the Prophets Be Wrong about Trump?," *Christianity Today*, June 21, 2021, accessed June 2, 2022, https://www.christianitytoday.com/ct/2021/july-august/trump-prophets-election-jeremiah-johnson-reckoning-charisma.html.

73 Jerimiah Johnson, "Jerimiah Johnson: My Public Apology and Process," *Charisma News*, January 7, 2021, accessed June 2, 2022, https://www.charismanews.com/opinion/83947-jerimiah-johnson-my-public-apology-and-process.

74 Henry H. Leon Festinger and Stanley Schachter Riecken, *When Prophecy Fails: A Social and Psychological Study of a Modern Group That Predicted the Destruction of the World* (Mansfield Center, CT: Martino Publishing, 2009), 3.

75 Diana Tumminia, *When Prophecy Never Fails: Myth and Reality in a Flying Saucer Group* (New York: Oxford University Press, 2005), 156.

76 Ibid., 157.

77 Daniel Bar-Tal, *Shared Beliefs in a Society: Social Psychological Analysis* (Thousand Oaks, CA: SAGE Publications, Inc, 2000), xiv.

78 Tumminia, *When Prophecy Never Fails*, 160.

79 Ibid., 161.

80 Emily McFarlan Miller, "Trump Prophet Enraged His Followers by Apologizing. Now He's Shutting Down His Ministry," *Christianity Today*, March 8, 2021, accessed June 2, 2022, https://www.christianitytoday.com/news/2021/march/jeremiah-johnson-trump-prophecy-apology-shut-down-ministry.html.

81 Jeff Struss, "Key Faith Leaders Release, Endorse Prophetic Standards Statement," *Charisma News*, April 29, 2021, accessed June 3, 2022, https://www.charismanews.com/culture/85267-key-faith-leaders-release-endorse-prophetic-standards-statement.

82 "Prophetic Standards Statement," accessed June 2, 2022, https://propheticstandards.com/.

83 Holy Bible, Deuteronomy 18: 20, New King James Version.

Conclusion

1. Jack Jenkins, "Trump and His Religion Advisers Launch New National Faith Advisory Board," *Religion News Network*, September 4, 2021, accessed June 3, 2022, https://religionnews.com/2021/09/04/trump-and-his-religion-advisors-launch-new-national-faith-advisory-board/.
2. "Home," National Faith Advisory Board, accessed June 3, 2022, https://nationalfaithadvisoryboard.org/.
3. "About Us," National Faith Advisory Board, accessed June 3, 2022, https://nationalfaithadvisoryboard.org/about-us.
4. Jack Jenkins, "Trump and His Religion Advisers Launch New Advisory Board," *Religion News Service*, September 4, 2021, accessed October 1, 2022, https://religionnews.com/2021/09/04/trump-and-his-religion-advisors-launch-new-national-faith-advisory-board/.
5. Treva Bowdoin, "Twitter Isn't Holding Back on Donald Trump's Comments about the Roe V. Wade Decision," *MSN*, accessed June 15, 2022, https://www.msn.com/en-us/news/politics/twitter-isn-t-holding-back-on-donald-trump-s-comments-about-the-roe-v-wade-decision/ar-AAYQn1j?ocid=msedgntp&cvid=9d6ac1ac9b27449b816f0eb9180b6e24.
6. Brooke Singman, "Trump Praises Supreme Court Decision Overturning Roe v. Wade, Says Ruling 'Will Work Out for Everybody,'" *Fox News*, June 24, 2022, accessed June 24, 2022, https://www.foxnews.com/politics/trump-praises-supreme-court-decision-overturning-roe-v-wade.
7. Jerimiah Johnson, "The Ending of Roe v Wade," *The Altar*, accessed June 24, 2022, https://app.getresponse.com/view.html?x=a62b&m=BJCoOU&mc=ro&s=BRf9BvS&u=MPtYp&z=EVAQVfP&. In this letter, Johnson claims that the dream was from June 2020, but in his book *The Altar: Preparing for the Return of Jesus* (2022), which he references in the letter, he claims that he had the dream in September of 2020.
8. Charisma House, "Jonathan Cahn Celebrates the Overturning of Roe v. Wade with New SCOTUS Ruling," Charisma House, June 24, 2022, accessed June 24, 2022, https://charismahouse.com/jonathan-cahn-celebrates-the-overturning-of-roe-v-wade-with-new-scotus-ruling/.
9. Laura Bailey, "Franklin Graham: 'The Battle Is Not Over' in Roe v. Wade," Billy Graham Evangelistic Association, May 3, 2022, accessed June 24, 2022, https://billygraham.org/story/franklin-graham-responds-to-potential-overturn-of-roe-v-wade/.

10 Maureen Mackey, "Roe v. Wade Overturned: Rev. Franklin Graham, Other Faith Leaders React to 'Significant' Abortion Ruling," *Fox News*, June 24, 2022, accessed June 24, 2022, https://www.foxnews.com/lifestyle/franklin-graham-faith-scotus-abortion-ruling.

11 Michael L. Brown, "The Significance of the Overturning of Roe," *Ask Dr. Brown*, June 24, 2022, accessed June 24, 2022, https://askdrbrown.org/library/significance-overturning-roe.

12 Michael Brown, *Evangelicals at the Crossroads: Will We Pass the Trump Test?* (Concord, NC: Equal Tine Books, 2020), 211.

13 Ibid., 211–12.

14 Ibid., 212.

15 Michael Brown, *Donald Trump Is Not My Savior: An Evangelical Leader Speaks His Mind about the Man He Supports as President* (Shippensburg, PA: Destiny Image Publishers, Inc., 2018), 323.

16 Ibid., 325.

17 ElijahClips, "Johnny Enlow: Prophetic Vision of 45 | Aug 26 2021," YouTube Video, August 30, 2021, accessed June 10, 2022, https://www.youtube.com/watch?v=ZNobgg_HoEc&t=2s.

18 Johnny Enlow, "AN APOSTOLIC REBUKE AND ENTREATY FOR THOSE BLAMING THE PROPHETS," *Restore7*, February 11, 2021, accessed June 10, 2022, https://restore7.org/blog/2021/2/11/an-apostolic-rebuke-and-entreaty-for-those-blaming-the-prophets.

19 R.T. Kendall, *Prophetic Integrity: Aligning Our Words with God's Word* (Nashville, TN: Thomas Nelson, 2022), 70.

20 Ibid., 70–1.

21 Ibid., 162.

22 Ibid., 162–3.

23 Ibid., 165.

24 Ibid., 171.

25 Amos Yong, "Pentecostalism, Politics, and the Prophetic: Renewing the Public Square II," *Reverberations*, January 21, 2014, accessed October 16, 2021, http://forums.ssrc.org/ndsp/2014/01/21/pentecostalism-politics-and-the-prophetic-renewing-the-public-square-ii/.

26 David Roach, "A Year after the Election, Trump's Effect on Evangelical Churches Lingers," *Christianity Today*, November 1, 2021, accessed June 12, 2022, https://www.christianitytoday.com/news/2021/november/trump-effects-evangelical-churches-witness-survey-election.html.

27 Gregory A. Smith, "During Trump Presidency, More White Americans Adopted than Shed Evangelical Label," Pew Research Center, September 15, 2021, accessed June 20, 2022, https://www.pewresearch.org/fact-tank/2021/09/15/more-white-americans-adopted-than-shed-evangelical-label-during-trump-presidency-especially-his-supporters/?amp=1.

28 Michelle Boorstein, "As Southern Baptists Gather, Right-Wing Faction Sounds Alarms," *The Washington Post,* June 12, 2022, accessed June 20, 2022, https://www.washingtonpost.com/religion/2022/06/13/southern-baptists-john-macarthur/?fbclid=IwAR1R6stKXHJBxXbV0veNPJlhyh19iUP37oMNTsT6oyNEQKkziVUYHTrR3f4.

29 Anthea Butler, "From Republican Party to Republican Religion: The New Political Evangelists of the Right," *Political Theology* (2012), 635–51, 650. https://doi.org/10.1558/poth.v13i5.634.

30 "Watch Meet the Press Excerpt: Russell Moore: '"Evangelical '… Merely A Political Word,'" *NBC.com*, October 14, 2021, accessed June 20, 2022, https://www.nbc.com/meet-the-press/video/russell-moore-evangelical-merely-a-political-word/565637796.

31 Jason Lemon, "Adam Kinzinger Warns Churches Have Become 'House of Worship' to Trump," *Newsweek*, June 17, 2022, accessed June 20, 2022, https://www.msn.com/en-us/news/politics/adam-kinzinger-warns-churches-have-become-house-of-worship-to-trump/ar-AAYABUR?ocid=msedgdhp&pc=U531&cvid=9886dfa068894abadc0d368678105ea5.

32 Tim Alberta, "How Politics Poisoned the Evangelical Church," *The Atlantic*, May 10, 2022, accessed June 20, 2022, https://www.theatlantic.com/magazine/archive/2022/06/evangelical-church-pastors-political-radicalization/629631/.

33 Mark Silk, "Is American Conservatism De-Christianizing? No More than Usual," *Religion News Service*, June 8, 2022, accessed June 20, 2022, https://religionnews.com/2022/06/08/is-the-religious-right-defunct/?fbclid=IwAR0rojSqWcRGnuDjLiqrVRJ_0R6UJ1nr6nfXnHq-jgZkXhdmUnBQ06ZZRhM.

34 See Amanda Taheri, "Rep. Lauren Boebert Calls Sereation of Church and State 'Junk,' Says Church Should Direct Government," *People*, June 29, 2022, accessed October 1, 2022. https://people.com/politics/rep-lauren-boebert-denounces-separation-of-church-state/ & Darragh Roche, "Greene Launches Self Defense of Christian Nationalism—'Nothing to Be Ashamed Of,'" *Newsweek*, https://www.newsweek.com/marjorie-taylor-greene-launches-defense-christian-nationalism-1731500.

35 D. Michael Lindsay, *Faith in The Halls of Power: How Evangelicals Joined the American Elite* (New York: Oxford University Press, 2007), 216.
36 Ibid., 216–17.
37 Ibid., 217.
38 Ibid., 218.
39 Richard A. Oppel Jr. and Erik Eckholm, "Prominent Pastor Calls Romney's Church a Cult," *New York Times*, October 7, 2011, accessed June 10, 2022, https://www.nytimes.com/2011/10/08/us/politics/prominent-pastor-calls-romneys-church-a-cult.html.
40 Quoted in Oppel and Eckholm, "Prominent Pastor Calls Romney's Church a Cult."
41 Anthea Butler, "Beyond Alarmism and Denial in the Dominionism Debate," Religion Dispatches, April 17, 2012, accessed July 12, 2020, https://religiondispatches.org/beyond-alarmism-and-denial-in-the-dominionism-debate/.
42 Michael Wilkinson, "Charismatic Christianity and the Role of Social Networks," *Pneuma*, Vol. 38, No. 33–49 (2016): 35.
43 Chris Stirewalt, *Broken News: Why the Media Rage Machine Divides America and How to Fight Back* (New York: Hatchett Book Group, 2022), 7.
44 Paul Steinhauser, "Trump Stayed Neutral, but MAGA-Republicans, Meddling Democrats, Win Big New Hampshire's Fiery GOP Primaries," *Fox News*, September 14, 200, accessed October 2, 2022. https://www.foxnews.com/politics/trump-stayed-neutral-maga-candidates-still-swept-fiery-gop-primaries-battleground-new-hampshire & Brittany Shephard, "Voters Just Booted Liz Cheney from Office—Could She Run for President as a Republican? (Analysis)," *ABC News*, August 17, 2022, accessed October 2, 2022. https://abcnews.go.com/Politics/analysis-voters-booted-liz-cheney-office-run-republican/story?id=88493217.
45 William Bender, "New 'Prophet' on the Campaign Trail with Doug Mastriano Is a Prayer-Coin Salesman Who Calls Biden 'AntiChrist,'" *Pittsburgh Post-Gazette*, September 22, 2022, accessed September 23, 2022. https://www.post-gazette.com/news/election2022/2022/09/22/doug-mastriano-lance-wallnau-preacher-prophet-prayer-coin-salesman-pa-governors-race-2022/stories/202209220134.
46 Lance Wallnau, "Is America under Judgement?." Email. September 28, 2022.
47 "Fire & Glory Tour," accessed October 1, 2022. https://fireandglorytour.com/?inf_contact_key=6c688c94810facfab37362f836dd2586842e902fbefb79ab9abae13bfcb46658.

48 See Jeffery M. Jones, "How Religious Are Americans?," *Gallup*, December 23, 2021, accessed October 1, 2022, https://news.gallup.com/poll/358362/religious-americans.aspx; Pew Research Center, "In U.S., Decline of Christianity Continues at Rapid Pace," October 17, 2019, accessed October 1, 2022. https://www.pewresearch.org/religion/2019/10/17/in-u-s-decline-of-christianity-continues-at-rapid-pace/.

Index

abortion 3, 5–6, 8, 63, 65, 71, 93, 97, 100, 116–17, 120, 135, 137–9, 142, 157–8, 165–6
Ahab spirit 117. *See also* King Ahab
Ahn, Ché 63, 129–30, 142, 146
   Modern-Day Apostles: Operating in Your Apostolic Office and Anointing 22, 29
   "Promises Made, Promises Kept" 129
Alberta, Tim 164–5
Amedia, Frank 77–8, 111–19, 123–4, 140–1, 147–9, 153, 158–9, 162, 165
American Adversaries Radio 76
American civilization 91
American exceptionalism 87
American Religious Right. *See* Religious Right in America
American Revolution 109–10
Anderson, Troy
   The Babylon Code: Solving the Bible's Greatest End-Times Mystery 109
   Trumpocalypse: The End-Times President, a Battle against the Globalist Elite, and the Countdown to Armageddon 109
anti-communism 58
antigay agenda 16
apocalypticism 44–6, 50, 57, 60, 62, 67, 168
   apocalyptic literature 51–2
   avertive 12, 55, 62, 65, 69, 71, 74, 102, 112, 135
   diversity 51
   narrative function of 52
   rhetorical value of 55
apostles 1, 7, 9–10, 12, 15, 17, 20, 24, 26, 40–1, 43, 51, 61, 65, 68, 83–4, 97, 110, 160. *See also* prophets
   horizontal 27
   vertical 27
   workplace 27–30, 33

The Apostolic Council Prophetic Elders 33
Ashcraft, W. Michael 50
Asprem, Egil, *Handbook of Conspiracy Theory and Contemporary Religion* 55
The Atlantic magazine 6, 164
avertive apocalypticism 12, 55, 62, 65, 69, 71, 74, 102, 112, 135
avertive millennialism 50

"Baby Boomers" 139
Babylon's system 33
Bachmann, Michelle 16, 128
Bakker, Jim 84, 119. *See also Jim Bakker Show*
Barkun, Michael
   A Culture of Conspiracy: Apocalyptic Visions in Contemporary America 56
   stigmatized knowledge 150
Barret-Fox, Rebecca 96
Barrett, Amy Coney 156
Bar-Tal, Daniel 151
Batholomew, Craig G. 178 n.80
Bauer, Gary 128
Beverley, James A. 76
Bickle, Mike 21–2, 128
Biden, Hunter 123
Biden, Joe 76, 123, 141, 145–6, 150, 160
Bieber, Justin 138–9
Billy Graham Evangelistic Society 60, 194 n.3
bin-Laden, Osama 94
Black Lives Matter 61
Bolsonaro, Jair 144
Book of Isaiah 88, 101, 119, 133
Bossie, David N., *Trump's Enemies: How the Deep State Is Undermining the Presidency* 109
Boykin, William "Jerry" 112–13
Bright, Bill 29

Brown, Michael L. 20–1, 133, 135, 152, 157, 159–61
   Ask Dr. Brown 133–5
   Donald Trump Is Not My Savior: An Evangelical Leader Speaks His Mind about the Man He Supports as President 159
   Evangelicals at the Crossroads: Will We Pass the Trump Test? 158
   Jezebel's War with America 138
Butler, Anthea 18–19, 163, 167, 170
   "From Republican Party to Republican Religion: The New Political Evangelists of the Right" 13, 163
Byford, Jovan, *Conspiracy Theories: A Critical Introduction* 55–6

Cabal 83
Cahn, Jonathan 84, 90–1, 96, 99, 102, 109, 113, 116, 144, 157, 168
   apostasy in United States 92, 94–5, 100
   Democratic Party Platform 94
   "founding vision of America" 100
   Harbinger II 157
   The Harbinger: The Ancient Mystery That Holds the Secret of America's Future 65–7, 76, 89–90, 93–4, 99–101, 124, 157
   "The Paradigm of the King" 92
   "The Paradigm of the Warrior" 94–5
   The Paradigm: The Ancient Blueprint That Holds the Mystery of Our Times 76, 89–90, 94, 96, 100–1, 113
   worship of Baal 91–4, 97
Calvinism 10, 163
Chaffetz, Jason 68
   The Deep State: How an Army of Bureaucrats Protected Barack Obama and Is Working to Destroy the Trump Agenda 109–10
Charisma House Book Group 89
Charisma magazine 76, 109
Charisma News 117–18, 139–40, 151–2
Charisma Podcast Network 85, 88
charismatic Christian movements 1–3, 9, 15, 16, 17, 61, 72, 84, 110, 129, 133, 146, 165–7
   Charismatic renewal 22
   crisis of leadership 160

Pentecostal Christianity 18, 22–4
   Third and Fourth Wave 133
Cheney, Liz 168
Christerson, Brad 21, 167
Christian Broadcasting News (CBN) 79–81, 84, 104
Christianity Today magazine 6, 75, 123, 151, 163
Christian Reconstruction 31, 47
Christian Right in the United States 3–4, 68, 128
Christians/Christianity 1, 11, 25, 32, 34, 38, 46, 57, 61, 72, 75, 85, 88, 96, 99, 109, 145, 152, 155, 158, 161, 163, 166–7, 169–70
   communism and 57–62
   hypocrisy 158
   nationalism 8–9, 144–5
Christian World News 32
Civil Rights for the Unborn 128
Clement, Kim 75–6, 78, 85, 104, 134
Clinton, Bill 90, 92–3, 100, 158
Clinton, Hillary 6, 78, 89–90, 93–4, 96, 101, 106, 111, 127, 135, 143
Cohen, Michael 114–16, 137
Colbert, John 84
Colbert, Mary 84
Comey, James 121
conservative Christianity 1, 3–5, 7–10, 19, 65, 128, 137, 142, 148, 155, 157, 159, 166
conspiracism 3, 12–13, 20, 44–6, 57, 62, 68–9, 102, 104–6, 112, 114, 127, 131, 143, 168
   anatomy 55
   conspiracy belief 56
   demonic forces 41, 44, 113
   Manichean moral dualism 56
   naïve optimism 56
   optimistic millennialism 69, 71, 114
   paranoid style 55–6
Corsi, Jerome
   Killing the Deep State: The Fight to Save President Trump 109
   Obamanation: Leftist Politics and the Cult of Personality 68
   Where's the Birth Certificate? The Case Barak Obama Is Not Eligible to Be President 68

Costa, Paul, *The Power to Get Wealth* 33
counterfeit evangelism 86
Covid 19 crisis 104, 118, 129–30, 146, 164
Cruz, Ted 4, 78
Cubitt, Geoffrey 56
culture 32, 38, 47, 112, 142
    anti-cosmopolitan 93
    cultural issues/framework 7–8
    cultural Marxism 61
    culture wars 92
    seven molders of 28, 31, 35
    of Western civilization 90–1
Cunningham, Loren 29

Darby, John Nelson 47–8
Davis, Lanny 115
"Deep State" 44, 68, 82, 97, 104–10, 112, 115, 117, 122, 124, 143, 158, 168
Defender Publishing 83–4
delegitimization 55, 106
demographic and cultural shifts 8–9, 93, 170
demonization 9–10
Devos, Betsy 129
disasters 45, 66, 96, 127
dispensational premillennialism 47
Dittmer, Jason, *Mapping the End Times: American Evangelical Geopolitics and Apocalyptic Visions* 47
Dobson, James 19, 47, 128
dominionism 2, 4, 11–12, 29–31, 35, 39–41, 43, 46, 49, 52, 55, 83, 102, 139, 165, 168
dominion mandate 2, 12, 20, 31, 34–9, 43–4, 69, 146
doubtful morality 6
Douglas, Lawrence 105–6
Du Mez, Kristin Kobes 7–10, 163
    Jesus and John Wayne: How White Evangelicals Corrupter a Faith and Fractured a Nation 7–8
Dyrendal, Asbjørn, *Handbook of Conspiracy Theory and Contemporary Religion* 55

economics 33, 36
ecumenism 166
election (2016) 4–5, 12, 39–40, 45–6, 55, 62, 65, 67–8, 75–6, 79–80, 86–9, 92, 94–5, 102, 104, 109–10, 113, 117, 121, 127, 129, 143
    Deep State (*see* "Deep State")
    demonic principalities 120
    eschatological importance 73
    prophecy voters 69, 71, 127
    prophetic significance 135–6
    Trump prophecies 78, 84–5, 111, 135
election (2020) 1, 3–4, 10–13, 40, 44–6, 60–1, 65, 76, 86, 105, 118, 123–4, 133, 136, 138, 142–8, 164, 166
    prophecy voters 146
    spiritual warfare 128, 139
    Trump prophecies for 159
The Elijah List 73, 104, 123
End Times theology 10, 49, 163
Engle, Lou 36, 63, 112–13
Enlow, Johnny 36, 104, 124, 159, 161, 165
    "An Apostolic Rebuke and Entreaty for Those Blaming the Prophets" 160
    "God Says, 'I Played My Trump Card, I Will Win the Hand'" 120–1
    The Seven Mountain Mantle 48, 52
    The Seven Mountain Prophecy: Unveiling the Coming Elijah Revolution 33, 40
    "Trump Quake! What's Next!" 119–22
escapism 48–9
eschatology/eschatological optimism 20, 25, 28, 30, 40–1, 46–7, 49–50, 57, 60, 65, 73, 122, 135, 166
evangelicalism/evangelism 17–18, 23, 25, 37, 39, 65, 72, 86, 159, 164, 167, 170
    American 166
    evangelical Protestants 1, 6–7, 59, 163
    politicization 165
    secularization of 164
    white 9
exalt demonic spirits 38

Falwell, Jerry 19, 47, 50, 63–4, 66–7, 168
Feinstein, Dianne 116
feminism 137–9, 165
Festinger, Leon, *When Prophecy Fails* 150
First and Second Amendment rights 158
The First Apostolic Age 24
Flory, Richard 21, 167
Floyd, George 146
Ford, Christine Blasey 116

Fox News 123
Franklin, Jentezen 132
free-market capitalism 33
Frykholm, Amy 47

Gagné, André 15, 49, 72
Gates, Bill 75
gay marriage 6, 8, 71, 142, 166
Geivett, R. Douglass 17–18, 20–1
Godin, Mark 73
Graham, Billy 57–62, 86, 168
   devices of Satan 59
   "How to Combat Communism" 58–9
   North Korea's education system 60
   "Why Communism Is Gaining Ground" 58
Graham, Franklin 60, 133, 157
   "Special Day of Prayer" 128
Greenwood, Lee 132

Hagee, John, Christian Zionism 20
Haggard, Ted 19
Haley, Nikki 136–7
Hannity, Sean 106
Hart, Christopher 76
Hebrew Bible 113
Hickey, Marilyn 90
Hinn, Benny 17
Hinn, Costi 17–18
Hofstadter, Richard 105
   "The Paranoid Style in American Politics" 55–6
Holding, John Patrick 90
Holy Spirit 2, 12, 22–3, 25, 31–2, 38, 41, 48, 64–5, 72, 81, 122, 146, 150, 152
homosexuality 32, 39, 50, 91–3, 97, 100, 135, 165
horizontal apostles 27
Horn, Thomas R. 83–4, 108
   Saboteurs: Shadow Government in Quest of the Final World Order 83, 108
   Shadowland 108
Horowitz, David 145
   Dark Agenda: The War to Destroy Christian America 142
Horwitz, Robert B. 105
The Hour of Decision (radio program) 58
Howell, Donna 84

Huckabee, Mike 67
Huckabee, Sarah 136–7
Human Rights Campaign 87
Hunter, James Davidson, *To Change the World: The Irony, Tragedy, & Possibility of Christianity in the Late Modern World* 15
Hunt, Stephen 47

Illuminati 82–3
Independent Network Christianity/INC Christianity 21
intersectionality 61
Israel 7, 64–6, 74, 77–80, 90–2, 94–6, 99–100, 104–5, 124, 140–1, 166, 169

Jackson, Harry 128
Jackson, Natalie 103
Jacobs, Cindy 37, 52, 117
   ideological strongholds 53
   occultic strongholds 53
   personal strongholds 53
   Possessing The Gates of the Enemy: A Training Manual for Militant Intercession 33, 36
   social strongholds 53–4
Jeffress, Robert 133, 166–7
Jehu 77, 101, 131
   vs. Jezebel 88–96
Jeroboam 100
Jesus Christ 8, 27–8, 31–2, 35, 38, 44, 47, 59, 62, 150, 156, 159, 164, 166–7
Jezebel
   Jehu *vs.* 88–96
   spirit 117, 169
   witchcraft 123
Jim Bakker Show 112, 119, 128, 195 n.4
Johnson, Bill, *Invading Babylon: The 7 Mountain Mandate* 30
Johnson, Jeremiah 124, 133–8, 140, 148–51, 153, 156–7, 162, 165
   The Altar 162
   "The Antichrist Spirit" 138
   "Entertainment Mountain" 138–9
   Johnson Amendment 129, 155
   "The Nebuchadnezzar Warning" 136–7
   Trump and the Future of America 135, 137, 149
   Trump, 2019, & Beyond 135–7, 140, 149

Jones, Alex, *InfoWars* 110
Jones, Robert P., *The End of White Christian America* 6
Joram 94–5
Joyner, Rick 84, 147–9, 153
judgments of God 41, 46–7, 50, 59, 124, 170
　on wayward nation 62–7

Kansas City Prophets movement 22
Kavanagh, Brett 114, 116
Kelly, John, *The Power to Get Wealth* 33
Kendall, R.T., *Prophetic Integrity: Aligning Our Words with God's Word* 160–1
Kerr, Kat 73–6, 78, 96
King Ahab 90, 92–4, 100
King, Alveda 128
King Cyrus 3, 88–9, 101, 128, 131, 134, 142, 144, 156–7
Kingdom of God 9, 12, 22, 25, 28–9, 31–3, 37–8, 40, 43–4, 48–50, 52, 54, 57, 86–7, 120, 130, 133, 147–8, 159, 170
　spiritual and social activism 32
　transfer of wealth 33–4, 36
Kingdom values 34–5
King, Martin Luther 128
Kinzinger, Adam 164
Kurtzleben, Danielle 7, 9
Kuyper, Abraham, sphere sovereignty 31, 178 n.80

LaHaye, Tim 47–8, 50
Latter Rain movement 17, 22
Left Behind series 20, 46–7, 72
Lewandowski, Corey 68, 109, 148
　Trump's Enemies: How the Deep State Is Undermining the Presidency 109
liberal media 74
Lincoln, Abraham 137, 139
Lincoln, Bruce, "Theses on Method" 11
Lindsay, D. Michael
　elastic orthodoxy 166
　Faith in The Halls of Power: How Evangelicals Joined the American Elite 166
Lindsay, Hal 48
　The Late Great Planet Earth 47
Lord of the Rings 57, 73
Luther, Martin 24

MacArthur, John 17
　Charismatic Chaos 17
　The Charismatics 17
　Strange Fire: The Danger of Offending the Holy Spirit with Counterfeit Worship 18
MacDonald, Andrew 6–7, 9
MAGA Republicans 168–9
Maginnis, Robert 84, 108
Maldonado, Apostle 133
Malloch, Theodore Roosevelt, *The Plot to Destroy Trump: How the Deep State Fabricated the Russian Dossier to Subvert the President* 110
Mansfield, Stephen 6
Marno, David 67
Marshall, Rich, *God @ Work* series 28
Marxist infiltration 61
Masistrano, Doug 169
master blueprint 90
Mattera, Joseph 152
McAllister, Colin, *The Cambridge Companion to Apocalyptic Literature* 51
McCloud, Sean, *American Possessions: Fighting Demons in the Contemporary United States* 71
McGinn, Bernard 52
McGuire, Paul
　The Babylon Code: Solving the Bible's Greatest End-Times Mystery 109
　Trumpocalypse: The End Times, A Battle against the Globalist Elite, and The Countdown to Armageddon 109
McMahon, Vince 4
McQueen, Alison 45
McVicar, Michael J., *Christian Reconstruction: R.J. Rushdoony and American Religious Conservatism* 31, 178 n.80
Meet the Press Reports 163
metamorphosis 91, 93
Metaxas, Eric 142
"Me Too Movement" 116
millennialism 12, 44, 46–7, 55, 69, 102, 112
　apocalyptic and 44, 51, 57
　avertive 50
　catastrophic 48, 50

optimistic 69, 71, 81
progressive 50, 52, 54, 86
rapture and 48
Wessinger's description 49–50
Miller, Stephen 106
Moore, Russell 163–4
Mormonism 166–7
Moses 117, 124
Mueller, Robert 106, 109, 123, 127
Muirhead, Russell, *A Lot of People Are Saying: The New Conspiracism and the Assault on Democracy* 106
Murillo, Mario 169

national and corporate transformation 34
National Faith Advisory Board 155
NATO 104, 129
Netanyahu, Benjamin 77, 79, 141
New Apostolic Reformation (NAR) 1, 11, 13, 15, 18, 21, 25, 43, 102–4, 130–1, 135–6, 145, 151, 159, 162, 165, 167–70
   cultural conquest mission 34
   ecclesiastical reform 16–17, 19, 22, 167
   extra-denominational networks 1, 20, 25
   like-minded individuals 2, 20
   origins of 20–5
   theological perspectives 11, 72
New Testament 2, 9, 17, 22, 26
nostalgia voters 6
Nunes, Devin 106

Obama, Barack 6, 68, 77, 80, 90, 94–5, 99–101, 107, 111, 166–7
   administration 68, 94, 101–2, 109, 141
   Obamacare 4
Ocasio-Cortez, Alexandria 138
Olmsted, Katheryn S. 55
Operation Warp Speed 129
Orbán, Viktor 144
Otis, George, Jr. 32, 37–8

Papadopoulos, George 68
   Deep State Target: How I Got Caught in the Crosshairs of the Plot to Bring Down President Trump 110

partisan politics 13, 165
patriotism 148, 159
Paul the Apostle 27
Pelosi, Nany 138
Pence, Mike 129, 136
Pendleton, Les, *1600 Trump Avenue: Against All Odds* 107–8
Pentecostal-Charismatic movement 21
Pentecostalism 2, 15, 19, 22, 47
Peretti, Frank 72–3
Perry, Rick 16, 112, 166
Perry, Samuel L. 9
   Taking Back America for God: Christian Nationalism in the United States 8
Pew Research 5, 7, 103, 163
Pierard, Richard V. 58
Pierce, Chuck 76–9, 117
Pittsburgh Post-Gazette 169
Pivec, Holly 17–18, 20–1
political correctness 38, 85, 100, 107, 158
   Babylon 87
political prophecy 107
Pompeo, Mike 129
Posner, Sarah, cross-pollination 16, 19
post-millennialism 49
post-Second War Evangelicalism 57
POTUS Shield 77, 110–19, 128, 140
premillennialism 47, 49, 60
pro-Christian policies 159
progressive millennialism 50, 52, 54, 86
prophecy voters 2, 4–12, 14, 39, 44, 69, 71, 97, 118, 120, 122, 125, 127, 131–2, 146, 153, 156, 162, 164–5, 170
   churchgoing Republicans 5
   flaws and loss 14
   GOP nomination 4–5
   political agenda 164
prophetic accountability 160
"Prophetic Standards Statement" 152, 159–60
prophets 1–4, 7, 9–10, 12–13, 15, 17, 24, 33, 39–41, 44, 50–1, 65, 68, 73, 75, 78, 83–4, 86, 96–7, 110–11, 124–5, 129–31, 133, 136, 147, 153, 160–2, 165
prosperity gospel movement 1–2, 17, 23, 80, 133, 167

Public Religion Research Institute (PRRI) 6, 103
Puritans 62, 91

QAnon conspiracy theories 103

radical feminism 137–9
Reagan, Ronald 4
reelection 12, 44–5, 75, 127, 129–30, 132–3, 136, 138–41, 143–4, 151, 156, 159
Religion & Ethics Newsweekly (TV show) 111
religious freedom/liberty 7, 87, 129, 142, 155, 158
Religious Right in America 4, 11, 13, 15–16, 19, 45–7, 62, 155, 163, 165, 170
Republican Party 13, 163, 167
Riecken, Henry W., *When Prophecy Fails* 150
Riedel, Matthias, *The Apocalyptic Complex: Perspectives, Histories, Persistence* 67
Roach, David 163
Robertson, David, *Handbook of Conspiracy Theory and Contemporary Religion* 55
Robertson, Pat 47, 50, 63–4, 66–7, 168
Rodham, Hillary 93
Roe v. Wade 5–6, 14, 99, 138–9, 155–8
Romney, Mitt 166–7
Rosenbaum, Nancy L., *A Lot of People Are Saying: The New Conspiracism and the Assault on Democracy* 106
Rushdoony, Rousas John (R.J.) 31, 47

Satan 12, 25, 30–2, 38, 52–3, 57, 69, 87, 124, 160
Schachter, Stanley, *When Prophecy Fails* 150
Schultz, Steve 104, 123. See also The Elijah List
Scofield, C. I. 47
Second Apostolic Age 24, 26, 32
Second Corinthians 7
Seven Mountains Mandate (Dominion Mandate) 2, 12, 16, 29–35, 36, 41, 43, 52, 97, 122, 144, 170

sexual immorality 32, 92, 94, 97, 99, 135
Sheets, Dutch 64, 84, 123
Sid Roth's It's Supernatural! (TV show) 79
Silk, Mark 165
Silliman, Daniel 5–6
  Reading Evangelicals: How Christian Fiction Shaped a Culture and a Faith 72
Silva, Ken 17
Simpson, Sandy 17
social and political issues 8, 10, 15, 29, 36, 43, 51, 91, 163–5
social justice 61
social transformation 3, 29, 31–3, 35, 39, 49, 150, 165
societal beliefs 151
sociologically verifiable transformation 32
Soros, George 142
Spirit of God 22, 24, 26, 32, 64, 79–82, 85, 89, 134
spirit of poverty 36
spiritual amnesia 99
spiritual mapping 9, 36–9, 71
spiritual stronghold 37, 114
spiritual warfare 2, 9, 11, 13, 23, 26, 31, 33, 36–40, 43–4, 46, 53–4, 57, 68–9, 71–2, 74, 81, 83, 87, 110, 112–16, 128, 141, 143–4, 146, 162
  demonic forces 104, 170
  as dualistic forces 120, 136
  and intercessory prayer 10, 19–20, 30, 40, 113–14
  manifestation 158
  political activism and 51
  POTUS Shield 116–17
Sproul, R. C. 18
Stetzer, Ed 6–7, 9
Stirewalt, Chris, *Broken News* 168
Stone, Roger 110
"Stop the Steal" rally 131
Strang, Stephen 76–8, 84, 116, 140, 142–3, 145–6
  God and Donald Trump 76, 78
  God, Trump, and Covid-19: How the Pandemic Is Affecting Christians, The World, and America's 2020 Election 142–3, 146

Strang, Steven 117–19, 152, 157
Sturm, Tristan 51
   Mapping the End Times: American Evangelical Geopolitics and Apocalyptic Visions 47
Sunstein, Cass 55
Sutton, Matthew Avery 57

Tabachnick, Rachel 16–17
Tada, Joni Eareckson 18
Taylor, Mark 76–80, 83–5, 117, 135, 144
   "America, America" 82
   "Commander in Chief" prophecy 79
   "The Fourth Reich, ISIS" 82
   The Trump Prophecies: The Astonishing True Story of the Man Who Saw Tomorrow ... And What He Says Is Coming Next 79, 81, 84
Teigen, Arne Helge 15
theocracy and dominion 35
theology and eschatology 122
Third Reich 53
Thomas, John E. 161
Thompson, Bennie 105
Todd, Chuck 163
Toronto Blessing 23
Trump, Donald 1–2, 4, 6, 39, 44–5, 61, 68, 75, 89, 95, 101, 105, 108–9, 124, 128, 134, 142, 144, 149, 158, 161, 163–4, 167
   on abortion and social issues 3, 5–6, 8, 71
   anger, accountability, and apologies 146–50
   anointing and mission 44, 67–9
   belligerence 7
   chaos candidate 85–8, 96, 109
   Christian support 1, 3, 5–11, 15, 19, 52, 57, 103–4, 112, 128, 133, 141, 143, 155, 157
   "Christian Support for Trump" 46
   as Cyrus phenomenon 96–7
   deregulation 129
   "Frank Amedia: God Has Shown Me What Will Happen With This Election if We Do Our Part" 118
   on gay marriage 6, 8, 71
   as God's chosen leader 3, 12–14, 69, 88, 96–7, 103, 137
   imaginative world-building 73
   "Make America Great Again" 127
   "My Public Apology and Process" 149
   presidency 5, 7, 13, 15, 40, 46, 68, 84, 97, 109, 113, 122–3, 127, 131, 136, 158, 162, 166
   prophecies 3, 7, 12–13, 15, 71–3, 75–6, 78–84, 87, 122, 131–8, 148, 151, 159–61
   prophesying victory 73–8
   racial and xenophobic anxieties 9
   "Voting in The Kingdom: Prophecy Voters, the New Apostolic Reformation" 46
Tumminia, Diana G., *When Prophecy Never Fails* 150–1

Unarians' mythology 151
Urban, Hugh B. 11

values voters 4, 6
vertical apostles 27

Wagner, C. Peter 1–2, 16–17, 20–2, 30–2, 36, 43, 46, 48, 71–2, 80, 164
   Apostles Today: Biblical Government for Biblical Power 26–7
   Breaking Spiritual Strongholds in Your City 37–8, 52
   church in the workplace 27–8, 33
   Churchquake! How The New Apostolic Reformation Is Shaking Up the Church as We Know It 23–5, 49
   Dominion! How Kingdom Action Can Change the World 2, 31, 34, 48, 178 n.91
   dominion theology 31, 34–5
   "The Great Transfer of Wealth" 33, 74, 80
   The New Apostolic Churches: Rediscovering the New Testament Model of Leadership and Why It Is God's Desire for The Church Today 23, 27
   "The New Apostolic Reformation" 23
   phenomenological approach 27
   power evangelism 17

The Third Wave of the Holy Spirit: Encountering the Power of Signs and Wonders 22–3
Warfare Prayer: What the Bible Says about Spiritual Warfare 40
Wallnau, Lance 6, 29–31, 48, 51–2, 57, 61–4, 67, 76, 78, 85, 87–9, 96–7, 101, 109, 111–12, 115, 117, 122–4, 128, 134, 144–9, 153, 158, 162, 165, 168–9
"The Crimes of Our Educators: Brainwashing America's Kids into Communists" 61
"era of Cyrus Trump" 122–5
God's Chaos Candidate 68, 85–6, 144
God's Chaos Code: The Shocking Blueprint That Reveals 5 Keys to the Destiny of Nations 144, 146
Invading Babylon: The 7 Mountain Mandate 30
"Jezebel witchcraft" 123
political cosmology 86
"The Seven Mountain Mandate" 30
Sheep Nations Rising 57
warfare strategy 29
Warren, Rick 16–17
Weaver, John 15, 22, 33–4
Wesley, John 24

Wessinger, Catherine 49
catastrophic millennialism 50
"Millennialism With and Without the Mayhem" 50
Western civilization culture 90–1
West, Kanye 138–9
Whacker, Grant 58
white evangelicalism 9
Whitehead, Andrew L. 9
Taking Back America for God: Christian Nationalism in the United States 8
White, Paula 1, 102, 110, 129, 132–3, 141–3, 155, 167
"I hear the sound of victory" 141–6
wild conspiracy theories 104
Wilder, Forrest, *The Texas Observer* 16
Wilkinson, Michael 167
Wimber, John 23
Winthrop, John 63, 99–100
Wojcik, Daniel 50, 62
Wommack, Andrew 144
Wood, Anthony G. 18
workplace apostles 27–30, 33
Wright, N. T. 51

Yong, Amos 162
In The Days of Caesar: Pentecostalism and Political Theology 9
prophetic politics 162

www.ingramcontent.com/pod-product-compliance
Lightning Source LLC
Chambersburg PA
CBHW052111300426
44116CB00010B/1616